The Soul
of the
Apostolate

The Soul
of the
Apostolate

By

DOM JEAN-BAPTISTE CHAUTARD, O.C.S.O.

(Abbot of Notre Dame de Sept-Fons)

Translated by

A MONK OF OUR LADY OF GETHSEMANI

TAN Books

An Imprint of Saint Benedict Press, LLC

Charlotte, North Carolina

Nihil Obstat:	M. Maurice Molloy, O.C.S.O.
	M. Alberic Wulf, O.C.S.O.
Imprimi Potest:	M. Fredericus Dunne, O.C.S.O.
	Abbas B.M. de Gethsemani
Imprimatur:	✠ Joannes A. Floersh, D.D.
	Archiepiscopus Ludovicopolitanus
	Die 16a Septembris, 1946

First published in 1946. Published by TAN Books, an Imprint of Saint Benedict Press, LLC, in 1974. Retypeset and republished by TAN in 2008 and 2012.

ISBN: 978-0-89555-031-6

Cover photo credits—left to right, top and bottom:
Minor Elevation at the Tridentine Mass, courtesy of The Institute of Christ the King, Chicago, IL.
Cathedral of the Blessed Sacrament, Sacramento, CA, photo copyright © Milo Persic.
Sister Adorers of the Royal Heart of Jesus, courtesy of The Sister Adorers, Sieci, Italy.
Grandmother's 90th Birthday, photo copyright © Ann Marie Kurtz; iStockphoto.
The Hands of the Poor, photo copyright © Sean Warren; iStockphoto.
Schoolboys, photo copyright © Steven Stone; iStockphoto.

Cover design by Milo Persic.

Published in the United States by
TAN Books
P.O. Box 410487
Charlotte, NC 28241
www.tanbooks.com

Printed and bound in the United States of America.

DOM CHAUTARD

A Biographical Note

It is surely significant that the day on which the author of this modern spiritual classic, the *Soul of the Apostolate*, was born in the French Alps, was the feast of St. Gregory the Great, March 12, 1858. For it is one of the cardinal principles of St. Gregory's mystical and ascetical teaching that there exists an inseparably close relation between the so-called "active" and "contemplative" lives, so much so that though one may dominate over the other (and the most perfect state is that in which contemplation dominates) yet in the soul of anyone called by God to high sanctity the life is always essentially a mixture of contemplation (love of God) and action (love of neighbor).

Now it is precisely this problem which the brilliant and ardent Cistercian abbot of Sept-Fons, in central France sets himself to elucidate and discuss in this pamphlet, which has gone into many editions and hundreds of thousands of copies in many languages, and which was the bedside book of Pope Pius X. The reason why St. Gregory the Great was so perfect in expounding the relation of action and contemplation is that, called from the cloister to the Papacy in one of the crises in the history of the Church, he found out what that relation was in the crucible of trial and labor and distraction and struggle.

And the reason why Dom Chautard has been able to write so well on the same theme for our own age, intoxicated with the confusion of its own sterile and purely worldly activities, is that he too was so often torn, by the hand of God, from the cloister, and made an instrument of Divine Power and Providence and Love to protect the monks and nuns of the Cistercian Order, and to call priests, religious, and layworkers in Catholic Action to a life of closer union with God, in Whom is the only principle of vital and effective social action: divine charity, won for us by the Sacrifice of Christ, His Incarnate Word, upon the Cross.

The Chautards ran a little bookshop, and the father of the future monk was one of those purely nominal Catholics who sometimes go to Mass, but whose principles are entirely vitiated by the materialistic and utilitarian views of the middle class to which they belong. The mother was in a different category. She had more faith, and she saw to it that her children were educated as Catholics.

However, as their son grew into young manhood, neither he nor they had an idea of his entering religion. He went to Marseilles to study economics at the university, with a commercial career in mind. There was a relative in Chile. Perhaps the young man would join him and make a fortune there. The atmosphere of the University of Marseilles was scarcely Catholic, but in a footnote to one of the later sections of the *Soul of the Apostolate*, the author tells us how he was one day much affected by the simple devotion with which a priest was reciting his Breviary, and he began to ask himself why he did not pray more himself.

Soon he began to frequent a Catholic club, founded for the working and lower middle-class youth of the great Mediterranean port by the saintly Father Allemand.

When Dom Chautard describes his experience of this really vital and supernatural brand of Catholic Action in the *Soul of the Apostolate* he is referring to a later visit to Fr. Allemand's club, after his ordination.

But indeed it may be said that Dom Chautard's vocation, and the *Soul of the Apostolate* itself are both to be traced to Fr. Allemand's club, at Marseilles.

If this youth-club had been one of those more or less timid compromises with modern notions that make so much Catholic Action seem like no more than a Y.M.C.A. run by a couple of priests, Dom Chautard would have probably ended by exporting nitrates from Chile. But here he found something more than third-rate amateur dramatics and the atmosphere of a secular social club. This was more than a tame and sheepish attempt to rival the attractions of the dance hall and the *cafe* by vainly trying to beat them at their own game of pleasing and entertaining human nature. There was something more, something that appealed to a much deeper and more urgent and more vital necessity: faith, supernatural charity, a deep and simple and unbreakable solidarity among souls united, as he was to discover, in Christ. And, as a result of all this, he began to taste "that peace which the world cannot give."

It was when he was kneeling in prayer, one day, in the chapel of the club, at the tomb of its saintly founder, that he received the grace of his vocation to religion.

He countered the violent and embittered opposition of his father's *bourgeois* hatred of religious orders, by a barefoot pilgrimage up the stony Alpine roads to Our Lady's Mountain Shrine at Laus, and in answer to his prayers, he was admitted as a postulant to the Trappist Abbey of Aiguebelle, near the Rhone, north of Avignon, in 1877.

Here he began to learn, with inexpressible joy, how to live

the contemplative life as it had been practiced for centuries according to the Rule of St. Benedict and the Usages of the Cistercians. He began to live the life of a White Monk, that life of obscurity, obedience, silence, poverty, solitude, hidden in the "secret of God's face," that is, of His presence and of His will. But it is above all, a life of ceaseless praise.

Dom Gabriel, the abbot of this ancient monastery, was a friend of the great Benedictine Dom Guéranger and he stressed the liturgical character of the Cistercian life above all. That is one reason why a most valuable section of the *Soul of the Apostolate* is the one devoted to the liturgical life. Surely there is nothing more fundamental and nothing that is more closely interconnected with Dom Chautard's conception of Catholic Action as a reproduction of the life of the early Christians: and it was the earliest ages, especially the Patristic age, that were the most purely liturgical and, as we see from the writings of the Fathers, the fullest of pure charity, based on sacrifice, without which Catholic Action is a mockery.

But like so many White Monks before him, like St. Bernard and St. Peter of Tarentaise, Jean-Baptiste Chautard was not destined to taste for long the unmixed joys of contemplation. He was not yet solemnly professed, being still in the midst of his studies, and just ordained deacon, when Aiguebelle was faced with complete ruin.

Dom Gabriel had had some opportunity to estimate the young monk's practical ability, since Fr. Jean-Baptiste had been serving for some time as guest-master. The abbot took the bold step of sending him to Paris to try and use his ingenuity to save his community. But all Fr. Chautard's native ability and eloquence and learning and economics proved useless. Finally he threw himself down in prayer at the shrine of Our Lady of Victories. When, a half hour later, he emerged into the street, a stranger came up to him saying: "Are you not a Trappist? What brings you to Paris, Father? Can I be of any assistance to you?" The rest of the story can be guessed. Aiguebelle was saved. And Dom Chautard had his first real practical experience of the relative worth of natural activity, and activity aided by, and based on prayer.

The rest of the story of his life is a catalogue of activities that might appall a member of the most active Order in the Church.

After directing, as cellarer, the rebuilding of practically the whole monastery of Aiguebelle and the establishment of a chocolate factory there to provide a little revenue, he became abbot of Chambarand near Grenoble.

After the reunion of the various Trappist congregations in 1892 he was commissioned by the Abbot General, Dom Sebastian Wyart, to see to the repurchase of the old Mother House of the Cistercian Order, Citeaux, which he bought and made ready for occupancy. When Dom Sebastian moved into the Mother House, one of the most important abbeys of the Order, Sept-Fons, needed a new abbot. Dom Chautard was elected.

He made use of his right to refuse, but when Dom Sebastian appealed to the Pope, Leo XIII expressed his desire that Dom Chautard accept, and he yielded to the will of God.

Thus he became abbot of a house at once important and impoverished, and responsible for daughterhouses not only in France and Belgium, but in China, Japan, Palestine, and Australia. Soon he was to add another in Brazil. And the constitutions of the Order require that all such houses be often visited by their Father Immediate, though obviously he could not visit them all each year in person.

In 1901, when one of the frequent attacks against the

Church burst out again in France, Dom Chautard was chosen to represent the Cistercians of the Strict Observance in Paris. He put up such a good fight that Clemenceau, who was no friend of the Church, was nevertheless impressed with his sincerity and fearlessness, and the Order at large was spared. Others were by no means so fortunate.

During the First World War, besides his frequent visits to the monks who had been conscripted and sent to the front, Dom Chautard gave shelter at Sept-Fons to a community of Belgian Cistercians, another community from Palestine, the orphans from an asylum at Arras, and the inmates of an old men's home.

At the same time, Dom Chautard added to this a much more important work of mercy in the spiritual order. A magazine for French priests, conscripted and sent to the front, directed by him, attained such popularity and influence that it was continued with even greater fruit in the difficult period of readjustment that followed the war's end. At that time, these priests, exposed to great spiritual dangers by the moral and physical disintegration which they had seen at such close range, and by the unsettled state of the society to which they returned, needed nothing so much as the consolations and medicine of a doctrine like Dom Chautard's, which placed the greatest emphasis on the one source of all our strength: God's grace, obtained in ever greater abundance by a life of prayer and mortification.

No one was better qualified to help these priests adjust themselves to their difficult situation, and no one was better equipped to train them as good soldiers of Christ, in the active ministry, than this contemplative abbot who had been compelled, as it were, by Providence, to learn from experience the fruitfulness of an active life that had its roots deep in prayer and penance.

But Dom Chautard had long since arrived at the conclusions to which he was now giving his maturest expression.

In the persecution of the Church in France, under Clemenceau, in the early days of the century, Dom Chautard's keen eye had discovered a glaring inconsistency in the reaction of a certain type of Catholic leader. He observed that some priests, some organizers of Catholic Action, imagined that they could fight political enemies with more or less worldly and political weapons. In defending the Church against state persecution, they thought the most important thing was to gain and preserve political and social power. They believed that these gains could best be consolidated by a great material expansion. They expended all their efforts in running newspapers, holding conventions, publishing pamphlets and magazines, and above all, they measured the growth of Catholic life by the number of new school buildings, new Church buildings, new hospital buildings, new orphanages, new social centers. . . . As if the Church of God were built exclusively of bricks and mortar!

Such apostles tended to congratulate themselves when they had raised large sums of money, or when their Churches were filled with great throngs of people, without reference to what might be going on in the souls of all those who were present.

To the eyes of the Cistercian Abbot, a man who had learned his wisdom close to God, in the silence of the cloister, before the Tabernacle, there was a deep-seated and subtly pernicious error in all this. Were these the means to be emphasized in the defense of the King Whose Kingdom is not of this world, and Who said: "Seek ye first the Kingdom of God and His justice, and all these things shall be added unto you."[1]

---

1. *Matt.* 6:33.

Buildings, newspapers, meetings, conventions, all these things were important, vitally important. But they were not the one essential thing. And those who had become entirely absorbed in this work of more or less material growth, seemed to have lost sight of the fact that the Church is built of *living stones*. It is built of *saints*. And saints are made only by the grace of God and the infused virtues and the gifts of the Holy Ghost, not by speeches and publicity and campaigns which are all doomed to sterility without the essential means of *prayer and mortification*.

Dom Chautard saw, no doubt, that all this came from the subtle infection of Modernism and kindred heresies, bred of contact with a purely materialistic and secular culture. And he, like the saintly Pontiff under whose reign he was then living, saw that the only remedy was a return to the fundamentals of Christian Doctrine in all the power and beauty of their traditional presentation. The only thing that could save the Church was to base all work of reconstruction on the solid foundation of the Gospel as presented in the purity of Catholic Doctrine.

Consequently, Dom Chautard brought out, in 1907, a little pamphlet entitled *"L'Apostolat des Catechismes et de la Vie Interieure"* (*"The Apostolate of Catechism and the Interior Life"*). The title is self-explanatory. More important than all the methods based on modern publicity and display was the old traditional Christian technique of the formation of saints by personal contact and the teaching by word and example, in the charity of Christ. And the most vitally necessary thing in the regrowth of Christian life in countries where the Church was subject to state opposition and interference, was the solid and systematic teaching of the basic truths of our Faith by men and women deeply imbued with the interior life.

It was this little pamphlet that first presented the arguments that form the cornerstone of the present volume, and it was on this foundation that the holy abbot proceeded to build when his book was acclaimed on all sides by Catholic leaders, priests, bishops, and cardinals. The result was the first edition of *The Soul of the Apostolate*, which became one of the favorite spiritual books of Catholic priests, religious, and even laymen, in our time.

Not until after the First World War, however, did the book reach its present size, with the addition of the valuable sections on the Liturgical Life and Custody of the Heart. In its final form, it has been translated into all the most important languages of the world, and its multiple editions have run into many hundreds of thousands of copies.

Far from losing any of its popularity and usefulness, the *Soul of the Apostolate* recommends itself with ever more urgency in our time, when the world is barely recovering from the most frightful social cataclysm in the history of man, with no prospect of anything brighter in the future, if men do not learn to turn their steps in the directions pointed out in these pages: the path that was first shown to men by the incarnate Son of God.

What was Dom Chautard's own interior life? His book itself tells us enough on that score. In it we see the reflection of his own soul, a strong and simple faith and indomitable will to serve God in all things, profound and uninterrupted union with the Indwelling Trinity, an unconquerable love of Christ and of His Immaculate Mother: all these elements kept this sane and prudent and ardent priest on the safe and direct road to heaven, steering clear of the two equally noxious extremes of quietism (which he characterized as "perfumed jelly") and the heresy of works whose obstreperous addicts he condemned, characterizing them as "the heavyweights" (*les champions de boxe*).

The life of Dom Chautard was a life of labor, of sacrifice, in which perhaps the greatest sacrifice was to be constantly out of his beloved cloister, separated from his monastic community and above all from the delights of the liturgical life as lived from day to day by the Cistercian monks in their choir, which is the court of Jesus and Mary, the anteroom of heaven. In his later years, he was persecuted by ill-health, and spent many nights without sleep, in between his days of arduous work for his Order and for souls. But all this, far from breaking his morale and leading him into the morass of self-pitying discouragement, only intensified his union with God. What was his secret? A deep interior life, a profound and simple spirit of faith which was able to see God's will in all things— a charity, indeed, which was hungry, avid for that will, under whatsoever form it presented itself to him.

If there is one concept that is capable of summing up Dom Chautard's spirituality, it is one which is sometimes seen written, most appropriately, over the doors of Cistercian monasteries: "GOD ALONE." Not contemplation, not action, not works, not rest, not this or that particular thing, but God in everything, God in anything, God in His will, God in other men, God present in his own soul. To do whatever God willed, to suffer whatever He willed, that was enough for Dom Chautard, because all he asked was the opportunity to give himself, to give his will, utterly, without recall, to the infinite Wisdom and Love Who created and redeemed us all.

It is the spirit of St. Bernard, and the spirit of the White Monks. It is the spirit of Jesus Christ, the Son of God.

It is the spirit in which these pages were written.

WORDS OF POPE PIUS X

Pius X, in an audience granted in 1908 to Msgr. Cloutier, Bishop of Three Rivers, Canada, addressed the following words to the Bishop, who was laying before His Holiness his many projects for the good of his diocese:

"And now, my dear Son, if you desire that God should bless your apostolate and make it fruitful, undertake everything for His glory, saturate yourself and your devoted fellow-workers with the spirit of Jesus Christ, animating yourself and them with an intense interior lift. To this end, I can offer you no better guide than 'The Soul of the Apostolate,' by Dom Chautard, Cistercian Abbot. I warmly recommend this book to you, as I value it very highly, and have myself made it my bedside book."

AUTOGRAPH LETTER OF HIS HOLINESS POPE BENEDICT XV

to Dom J. B. Chautard, Abbot of the Trappist Monastery of Notre Dame de Sept-Fons, upon the receipt of his work entitled "L'Ame de Tout Apostolat."

Dearly Beloved Son:

We congratulate you sincerely upon having brought out so clearly the absolute necessity of the interior life for those engaged in good works, a life so necessary for the success of their ministry.

Expressing a wish that this work in which are found gathered together doctrinal lessons and practical advice suited to the needs of our times may continue to spend and do good.

We send with all Our heart to its esteemed author an affectionate Apostolic Blessing.

Given at the Vatican, March 18, 1915.

BENEDICT PP XV

OTHER TESTIMONIALS

His Eminence Cardinal VICO *sent, along with the letter of the Sovereign Pontiff, the following lines:*

I hasten to send you herewith the Parchment that our Holy Father, Pope BENEDICT XV, had kindly entrusted to me to transmit to you.

You will read in this revered autograph letter the great praise that His Holiness gives to your valuable book *L'Ame de Tout Apostolat*. The Holy Father has read this book with deep satisfaction.

Already PIUS X of holy memory had entrusted me with the care of expressing his warm congratulations to the pious prelate who translated your book into Spanish.

From His Eminence Cardinal SEVIN,

Your book is a golden book. I have read it eagerly. Never has Pius X met with a commentator more pious, more learned, more eloquent, more practical on the thoughts with which he has filled his Exhortation to the Clergy and twenty other Encyclicals.

You may be sure that I have made this treasure known around me. Your book is used in the spiritual readings of both my seminaries. To Bishops and to a number of priests I have expressed a sincere admiration for your work.

From His Eminence Cardinal MERCIER, *Archbishop of Mechlin*

The events in which I have just taken part did not allow me sufficient freedom of mind and the leisure that I should have had to read your book with the attention which it deserves and to fix my mind on the sublime thoughts that you have set forth with your apostolic ardour.

On looking over your book, I have been struck by the resemblance of your teaching with the main subject of a retreat that I preached in 1910 to the clergy of my diocese.

From His Eminence Cardinal VIVES,

It is no small merit to have been able in your excellent work on the interior life and the Apostolate to condense doctrine and practical methods. . . .

From His Eminence Cardinal FISCHER, Archbishop of Cologne

I fully approve of what you have written with so much learning, so much experience in this matter and so much unction.

From His Eminence Cardinal AMETTE, Archbishop of Paris

I read with much edification your book: *L'Ame de Tout Apostolat*, and I will be happy to recommend it to our priests and to zealous persons who devote themselves to good works. In Paris, especially, where the exterior work of the apostolate is so absorbing, it is of great importance to be always animated by that sap of the interior life which can alone assure its fecundity.

From His Eminence Cardinal LUCON, Archbishop of Reims

I appreciate the truth of the thesis which you develop and completely approve of it. . . .

From His Eminence Cardinal ARCOVERDE,
Archbishop of Rio de Janeiro

To put on Jesus Christ, to live the life of Jesus Christ, is the soul of every apostolate as you say in your excellent book. . . .

From His Excellency D. PENON,
Bishop of Moulins

Fresh and profound thoughts, impressive comments on several well known texts and on new texts taken from Holy Scripture and the Fathers, striking examples, most of them collected and vouched for by yourself in the good works with which you have been intimately connected, in fine and above all, the personal note, with which you show forth the fecundity of an apostolate, which results from the union of zeal and *piety by the Eucharistic and liturgical life,* add a more powerful attraction and assure a fuller efficacy to what you have already said so well in the first development of your fundamental thesis.

Priests, religious, both men *and women,* lay people interested in the apostolate, will have no pretext for doing without this *vade mecum. Zealous souls* especially may distribute it widely so that it may be for everyone's use, not for reading once only, but *habitually,* so that they may go back to it, employ it for *meditation,* that it may serve for annual and monthly retreats and also for the training of *seminarists* or *novices.* . . .

From His Excellency DR. MARRE,
*titular Bishop of Const., Abbot General
of the Reformed Cistercians*

Nothing has pleased me more than to hear about the new edition of your excellent book, *"L'Ame de Tout Apostolat."*

TABLE OF CONTENTS

PART ONE

ACTIVE WORKS AND THE INTERIOR LIFE: WHAT THEY MEAN

PART TWO

UNION OF THE ACTIVE LIFE AND THE INTERIOR LIFE

PART THREE

WITHOUT THE INTERIOR LIFE THE ACTIVE LIFE IS FULL OF DANGER: WITH IT, IT WILL GUARANTEE PROGRESS IN VIRTUE

PART FOUR

ACTION MADE FRUITFUL BY THE INTERIOR LIFE

PART FIVE

PRINCIPLES AND HINTS FOR
THE INTERIOR LIFE

The Soul
of the
Apostolate

PROLOGUE

EX QUO OMNIA,
            PER QUEM OMNIA,
                        IN QUO OMNIA[1]

O God, infinitely good and great, wonderful indeed are the truths that faith lays open to us, concerning the life which Thou leadest within Thyself: and these truths dazzle us.

Father all holy, Thou dost contemplate Thyself forever in the Word, Thy perfect image—Thy Word exults in rapt joy at Thy beauty—and, Father and Son, from Your joint ecstasy, *leaps forth* the strong flame of love, the Holy Spirit.

You alone, O adorable Trinity, are the interior life, perfect, superabundant, and infinite.

Goodness unlimited, You desire to spread this, Your own inner life, everywhere, outside Yourself. You speak: and Your works spring forth out of nothingness, to declare Your perfections and to sing Your glory.

Between You and the dust quickened by Your breath, there is a deep abyss: and this, Your Holy Spirit wishes to bridge. Thus He will find a way of satisfying His immense need to love, to give Himself.

---

1. Liturgy. Fifth antiphon of Matins for the Feast of the Most Holy Trinity—Quoted from *1 Cor.* 8:6.

And therefore He calls forth, from Your bosom, the decree that *we become divine*. Wonder of wonders! This clay, fashioned by Your hands, will have the power to be *deified*, and share in Your eternal happiness.

Your Word offers Himself for the fulfillment of this work. And He is made flesh, that we may become gods.[2]

And yet, O Word, Thou hast not left the bosom of Thy Father. It is there that Thy essential life subsists, and it is from this source that the marvels of Thy apostolate are to flow.

O Jesus, Emmanuel, Thou dost hand over to Thy apostles Thy Gospel, Thy Cross, Thy Eucharist, and givest them the mission to go forth and beget for Thy Father, sons of adoption.

And then Thou dost return, ascending, to Thy Father.

Thine, henceforth, O Holy Spirit, is the care of sanctifying and directing the Mystical Body of the God-man.[3]

Thou deignest to take unto Thyself fellow-workers, in Thy function of bringing, from the Head, divine life into the members.

Burning with Pentecostal fires, they will go forth to sow broadcast in the minds of all, the word that enlightens, and in all hearts the grace that enkindles. Thus will they impart to men that divine life of which Thou art the fullness.

*   *   *

O Divine Fire, stir up in all those who have part in Thy apostolate, the flames that transformed those fortunate retreatments in the Upper Room. Then they will be no longer mere preachers of dogma or moral theology, but men living to

---

2.   *Factus est homo ut homo fieret deus* (St. Augustine, Serm. 2 de Nativ.).
3.   *Deus, cujus Spiritu totum corpus sanctificatur et regitur*. Liturgy.

transfuse the Blood of God into the souls of men.

Spirit of Light, imprint upon their minds, in characters that can never be erased, this truth: *that their apostolate will be successful only in the measure that they themselves live that supernatural inner life of which Thou art the sovereign PRINCIPLE and Jesus Christ the SOURCE.*

O infinite Charity, make their wills *burn with thirst* for the interior life. Penetrate and flood their hearts with Thy sweetness and strength, and show them that, even here on this earth, there is no *real happiness* except in this life of imitation and sharing in *Thine own life* and in that of the *Heart of Jesus* in the bosom of the Father of all mercy and all kindness.

* * *

O Mary Immaculate, Queen of apostles, deign to bless these simple pages. Grant that all who read them may really *understand* that, if it please God to use their activity as an ordinary instrument of His Providence, in pouring out His heavenly riches upon the souls of men, this activity, if it is to produce any results, will have to *participate, somehow, in the nature of the Divine Act* as Thou didst behold it in the bosom of God when He, to Whom we owe the power of calling thee our Mother, became incarnate in the virginal womb.

PART ONE

ACTIVE WORKS AND THE INTERIOR LIFE: WHAT THEY MEAN

1. GOD WANTS GOOD WORKS AND, THEREFORE, HE WANTS ZEALOUS ACTION

Sovereign liberality is inseparable from the divine Nature. God is infinite goodness. Goodness seeks nothing except to *give itself* and to communicate the riches which it enjoys.

The mortal life of Our Lord was nothing else but a continual manifestation of this inexhaustible liberality. The Gospel shows us the Redeemer scattering along His way the treasures of love of a Heart eager to draw all men to truth and to life.

This apostolic flame has been passed on by Jesus to His Church, which is the gift of His love, which diffuses His life, manifests His truth, and shines with the splendor of His sanctity. Burning with the selfsame love, the Mystic Spouse of Christ carries on, down through the ages, the apostolic work of her divine Model.

How admirable the plan, the universal law laid down by

Providence, *that it is through men, that men* are to find out the way to salvation.[1] Jesus Christ alone has shed the Blood that redeems the world. Alone, too, He might have put its power to work, and acted upon souls directly, as He does in the Holy Eucharist. But He wanted to have others co-operate in the distribution of His graces. Why? No doubt His divine Majesty demanded that it be so, but His loving affection for men urged Him no less. And if it is seemly for the most exalted king to govern, more often than not, through ministers, what condescension it is for God to deign to give poor creatures a share in His work and in His glory!

Born, upon the Cross, from the pierced side of the Savior, the Church, by its apostolic ministry, carries on the bountiful and redeeming action of the man-God. This ministry, willed by Jesus Christ, becomes the essential factor in the diffusion of the Church among all nations, and the ordinary instrument of its great achievements.

In the front rank of this apostolate, stands the *clergy*, with its hierarchy forming the main body of the army of Christ, a clergy distinguished by so many holy, zealous bishops and priests, and covered with honor and glory by the recent canonization of the saint who was Curé of Ars.

Next to the official clergy, have risen, since the beginnings of Christianity, companies of *volunteers*, shock-troops, whose continued and abundant growth will always be one of the clearest signs of the vitality of the Church.

First of all, in the earliest centuries, came the contemplative orders, whose ceaseless prayer and fierce penances were

---

1. *Ad communem legem id pertinet qua Deus providentissimus, uti homines plerumque fere per homines salvandos decrevit . . . ut nimirum, quemadmodum Chrysostomus ait, per homines, a Deo discamus.* (Letter of Pope Leo XIII to Cardinal Gibbons, January 22, 1899.)

such a powerful aid in the conversion of the pagan world. In the Middle Ages, the preaching orders sprang up, with the mendicant and military orders, and those vowed to the ransom of captives in the powers of infidels. Finally, modern times have seen the birth of crowds of teaching institutes, missionary societies, congregations of all sorts, whose mission is to spread abroad every kind of spiritual and material good.

Then, too, at every stage of her history, the Church has received valuable help from the whole body of the faithful, like those fervent Catholics, whose name today is legion, tireless workers, ardent souls who know how to unite their forces and to devote, without stint, to the cause of our common mother, their time, abilities, and fortune, often sacrificing their liberty or their very lives.

A wonderful and encouraging sight, indeed, this providential harvest of works springing up just when they are most needed and in precisely the way that the situation seems to demand! Church history clearly proves that each new need, each new emergency to be faced, has invariably meant the appearance of the institution that the circumstances required.

And so, in our own day, we see a multitude of works that were scarcely even heard of, a generation ago, rise up in opposition to evils of the most serious kind: Catechism classes for first communicants and converts, as well as for abandoned children, all types of Catholic societies, sodalities, and confraternities, laymen's retreats for young and old of both sexes, Apostleship of Prayer, the Work of the Propagation of the Faith, Catholic action in student and military circles, Catholic press association and other works of both general and local usefulness. All these forms of apostolate are called into being by the spirit that burned in the soul of St. Paul: "But I most gladly will spend and be spent for your souls,"[2] the spirit that wishes to spread abroad, everywhere, the benefits of the Blood of Christ.

May these humble pages go out to the soldiers of Christ, who, consumed as they are with zeal and ardor for their noble mission, might be exposed, because of the very activity they display, to the danger of *not being, above all, men of interior life!* For such men, when the day comes for this deficiency in their lives, to be punished, by failures no one seems able to explain and by serious spiritual collapse, may well be tempted to give up the fight and retire, in discouragement, behind the lines.

The thoughts developed in this book have helped us, ourselves, to fight against an excessive exteriorization through good works. May they help others, also, to escape such a mishap, and lead the stream of their courageous action into better channels. May they show that we must never leave the God of works, for the works of God, and that St. Paul's: "Woe unto me if I preach not the Gospel"[3] does not entitle us to forget: "What does it profit a man, if he gain the whole world and suffer the loss of his own soul?"[4]

May these modest pages also reach those fathers and mothers of families who do not consider the *Introduction to the Devout Life* out of date, Christian husbands and wives who feel obligated to an apostolate towards one another as well as towards their children, in order to form them in the love and imitation of the Savior. For then they will better understand

---

2. *Ego autem libentissime impendam et superimpendar ipse pro animabus vestris* (*2 Cor.* 12:15).
3. *Vae mihi si non evangelizavero* (*1 Cor.* 9:16).
4. *Quid prodest homini si mundum universum lucretur, animae vero suae detrimentum patiatur?* (*Matt.* 16:26).

the need not only of a pious, but of an interior life, if their zeal is to have any success, and if they are to fill their homes with the unction of the spirit of Jesus Christ, and with that unchanging peace which in the face of every trial will always be a characteristic of the truly Christian family.

2. GOD WILLS THAT THE LIFE-PRINCIPLE OF OUR WORK BE CHRIST HIMSELF

Science is proud of its immense success, and justly so. And yet there is one thing which always has been, and always will be, impossible to it: to create life, to produce, from a chemical laboratory, a grain of corn, a larva. The wholesale discomfiture of the defenders of spontaneous generation shows us, clearly enough, how little there is in these claims. God reserves for Himself the power of creating life.

In the vegetable and animal order, living beings can grow and multiply: but still, their fecundity only operates under definite conditions laid down by the Creator. But as soon as there is question of intellectual life, God reserves this to Himself, and He is the One who directly creates the reasoning soul. And yet there is one other realm which he guards even more jealously still, that of *Supernatural life*, which flows from the divine life communicated to the humanity of the Incarnate Word.

Per Dominum nostrum Jesum Christum, Per Ipsum et cum Ipso et in Ipso.[5]

The Incarnation and Redemption establish Jesus as the Source, and the *only Source*, of this divine life which all men

---

5. Liturgy.

are called upon to share. The essential activity of the Church consists in spreading this life through the Sacraments, Prayer, Preaching, and all other works connected with these.

God does nothing except through His Son. "All things were made by Him and without Him was nothing made that was made."[6] True as this is in the natural order, how much more so is it in the supernatural order, when it is a question of imparting His inner life, and causing men to share in His own nature, making them children of God.

"I am come that they may have life. In Him was life. I am the life."[7] What precision there is in these words! And what light, in the parable of the vine and the branches, in which the Master develops this truth! With what insistence he strives to impress upon the minds of the Apostles the fundamental principle that HE ALONE, JESUS, IS THE LIFE, and the consequence that, in order to *share* in that life and *communicate* it to others, they must be grafted on to the God-man.

Men, called to the honor of working with the Savior in transmitting this divine life to souls, ought to consider themselves mere channels, whose function it is to draw from this one and only source.

Failure, on the part of the apostle, to realize this principle, and the illusion that he could produce the slightest trace of supernatural life without borrowing every bit of it from Jesus Christ, would lead us to believe that his ignorance of theology was equaled only by his stupid self-conceit.

If the apostle, while recognizing in theory that the Redeemer is the primary cause of all divine life, were to forget this truth

---

6. *Omnia per Ipsum facta sunt, et sine Ipso factum est nihil quod factum est* (*Joan.* 1:3).

7. *Veni ut vitam habeant. In Ipso vita erat. Ego sum vita* (*Joan.* 10:10; 1:4; 14:6).

in his actions and, blinded by insane presumption, were to insult Jesus Christ by relying on his own powers, it would be a lesser disorder than the preceding, but one just as insufferable in the sight of God.

To reject the truth, or to ignore it in one's actions, always constitutes an *intellectual disorder* in doctrine or in practice. It is the denial of a principle on which our conduct ought to be based. Obviously, the disorder will be still further aggravated if the clear light of truth is obscured and obstructed, in the heart of the active laborer, by his opposition, through sin or voluntary lukewarmness, to the God of all light.

Now for a man, in his practical conduct, to go about his active works as if Jesus were not his one end only life-principle, is what Cardinal Mermillod has called the "HERESY OF GOOD WORKS." He uses this expression to stigmatize the apostle who so far forgets himself as to overlook his secondary and subordinate role, and look only to his own personal activity and talents as a basic for apostolic success. Is this not, in practice, a *denial of a great part of the Tract on Grace?* This conclusion is one that appalls us, at first sight. And yet a little thought will show us that it is only too true.

HERESY IN GOOD WORKS! Feverish activity taking the place of God; grace ignored; human pride trying to thrust Jesus from His throne; supernatural life, the power of prayer, the economy of our redemption relegated, at least in practice, to the realm of pure theory: all this portrays no merely imaginary situation, but one which the diagnosis of souls shows to be very common though in various degrees, in this age of naturalism, when men judge, above all, by appearances, and act as though success were primarily a matter of skillful organization.

Even setting aside revelation altogether, the plain light of sane philosophy makes it impossible for us not to pity a man who, for all his remarkable gifts, refuses to recognize God as the principle of the marvelous talents that all observe in him.

What would be the feelings of a Catholic, thoroughly instructed in his religion, at the sight of an apostle who would boast, at least implicitly, that he could do without God in communicating to souls even the smallest degree of divine life?

"He is crazy!" we would say, if we heard an apostolic worker using such words as these: "My God, just do not raise any obstacle to my work, just keep out of my way, and I guarantee to produce the best results!" Our feelings would be a mere reflection of the aversion excited in God by the spectacle of such disorder: by the spectacle of presumption carrying its pride to such limits as to wish to impart supernatural life, to produce faith, to put an end to sin, incite men to virtue, and without attributing these effects to the direct, unfailing, universal, and overwhelming action of the Blood of God, the price, the cause, and the means of all grace and of all spiritual life.

Therefore, God owes it to the Humanity of His Son to make fools of these false Christs by paralyzing the works of their pride, or by allowing them to pass away as a momentary mirage.

Setting aside everything that works upon souls *ex opere operato*, God owes it to the Redeemer to withdraw from the apostle who is inflated with his own importance, all His best gifts, and to reserve these for the branch that humbly recognizes that all its life-sap comes from the Divine stock.

Otherwise, if He were to bless with deep and lasting results the work filled with the poison of this virus we have called the *Heresy of Good Works*, God might seem to be encouraging this abuse and favorings its contagious spread.

3. WHAT IS THE INTERIOR LIFE?

In this book the words *life of prayer, contemplative life* will be applied, as they are in the *Imitation of Christ* to the state of those souls who have dedicated themselves to a Christian life which is at the same time out of the common, and accessible to all, and, in substance, obligatory for all.[8]

Without embarking upon a study of asceticism, let us at least remind the reader that EVERYONE *is obliged to accept the following principles as absolutely certain, and base his inner life upon them.*

FIRST TRUTH. Supernatural life is the life of Jesus Christ Himself *in my soul*, by Faith, Hope, and Charity; for Jesus is the meritorious, exemplary, and final cause of sanctifying grace, and, as Word, with the Father and the Holy Ghost, He is its *efficient* cause in our souls.

The presence of Our Lord by this supernatural life is not the real presence proper to Holy Communion, but a presence of *vital action* like that of the action of the head or heart upon the members of the body. This action lies deep within us, and God ordinarily hides it from the soul in order to increase the merit of our faith. And so, as a rule, my natural faculties have no feeling of this action going on within me, which, however, I am formally obliged to believe by faith. This action is divine, yet it does not interfere with my free will, and makes use of all secondary causes, *events, persons*, and *things*, to teach me the will of God and to offer me

---

8. Although we are not here concerned with the phenomena that accompany certain extraordinary states of union with God, we are firmly persuaded that God, quite apart from such phenomena, frequently grants special graces of prayer to generous souls who thirst after a life of intimacy with Him.

an opportunity of acquiring or increasing my share in the divine life.

This life, begun in Baptism by the *state of grace*, perfected at Confirmation, recovered by Penance and enriched by the Holy Eucharist, is *my Christian life.*

SECOND TRUTH. By this life, Jesus Christ imparts to me *His Spirit.* In this way, He becomes the principle of a superior activity which raises me up, provided I do not obstruct it, to think, judge, love, will, suffer, labor with Him, by Him, in Him, and like Him. My outward acts become the manifestations of this life of Jesus in me. And thus I tend to realize the ideal of the INTERIOR LIFE that was formulated by St. Paul when he said: "I live, now not I, but Christ liveth in me."

Christian life, piety, interior life, sanctity: in all these we find no essential difference. They are only different degrees of one and the same love. They are the half-light, the dawning, the rising, and the zenith of the same sun.

Whenever the expression *"interior life"* is used in this book, the reference is not so much to *habitual* interior life, which we may call the "principal" or "capital" of the divine life deposited in us, by sanctifying grace, as to the *actual* interior life, which invests this capital and puts it to work in the activity of our soul, and in our fidelity to actual graces.

Thus I can define it as the *state of activity of a soul which strives against its natural inclinations in order to REGU-LATE them,* and *endeavors to acquire the HABIT of judging and directing its movements IN ALL THINGS according to the light of the Gospel and the example of Our Lord.*

Hence: a twofold movement. By the first, the soul withdraws from all that is opposed to the supernatural life in created things, and seeks at all times to be recollected: *aversio a creaturis.* By the second, the soul tends upwards to God, and unites itself with Him: *conversio ad Deum.*

The soul wishes in this way to be faithful to the grace which Our Lord offers to it *at every moment.* In a word, it lives, united to Jesus, and carries out in actuality the principle: "He that liveth in Me, and I in him, the same beareth much fruit.[9]

THIRD TRUTH. I would be depriving myself of one of the most effective means of acquiring this interior life if I failed to strive after a *precise* and *certain* faith in the active presence of Jesus within me, and if I did not try to make this presence within me, not merely a living, but an *extremely vital* reality, and one which penetrated more and more into all the life of my faculties. When Jesus, in this manner, becomes my light, my ideal, my counsel, my support, my refuge, my strength, my healer, my consolation, my joy, my love, in a word, my life, I shall acquire all the virtues. Then alone will I be able to utter, with sincerity, the wonderful prayer of St. Bonaventure which the Church gives me for my thanksgiving after Mass: *Transfige dulcissime Domine Jesu.*

FOURTH TRUTH. In *proportion* to the intensity of my love for God, my supernatural life may increase at *every* moment by a *new* infusion of the grace of the active presence of Jesus in me; an infusion produced:

1. By each *meritorious act* (*virtue,* work, suffering under all its varying forms, such as privation of creatures, physical or moral pain, humiliation, self-denial; prayer, Mass, acts of devotion to Our Lady, etc.).

2. By the *Sacraments* especially the Eucharist.

---

9.   *Qui manet in Me et Ego in eo, hic fert fructum tum (Joan.* 15:5).

It is certain, then (and here is a consequence that over-whelms me with its sublimity and its depth, but above all, fills me with courage and with joy), it is certain that, by *every* event, person or thing, Thou, Jesus, *Thou Thyself*, dost present Thyself, objectively, to me, at *every* instant of the day. Thou dost hide Thy wisdom and Thy love beneath these appear-ances and dost *request my co-operation to increase Thy life in myself.*

O my soul, at every instant Jesus presents Himself to you by the GRACE OF THE PRESENT MOMENT—every time there is a prayer to say, a Mass to celebrate or to hear, read-ing to be done, or acts of patience, of zeal, of renunciation, of struggle, confidence, or love to be produced. Would you dare look the other way, or try to avoid His gaze?

FIFTH TRUTH. The triple concupiscence caused by original sin and increased by every one of my actual sins establishes *elements of death* that militate against the life of Jesus in me. Now in *exact proportion* as these elements develop in me, they diminish the exercise of that life. Alas! They may even go so far as to destroy it outright.

Nevertheless, inclinations and feelings contrary to that life, and temptations, even *violent and prolonged* can do it no harm whatever as long as my will *resists them.* And then (what a consoling truth!) like any other elements in the spiri-tual combat, they serve only to augment that life, in propor-tion to my own zeal.

SIXTH TRUTH. If I am not faithful in the use of certain means, my intelligence will become blind and my will too weak to co-operate with Jesus in the increase, or even in the maintenance of His life in me. And the result will be a pro-gressive diminution of that life: I shall find myself slipping into *tepidity of the will.*[10] Through dissipation, cowardice, self-delusion, or blindness, I tend to compromise with venial sin. But therefore my whole salvation is in danger, since I am paving the way to *mortal* sin.

Were I to have the misfortune to fall into this tepidity (and a *fortiori* if I were to go lower still), I would have to make every effort to get out of it.   1) I would have to revive the *fear of God* in my soul by imagining myself, as vividly as possible, face to face with my last end, with death, with the judgment of God, with hell, eternity, sin, and so forth.   2) And to revive *compunction* by the sweet science of Thy wounds, O my merciful Redeemer. Going, in spirit, to Calvary, I would throw myself down at Thy holy feet and let Thy living Blood run down upon my head and heart to wash away my blindness, melt the ice in my soul, and drive away the torpor of my will.

SEVENTH TRUTH. I must seriously fear that I do not have the degree of interior life that Jesus *demands* of me:

---

10. This tepidity is clearly distinct from the dryness and even disgust which fervent souls experience in spite of themselves. For in that case, no sooner are the venial faults that escape us, through weakness committed, than we fight back, and detest them, and consequently show no evidence of *tepidity of the will.*

But the soul that is poisoned with this kind of tepidity manifests two opposing wills: one good, the other bad. One hot, the other cold. On one hand, it wants salvation, and therefore it avoids evident mortal sin; on the other hand it does not want what is demanded by the love of God. On the contrary, it wants all the comforts of a free and easy life, and that is why it allows itself to commit deliberate venial sins.

When this tepidity is not resisted, the very fact goes to show that there is in the soul a partial, though not total, bad will. That is to say, one part of the will says to God: "On such and such a point I do not want to cease displeasing You." (Father Desurmount, C.SS.R., *Retour Continuel a Dieu.*)

1. If I cease to increase my *thirst* to live in Jesus, that thirst which gives me both the desire to please God in all things, and the fear of displeasing Him in any way whatever. But I necessarily cease to increase this thirst if I no longer make use of the means for doing so: morning mental-prayer, Mass, Sacraments, and Office, general and particular examinations of conscience, and spiritual reading; or if, while not altogether abandoning them, I draw no profit from them, through my own fault.

2. If I do not have that minimum of *recollection* which will allow me, during my work, to *watch over my heart* and keep it pure and generous enough *not to silence the voice of Our Lord* when He warns me of the elements of death, as soon as they show themselves, and urges me to fight them. Now I cannot possibly retain this minimum if I make no use of the means that will secure it: liturgical life, aspirations, especially in the form of supplication, spiritual communion, practice of the presence of God, and so on.

Without this, *my life will soon be crawling with venial sins, perhaps without my being aware of it*, self-delusion will throw up the smoke screen of a seeming piety that is more speculative than practical, or of my ambition for good works, to hide this state from me, or even to conceal a condition more appalling still! And yet my blindness will be imputed to me as sin since, by failing to foster the recollection indispensable to it, I shall have fomented and encouraged its very cause.

EIGHTH TRUTH. My interior life will be no better than my custody of my heart. "Before all things keep a guard over thy heart, for from it springs forth life."[11]

---

11. *Omni custodia serva cor tuum, quia ex ipso vita procedit* (*Prov.* 4:23).

This custody of the heart is simply *a HABITUAL or at least frequent anxiety to preserve all my acts, as they arise, from everything that might spoil their motive or their execution.*

It is a peaceful, unexcited anxiety, without any trace of strain, yet powerful because it is based on childlike confidence in God.

It is the work of the heart and the will, rather than of the mind, which has to remain free to carry out its duties. Far from being an impediment to activity, the custody of the heart perfects it, by ordering it to the Spirit of God, and adjusting it to the duties of our state of life.

It is an exercise that can be carried on at any hour. It is a quick glance, from the heart, over present actions and a peaceful attention to all the various phases of an action, as we perform it. It is carrying out exactly the precept, *"Age quod agis."* The soul, like an alert sentry, keeps watch over every movement of its heart, over everything that is going on within it: all its impressions, intentions, passions, inclinations; in a word, all its interior and exterior acts, all its thoughts, words, and deeds.

Custody of the heart *demands* a certain amount of recollection: there is no place for it in a soul given to dissipation.

By frequently following this practice, we will gradually acquire the habit of it.

Quo vadam et ad quid? Where am I going and why? What would Jesus do? How would He act in my place? What advice would He give me? What does He want from me, at this moment? Such are the questions that spring up spontaneously in the soul that is hungry for interior life.

For the soul that goes to Jesus through Mary, this custody of the heart takes on a still more affectionate quality, and recourse to this dear Mother becomes a continual need for his heart.

NINTH TRUTH. Jesus Christ reigns in a soul that aspires to imitate Him seriously, wholly, lovingly. This imitation has two degrees: 1) The soul strives to become indifferent to creatures, considered in themselves whether they suit its tastes or not. Following the example of Jesus, it seeks no other rule, in this, but the will of God: "I came down from heaven not to do my own will, but the will of Him that sent me."[12] 2) The soul shows more readiness in doing things that are contrary to its nature, and repugnant to it. And thus it carries out the *agendo contra* that St. Ignatius speaks of in his famous meditation on the reign of Christ. It is acting against natural inclination in order to tend, by preference, to what imitates the poverty of the Savior, and His love for sufferings and humiliations. "For Christ did not please Himself."[13]

Following the expression of St. Paul, the soul then truly knows our Lord: "You have learned Christ."[14]

TENTH TRUTH. No matter what my condition may be, if I am only willing to pray and become faithful to grace, Jesus offers me every means of returning to an inner life that will restore to me my intimacy with Him, and will enable me to develop His life in myself. And then, as this life gains ground within me, my soul will not cease to *possess joy*, even in the thick of trials, and the words of Isaias will be fulfilled in me: "Then shall thy light break forth as the morning, and thy health shall speedily arise, and thy justice shall go before thy face, and the glory of the Lord shall gather thee up. Thou shalt call, and the Lord shall hear, thou shalt cry and He shall say:

---

12. *Descendi de coelo non ut faciam voluntatem meam sed ejus qui misit me* (*Joan.* 6:38).
13. *Christus non sibi placuit* (*Rom.* 15:3).
14. *Didicistis Christum* (*Eph.* 4:20).

'Here I am.' And the Lord will give thee rest continually, and will fill thy soul with brightness and will deliver thy bones, and thou shalt be like a watered garden, and like a fountain of water whose waters do not fail."[15]

ELEVENTH TRUTH. If God calls me to apply my activity not only to my own sanctification, but also to good works, I must establish this firm conviction, before everything else, in my mind: Jesus has got to be, and wishes to be, the life of these works.

My efforts, by themselves, are *nothing*, absolutely nothing. "Without Me you can do nothing."[16] They will only be useful, and blessed by God, if by means of a genuine interior life I unite them constantly to the life-giving action of Jesus. But then they will become *all-powerful:* "I can do *all things* in Him who strengtheneth me."[17] But should they spring from pride and self-satisfaction, from confidence in my own talents, from the desire to shine, they will be rejected by God: for would it not be a sacrilegious madness for me to steal, from God, a little of His glory in order to decorate and beautify myself?

This conviction, far from robbing me of all initiative, will be my strength. And it will make me really feel the need to pray that I may obtain humility, which is such a treasure for my soul, since it is a guarantee of God's help and of success in my labors.

Once I am really convinced of the importance of this principle, I will make a serious examination of myself, when I am on retreat, to find out: 1) if my conviction of the nothingness

---

15. *Is.* 58:8, 9, 11.
16. *Sine me nihil potestis facere* (*Joan.* 15:5).
17. *Omnia possum in eo qui me confortat* (*Phil.* 4:13).

of my own activity, left to itself, and of its power when united
to that of Jesus, is not getting a little tarnished; 2) if I am ruthless in stamping out all self-satisfaction and vanity, all self-
admiration in my apostolate; 3) if I continue unwaveringly
to distrust myself; 4) and if I am praying to God to preserve
me from pride, which is the first and foremost obstacle to His
assistance.

This *Credo* of the interior life, once it has become for my
soul the whole foundation of its existence, guarantees to it,
even here below, a participation in the joys of heaven.

The interior life is the life of the elect.

It fits in with the end God had in view when He created
us.[18]

It answers the end of the Incarnation: "God sent His only
begotten Son into the world that we may live by Him."[19]

It is a state of complete happiness: "The end of human
creatures is union with God; and in this their happiness
consists."[20] In this happiness, if thorns are seen from the outside, yet roses bloom within: but with the joys of the world
it is just the reverse. "How pitiable they are, the poor people
out in the world," the Cure of Ars used to say, "they wear,
over their shoulders, a mantle lined with thorns; they cannot
make a move without being pierced. But true Christians have

---

18. *Ad contemplandum quippe Creatorem suum homo conditus fuerat
    ut ejus speciem quaereret atque in soliditate amoris illius habitaret*
    (St. Gregory the Great, *Moralia*, viii, 12).

    Man was created for the contemplation of his Creator, in order that
    he might ever seek the vision of Him and dwell in the stability of His
    love.
19. *Filium suum unigenitum Deus misit in mundum ut vivamus per eum*
    (*1 Joan.* 4:9).
20. *Finis humanae creaturae est adhaerere Deo: in hoc enim felicitas ejus
    consistit* (St. Thomas Aquinas).

a mantle lined with soft fur." *Crucem vident, unuctionem non vident.*[21]

Heavenly state! The soul becomes a living heaven.[22]

Then, like St. Margaret Mary, it can sing:

Je possède en tout temps et je porte en tout lieu
Et le Dieu de mon coeur et le Coeur de mon Dieu.

(I ever possess, and take with me everywhere, the God of my heart and the Heart of my God.) It is the beginning of eternal bliss, *Inchoatio quaedam beatitudinis.*[23]

Grace is the seed of Heaven.

4. IGNORANCE AND NEGLECT OF THIS INTERIOR LIFE

St. Gregory the Great, who was as skillful an administrator and as zealous an apostle as he was great in contemplation, sums up in two words, *Secum vivebat* (He lived with himself), the state of soul of St. Benedict, when, at Subiaco, he was laying the foundation for that Rule which was to become one of the most powerful apostolic instruments God has ever used upon this earth.

But we are forced to say exactly the contrary of the great majority of our contemporaries. *To live with oneself, within*

---

21. They see the cross, but do not see the consolations. (Said by St. Bernard, of those who took scandal at the austerity of the Cistercian life).

22. *Semper memineris Dei, et coelum mens tua evadit.* (St. Ephrem). Ever be mindful of God, and your mind will become His heaven.

    Mens animae paradisus est, in qua, dum coelestia meditatur quasi in paradiso voluptatis delectatur (Hugh of St. Victor). The mind is the paradise of the soul, wherein, while it meditates upon heavenly things, it rejoices as though in a paradise of delights.

23. St. Thomas Aquinas. 2a 2ae, q. 180, a. 4.

oneself; to desire *self-control,* and not allow oneself to be dominated by exterior things; to reduce the imagination, the feelings, and even the intelligence and memory to the position of *servants of the will* and to make this will conform, without ceasing, with the will of God: all this is a program that is less and less welcome to a century of excitement that has seen the birth of a new ideal: *the love of action for action's sake.*

Any pretext will serve, if we can only escape this discipline of our faculties: business, family problems, health, good reputation, patriotism, the honor of one's congregation, and the pretended glory of God, all vie with one another in preventing us from *living within ourselves.* This sort of frenzy for exterior life finally succeeds in gaining over us an attraction which we can no longer resist.

Is there any reason to be surprised, then, that the interior life is neglected?

"Neglected" is putting it mildly. It is often enough despised and turned to ridicule by the very people who ought to be the first to appreciate its advantages and its necessity. This situation even called forth the celebrated letter of Leo XIII to Cardinal Gibbons,[24] in protest against the disastrous consequences of an exclusive admiration for active works.

Priests are so anxious to avoid the *effort required to live an interior life* that they reach the point of overlooking the value of *living with Christ, in Christ and through Christ,* and of forgetting that everything, in the plan of Redemption, is based on the *Eucharistic life* as much as it is upon the rock of Peter. The unconscious preoccupation of these partisans of a spirituality that is all noise and fanfare, is to thrust what is *essential*

---

24. The Apostolical Letter *Testem Benevolentiae,* January 22, 1899, addressed to his Eminence Cardinal Gibbons, Archbishop of Baltimore, on "True and False Americanism in Religion."

into the background. True, the Church has not yet become for them a Protestant chapel; the Tabernacle is not yet empty. But in their eyes, the Eucharistic life can hardly be adapted to the needs of modern civilization, still less can it suffice for its needs. The interior life, which is a necessary consequence of the Eucharistic life, has had its day.

For the people steeped in these theories, and their number is legion, Holy Communion has lost the true meaning which the early Christians were able to see in it. They believe in the Eucharist, yes; but they no longer see in it something absolutely necessary, both to their works and to themselves. We must not be astonished, then, that since they have lost nearly all ability to converse intimately with Jesus in the Blessed Sacrament, as with a friend, they have come to consider the interior life as a memory of the Middle Ages.

To tell the truth, to hear these mighty men of works talking about their exploits, one might imagine that God Almighty, to Whom it is child's play to create worlds, and before Whom the universe is dust and nothingness, cannot get along without their cooperation. Imperceptibly, a number of the faithful, and even of priests and religious, follow this cult of action to the point of making it a *kind of dogma* which inspires their attitude and all their actions, and leads them to throw themselves without restraint into a life of extroversion. "The Church, the diocese, the parish, the congregation, the work has need of me," we can almost hear them say, "God finds me pretty useful." And if no one dares come right out with such a piece of stupidity, nevertheless there exists, deep down in the heart, the presumption on which it is based and the lack of faith which fomented it.

Neurasthenics are often ordered to give up all work, and to do so for long periods at a time. The remedy is, to them, unbearable, precisely because their sickness keeps them in a state of feverish excitement, which, having become a sort of *second nature*, drive them mercilessly on to pour out their energy and their motions and thus to aggravate their disease.

That is how it often is with the man of active works, when he has to consider the interior life. He disdains, or, rather, he *detests* it all the more because it is the only remedy to his morbid state. Rather than live a life of prayer he will do his best to *stupefy* himself under an ever-increasing avalanche of badly managed enterprises, and thus to set aside all hope of cure.

Full steam ahead! And while the helmsman is admiring the rapidity of his progress, God sees that, since the pilot does not know his job, the ship is off the course and is in danger of being wrecked. What Our Lord is looking for, above all, is adorers in spirit and in truth. But these activistic heretics, for their part, imagine that they are giving greater glory to God in aiming above all at external results.

This state of mind is the explanation why, in our day, in spite of the appreciation still shown for schools, dispensaries, missions, and hospitals, devotion to God in its interior form, by penance and prayer, is less and less understood. No longer able to believe in the value of immolation that nobody sees, your activist will not be content merely to treat as slackers and visionaries those who give themselves, in the cloister, to prayer and penance with an ardor for souls equal to that of the most tireless missionary; but he will also roar with laughter at those active workers who consider it indispensable to snatch a few minutes from even the most useful occupations, in order to go and purify and rekindle their energy before the Tabernacle and to obtain from its Divine Guest, better results for their work.

5. REPLY TO A FIRST OBJECTION: IS THE INTERIOR LIFE LAZY?

This book is addressed to such active workers as are animated with a burning desire to spend themselves, but who are liable to neglect the necessary measures to keep their devoted work fruitful for souls, without wreaking havoc on their own inner life.

It is not our object to wake up those pretended apostles who make a fetish of repose; nor to galvanize those souls whose egotism deludes them into thinking that laziness will foster piety; nor to shake up the apathy of those lazy, sleepy drones who will accept certain works, in the hope of material advantage or of honor provided their quietude and ideal of tranquillity are in no way disturbed. Such a task would require a special volume.

Leaving to others, then, the job of bringing home to this apathetic brood the responsibilities of an existence that God *willed to be active* and which the devil, in collusion with nature, makes barren by inaction and lack of ambition, let us return to those beloved and respected colleagues for whom these pages are destined.

There is no metaphor capable of giving any idea of the infinite intensity of the activity going on in the bosom of Almighty God. Such is the inner life of the Father, that it engenders a Divine Person. From the interior life of the Father and Son proceeds the Holy Ghost.

The inner life that was communicated to the apostles in the Cenacle at once aroused them to zealous action.

To anyone who knows anything about it and who does not contrive to disfigure the truth, this interior life is a principle of devoted and self-sacrificing action.

But even if it did not reveal itself by outward manifestations, the life of prayer is, intimately and of itself, a *source of activity* beyond compare. Nothing could be more false than to consider it as a sort of oasis, offering itself as a refuge to those who want to let their life flow by in tranquil ease. The mere fact that it is the shortest road to the Kingdom of Heaven means that the text: "The Kingdom of Heaven suffereth violence, and the violent bear it away,"[25] is applicable in a most special manner, to the life of prayer.

Dom Sebastian Wyart[26] was familiar with the labors of the ascetic as well as with the trials of army life, the cares of the student, and the responsibilities inseparable from the office of a superior, and he used to say that there were three kinds of works:

1. The almost exclusively physical work of those who live by manual labor, by a craft, or in the army. And he declares that, no matter what one may think about it, this kind of work is the easiest of the three.

2. The intellectual toil of the scholar, the thinker, in his often arduous pursuit of truth; that of the writer, of the professor, who put everything they have into the effort to communicate all they know to others; of the diplomat, the financier, the engineer and so on, as well as the intellectual labor required of a general during a battle if he is to foresee and direct everything

---

25. *Regnum coelorum vim patitur, et violenti rapiunt illud* (*Matt.* 11:12).

26. Having served as an officer in the Papal zouaves defending Rome under Pius IX, he made profession as a Trappist at N. D. du Mont, in northern France. When the various Trappist congregations were united as the Order of Cistercians of the Strict Observance, Fr. Sebastian was elected first Abbot-General of the Order, and held this position for twelve years until his death in 1904.

and make the proper decisions. This labor in itself is, he said, far more difficult than the first kind, for there is a saying that "the blade wears out its sheath."

3. Finally, there is the labor of the interior life. And he did not hesitate to declare that of the three, this kind, when it is taken seriously, is by far the most exacting.[27] But at the same time, it is this kind that offers us the most satisfaction here on earth. It is likewise the most important. It goes to make up not so much a man's profession as the man himself. How many there are who can boast of great courage in the first two types of labor, which lead to wealth and fame, but who, when it comes to the effort to acquire virtue, are totally deficient in ambition, energy, or courage.

A man who is determined to acquire an interior life must take, for his ideal, unremitting domination of self and complete control over his environment, in order to act in all things solely for the glory of God. To achieve this aim, he must strive, under all circumstances, to keep united with Jesus Christ and thus to keep his eye on the end he has in view, and to evaluate everything according to the standard of the Gospel. *Quo vadam, et ad quid?* he keeps saying, with St. Ignatius.[28] And so, everything in him, intelligence and will, as well as memory, feelings, imagination, and senses, depends on principle. But to *achieve this result, what an effort it will cost him!* Whether he is mortifying himself or permitting himself some legitimate enjoyment, whether he is thinking or acting, at work or at rest, loving what is good or turning away in

---

27. *Major labor est resistere vitiis et passionibus quam corporalibus insudare laboribus* (St. Gregory the Great). Greater effort is required to resist our vices and passions than to toil in manual labor.
28. Where am I going, and for what?

repugnance from what is evil, whether he is moved by desire or by fear, joy or sorrow, fear or hope, whether he feels indignation or is calm; in all things, and always, he endeavors to keep his course dead ahead, in the direction of *God's good pleasure*. At prayer, and especially before the Blessed Sacrament, he isolates himself more completely than ever from all visible things, that he may come to converse *with the invisible God as if he saw Him*.[29]

Even in the midst of his apostolic labors he will manage to realize this ideal, which St. Paul admired in Moses.

Neither the troubles of life, nor the storms aroused by passion, will succeed in turning him aside from the line of conduct, he has laid down for himself. But on the other hand, if he does weaken for a moment, he pulls himself together at once, and presses forward with even more determination than before.

What a job! And yet it is not hard to understand how God rewards, even here below, with *special joys*, those who do not flinch at the effort which this work demands.

"Idlers?" Dom Sebastian concludes, "Are these true religious, or these truly interior and zealous priests idlers? Nonsense! Let the busiest men of affairs in the world come and take a look at our life, and see how their labors compare with ours!"

Who does not know this from experience? There are times when we might be inclined to prefer long hours in some exhausting occupation to half an hour of serious mental prayer, to an attentive hearing of Mass, or to the careful and intelligent recitation of the Breviary.[30]

---

29. *Invisibilem enim tamquam visibilem sustinuit* (*Heb.* 11:27).
30. Quotation from Dom Festugiere, O.S.B.: "Whatever the difficulties of the active life may be, only the inexperienced will deny the gruelling

Father Faber expresses his grief in admitting that for some people "the quarter of an hour after Communion is the weariest quarter hour of the day." When we have to make a three days' retreat, how unwilling some of us are! To withdraw for three days from a life which, though full of things to be done, is easy, and to *live on the supernatural plane*, making the supernatural sink into every detail of our existence during this retreat; to compel one's mind to see everything, during this time, by the light of faith alone, and one's heart to forget everything in order to seek Christ alone, and His life; to remain face to face with one's self and lay bare the infirmities and weaknesses of one's soul; to throw the soul into the crucible, and turn a deaf ear to all its cries of complaint: all this is a prospect which makes some people, otherwise ready to face any fatigue, turn tail and flee when there is no longer a question of an expenditure of merely natural energy.

And if only three days of such occupation may seem already so exhausting, what does nature think of the idea of an *entire life* to be *gradually* made subject to the rule of the interior life?

No doubt, in this labor of detachment, grace shoulders a great part of the difficulty, making the yoke sweet and the burden light. But still, what efforts the soul has to make! It always costs something to get back on the right road, and return to the rule that "our conversation is in heaven."[31] St. Thomas explains this very well. Man, he says, is placed in between the things of this world and spiritual goods, in which eternal happiness is to be found. The more he clings

---

trials of the interior life. Many active workers, pious men, admit that what costs them the most, in their life, is not so much action as their prayers of obligation. It is a relief for them to go to work."

31. *Conversatio nostra in coelis est* (*Phil.* 3:20).

to one, the more he recedes from the other and *vice versa*.[32]
When one side of the scale goes down, the other goes up just
as much.

Now since the disaster of original sin has upset the whole
economy of our being, it has made this double movement of
adhesion and recession extremely difficult to carry out. To
re-establish order and balance in this "little world," which is
man, and to preserve it by the interior life requires, since the
fall, work, suffering, and sacrifice. The building has caved in,
and has to be rebuilt and preserved from fresh collapse.

By constant vigilance, self-denial, and mortification, we
have to tear away from thoughts of earth a heart made heavy
with all the weight of a corrupted nature, *gravi corde*.[33] We
have to remake our character, in detail, in all those points in
which it is most unlike the physiognomy of Our Lord's soul;
for instance in its dissipation, bad temper, self-satisfaction, its
hardness of heart, egoism, lack of pity and kindness, and so
forth. We have to resist the allurement of pleasures that are
both sensible and present, for the hope of a spiritual happiness which we shall only loose from everything that can cause
us to love this world. We have to take all creatures, desires,
longings, concupiscences, exterior goods, self-will, and self-
judgment, and offer them up in a holocaust without reserve.
What a task!

And yet this is only the *negative* side of the interior life.
After this hand-to-hand fight that made St. Paul[34] groan and

---

32. *Est homo constitutus inter res mundi hujus et bona spiritualia, in*
    quibus aeterna beatitudo consistit, ita quod quanto plus inhaeret uni
    eorum, tanto plus recedit ab altero, et e contrario (1ae 2ae, q. 108, a. 4).
33. *Psalm 4.*
34. *Condelector enim legi Dei secundum interiorem hominem: video autem*
    aliam legem in membris repugnantem legi mentis meae, et captivantem

which Father de Ravignan expressed as follows: "You ask me what I did during my novitiate? Well, there were two of us. I threw the other fellow out the window, and then I was alone;" after this unremitting fight against an enemy always liable to rise from the dead, we must protect, against the slightest movement of return of the natural spirit, a heart which, purified by penance, is now consumed with the desire to make up for its insults to God. We must devote all our energies to keeping that heart fixed upon the invisible beauty of the virtues to be acquired, that we may imitate those of Christ. We must endeavor to maintain, even in the smallest details of life, an absolute confidence in Providence. And this is the *positive* side of the interior life. Anyone can guess the unlimited field of work that it opens up.

This labor is personal, steady, and constant. And yet it is precisely by this work that the soul acquires a wonderful facility and an astonishing rapidity in carrying out the duties of an apostle. This secret belongs to the interior life alone.

The immense labors accomplished, in spite of precarious health, by a St. Augustine, a St. John Chrysostom, a St. Bernard, a St. Thomas Aquinas, or a St. Vincent de Paul amaze us. But we are still more astonished to see how these men, in spite of their almost unceasing work, kept themselves in the most constant union with God. Quenching, more than others, their thirst at the source of life, by contemplation, these saints drew from it the most unlimited capacity for work.

This truth was well expressed by one of our great bishops, overburdened as he was with work, when he replied to a statesman, himself hard-pressed with his affairs, who asked

---

me in lege peccati, quae est in membris meis. Infelix ego homo; quis me liberabit de corpore mortis hujus? (Rom. 7:22–24).

him the secret of his constant serenity and of the astonishing results of his enterprises. "To all your occupations, my dear friend," said the Bishop, "add half an hour of meditation every morning. Not only will you get through all your business, but you will find time for still more."

Finally, do we not see St. Louis, King of France, finding in the eight or nine hours a day which he was in the habit of devoting to the exercises of the inner life, the secret and the strength to apply himself with so much attention to the affairs of state and the good of his subjects that a socialist orator admitted that never, even in our own time, had so much been done for the working class, as under the reign of this king?

6. REPLY TO ANOTHER OBJECTION: IS THE INTERIOR LIFE SELFISH?

Let us not speak of the lazy man or the spiritual glutton for whom the interior life consists in the delights of a pleasurable idleness, and who are much more avid for the consolations of God than for the God of consolations. They have only a false piety. But anyone who, either offhand or through stubborn conviction, calls the inner life selfish, does not understand it any better than they do.

We have already said that this life is the pure and abundant source of the most generous works of charity for souls and of charity which seeks to alleviate the sufferings of this world. But let us consider the usefulness of this life from another point of view.

Was the interior life of Mary and Joseph selfish and sterile? What blasphemy, and what absurdity! And yet they are credited with not one external work. The mere influence upon the world of an intense inner life, the merits of prayers and sacrifices applied for the spread of the benefits of the Redemption were enough to make Mary Queen of the Apostles and Joseph Patron of the Universal Church.[35]

"My sister hath left me alone to serve,"[36] (in Martha's words) the presumptuous idiot who sees nothing but his own exterior works and their result.

His stupidity and lack of understanding of the ways of God do not go to such lengths as to make him suppose that God could not get along without him. And yet he still loves to repeat with Martha, incapable of understanding the excellence of the contemplation of Magdalen, "Speak to her that she help me,"[37] and goes so far as to cry out, "To what purpose is this waste?"[38] condemning as loss of time the moments that his apostolic colleagues, more spiritual than he, reserve for contemplation, in order to solidify their interior life with God.

"And for them do I sanctify myself *that they also may be sanctified* in truth,"[39] the soul that has realized all the implications of the Master's phrase, "that *they also*," and who, knowing the value of prayer and sacrifice, unites to the tears and Blood of the Redeemer the tears of his own eyes and the blood of a heart that purifies itself more and more each day.

With Jesus, the interior soul hears the voice of the world's crime rising up to heaven and calling down chastisement upon the guilty; and this soul delays the sentence by the omnipotence of suppliant prayer, which is able to stay the hand of

---

35. In another chapter, we shall see that it is this interior life which gives works their fruitfulness.
36. *Soror mea reliquit me solam ministrare* (*Luc.* 10:40).
37. *Dic illi ut me adjuvet* (*Luc.* 10:4).
38. *Ut quid perditio haec?* (*Matt.* 24:8).
39. *Pro eis ego sanctifico meipsum ut sint et ipsi sanctificati in veritate* (*Joan.* 17:19).

God, just when He is about to let loose His thunderbolt.

"Those who pray," said the eminent statesman Donoso Cortes, after his conversion, "do more for the world than those who fight, and if the world is going from bad to worse, it is because there are more battles than prayers."

"Hands uplifted," said Bossuet, "rout more battalions than hands that strike." And in the midst of their desert, the solitaries of the Thebaid often had burning in their hearts the fire that animated St. Francis Xavier. "They seemed to some," said St. Augustine, "to have abandoned the world more than they should have." *Videntur nonnullis res humanas plus quam oportet deseruisse.* But, he adds, people forget that their prayers, purified by this complete separation from the world, were all the more powerful and more *NECESSARY for a depraved society.*

A short but fervent prayer will usually do more to bring about a conversion than long discussions or fine speeches. He who *prays is in touch with the FIRST cause.* He acts directly upon it. And by that very fact he has his hand upon all the secondary causes, since they only receive their efficacy from this superior principle. And so the desired effect is obtained both more surely and more promptly.

A single burning prayer of the seraphic St. Theresa (as was learned through a highly creditable revelation) converted ten thousand heretics. And her soul, all on fire for Christ, could not conceive of a contemplative life, an interior life, which would take no interest in the Savior's intense anxiety for the redemption of souls. "I would accept Purgatory until the Last Judgment," she said, "to deliver but one of them. And what do I care how long I suffer, if I can thus set free a single soul, let alone many souls, for the greater glory of God?" Speaking of her nuns, she said: "Bring to bear, my children, your prayers, your disciplines, your fasts, and your desires upon this apostolic object."

This, indeed, is the whole work of the Carmelite, the Trappistine, the Poor Clare. See how they follow the advance of the apostle, supplying him with the overflow of their prayers and penances. All along the line of the Cross's march, or of the Gospel's shining progress over the earth, their prayers sweep down from on high upon souls, their divine prey. Better still, it is their secret but active love which awakens the voice of mercy in every part of a world of sinners.

No one in this world knows the reason for the conversions of pagans at the very ends of the earth, for the heroic endurance of Christians under persecution, for the heavenly joy of martyred missionaries. All this is invisibly bound up with the prayer of some humble, cloistered nun. Her fingers play upon the keyboard of divine forgiveness and of the eternal lights; her silent and lonely soul presides over the salvation of souls and the conquests of the Church.[40]

"I want Trappists in this apostolic vicariate," said Msgr. Favier, Bishop of Peking, "I even desire them to abstain from all exterior ministry in order that nothing may distract them from the work of prayer, penance, and sacred studies. For I well know what a help will be given to our missionaries by the existence of our poor Chinese people." And later on he declared: "We have succeeded in penetrating into a district hitherto unapproachable. I attribute this fact to our dear Trappists."

"Ten Carmelite nuns, praying," said a Bishop of Cochin-China to the Governor of Saigon, "will be of greater help to me than twenty missionaries, preaching."

---

40. *Lumière et Flamme*, P. Léon, O.M.

Secular priests, religious, both men and women, vowed to the active, *but also to the interior life*, share this same power, with the souls in the cloister, over the heart of God. Father Chevier, Don Bosco, Père Marie Antoine; are striking examples of this. Venerable Anne-Marie Taigi, in her duties as a poor housekeeper, was an apostle, as was St. Benedict-Joseph Labre, shunning the beaten track. M. Dupont, the holy man of Tours, Col. Paqueron, and so on, all consumed with the same ardor, were powerful in their works because they were interior souls. And General de Sonis, between battles, found the secret of his apostolate in union with God.

Was the life of the Curé d'Ars selfish and sterile? Such a statement would only be worthy of silent contempt. Anyone able to judge in such matters knows that it was precisely the perfection of his intimate union with God that was the reason for the zeal and success of this priest without natural talents, but who, as contemplative as a Carthusian, thirsted for souls with a thirst that his inner life had made unquenchable. And he received from Our Lord, in Whom he lived, as it were, a participation in the divine power to make converts.

Was his inner life barren? Let us imagine a St. Vianney in every one of our dioceses. Before ten years, our country would be regenerated, and much more completely regenerated than it could be by any number of enterprises without firm foundation in the interior life, even if they were supported by unlimited funds and by the talent and activity of thousands of apostles.

Nowadays, the whole power of hell seems more than ever bent upon fighting the moral power of the Church and suffocating the divine life in souls.

Beyond all doubt, our chief reason for hoping that our world will rise triumphant, in the teeth of all these onslaughts, is that at no other time (or so it seems) has there been what we now see: so great a proportion of souls, even among the simple faithful, filled with ardent desires to live united with the Heart of Jesus and to extend His Kingdom, by scattering around them the seeds of interior life. Granted that these chosen souls are a tiny minority. But what do numbers matter, where there is intensity of such life? The fact that France got back on her feet after the revolution must be accredited to a priesthood that learned the interior life the hard way, by persecution. But through these men a current of *divine life* came to enliven a generation which seemed condemned to death by apostasy and an indifference which no human power seemed able to overcome.

And yet now, after fifty years of freedom of education in France, after this half-century that has beheld the birth of works without number, and during which we have had, in our hands, the youth of the land, and have enjoyed the almost complete support of the various governments, how is it that, in spite of results that appear, outwardly, to be quite striking, we have been unable to form, in our nation, a majority with enough real Christianity in it to fight against the coalition of the followers of Satan?

No doubt, the abandonment of the liturgical life and the cessation of its influence upon the faithful have contributed to this impotence. Our spirituality has become narrow, dry, superficial, external, or altogether sentimental; it does not have the penetration and soul-stirring power that only the Liturgy, that great source of Christian vitality, can give.

But is there not another cause to be traced to the fact that we priests and educators, because we lack an intensive inner life, are unable to beget in souls anything more than a surface piety, without any powerful ideals or strong convictions?

Those of us who are professors: have we not, perhaps, been more ambitious for the distinction of degrees and for the reputation of our colleges than to impart a solid religious instruction to souls? Have we not worn ourselves out on less important things than forming of wills, and imprinting on well-tried characters the stamp of Jesus Christ? And has not the most frequent cause of this mediocrity been the *common banality of our inner life?*

If the priest is a saint (the saying goes), the people will be fervent; if the priest is fervent, the people will be pious; if the priest is pious, the people will at least be decent. But if the priest is only decent, the people will be godless. The spiritual generation is always one degree less intense in its life than those who beget it in Christ.

We would not go so far as to accept this proposition, but we consider that the following words of St. Alphonsus sufficiently well express the *cause* to which we may attribute the responsibility for our present situation:

"The good morals and the salvation of the people depend on good pastors. If there is a good priest in charge of the parish, you will soon see devotion flourishing, people frequenting the Sacraments, and honoring the practice of mental prayer. Hence the proverb: like pastor, like parish: *Qualis pastor, talis parochia.* According to this word of Ecclesiasticus (10:2) 'Those who dwell in the state, take after their ruler': *Qualis est rector civitatis tales et inhabitantes in ea.*" (Homo Apost., 7:16.)

7. NO CONFLICT BETWEEN THE INTERIOR LIFE AND THE SALVATION OF SOULS

But now the extrovert, in search of arguments against the interior life, will complain: how can I dare to curtail my active works? Can I possibly do too much, when the salvation of souls is at stake? Do I not make up for everything in my activity, and amply too, by my sublime self-sacrifice? Work is prayer. Sacrifice excels prayer. And does not St. Gregory call the zeal for souls the most pleasing sacrifice anyone could offer to God? *Nullum sacrificium est Deo magis acceptum quam zelus animarum?* (Hom. 12, in *Ezech.*)

First of all, let us fix the exact sense of St. Gregory's words, in the terms of the Angelic Doctor. "To offer sacrifice spiritually to God," he says, "is to offer Him something that gives Him glory." Now of all goods, the most pleasing that man can offer to God is, undeniably, the salvation of a soul. But every one must *first* offer *his own soul*, according to what is said in Scripture: 'If you wish to please God, have pity on your own soul.' When this first sacrifice has been consummated, *then* will it be permitted us to procure the same joy for others. The more closely a man unites first *his* own soul, and then that of another, to God, the more acceptable is his sacrifice. But this intimate and generous, as well as humble union, can only be effected *by prayer*. To apply oneself to a life *of prayer*, or to lead others to give themselves to it, is, therefore, more pleasing to God than to devote oneself to activity and good works, and lead others to practice these. "And so," the Angelic Doctor concludes, "when St. Gregory affirms that the most pleasing sacrifice to God is the salvation of souls, he does not mean by that *to give the active life preference over contemplation,*

but he is only saying that to offer to God one single soul gives
Him infinitely more glory and obtains, for ourselves, much
more merit than if we gave Him all that is most precious on
this earth."[41]

The necessity of the interior life is so far from being an
obstacle to zealous activity in generous souls, to whom the
clearly recognized will of God makes it a duty to accept the
responsibility for such works, that it would be the greatest
possible mistake for such persons to renounce this work, or
give themselves to it halfheartedly, or even desert the field of
battle under pretext of taking greater care of their souls and
arriving at a more perfect union with God. In some cases, such
a course would lead to grave danger. "Woe unto me," says
St. Paul, "if I preach not the Gospel."[42]

Once this reservation has been made, however, we must at
once add that it would be an even greater mistake to devote
oneself to the conversion of souls while forgetting one's own
salvation. God wants us to love our neighbor as ourselves, but
never more than ourselves, that is, never to such an extent that
we harm our own souls. And in practice, this is as much as if
He demanded that we take more care of our own soul than of
those others, since our zeal must be regulated by charity, and
"*Prima sibi charitas*"[43] is an axiom of theology.

"I love Jesus Christ," said St. Alphonsus Liguori, " and that
is why I am on fire with the desire to give Him souls, *first of
all my own*, and then an incalculable number of others." This
is a practical application of St. Bernard's *Tuus esto ubique*[44]
and that other principle of the holy abbot of Clairvaux:

41. St. Thomas Aquinas 2a 2ae, q. 182, a2, ad 3.
42. *1 Cor.* 9:16.
43. Charity for oneself first (Charity begins at home).
44. "In all places, belong to yourself."

"No man is truly wise, who is not wise for himself."[45]

St. Bernard, who was himself a rare miracle of apostolic zeal, followed this rule. Geoffrey of Auxerre, his secretary, depicts him as: *Totus primum sibi et sic totus omnibus.* "He belonged, first of all, entirely to himself, and thus he belonged entirely to all men."[46] "I do not tell you," writes the same saint to Pope Bl. Eugenius III, "to withdraw completely from secular operations. I only exhort you not to throw yourself entirely into them. If you are a man belonging to everybody, belong also to yourself. Otherwise what good would it do you to save everybody else, if you were to be lost yourself? Keep something, then, for yourself, and if everyone comes to drink at your fountain, do not deprive yourself of drinking there too. What! Must you alone go thirsty? Always begin with the consideration of yourself. *It would be vain for you to lavish care upon others, and neglect yourself.* May all your reflections, then, *begin with yourself, and end, also with yourself.* Be, for yourself, the first and last, and remember that in the business of winning salvation, no one is closer to you than your mother's only son."[47]

Very suggestive is this retreat note of Bishop Dupanloup, of Orleans: "My activities are so crushing that they ruin my health, disturb my piety and yet teach me nothing new. I have got to control them. God has given me the grace to recognize that the big obstacle to my acquiring a peaceful and fruitful interior life is my natural activity, and my tendency to be

---

45. *Non, ergo sapiens, qui sibi non est* (St. Bernard, *De Consideratione,* ii:3).

46. *Gaufridus*, Vita Bernardi.

47. *A te tua inchoetur consideratio ne frustra extendaris in alia, te neglecto . . . Tu tibi primus, tu ultimus . . . in acquisitione salutis nemo tibi gerinanior est unico matris tuae* (St. Bernard loc. cit.).

carried away by my work. And I have recognized, besides, that this *lack of interior life* is the source of all my faults, all my troubles, my dryness, my fits of disgust, and my bad health.

"I have therefore resolved to direct *all my efforts* to acquiring this interior life which I so badly need, and I have, with God's grace, drawn up the following points with that end in view:

"1. I will always take more time than is necessary, to do everything. This is the way to avoid being in a hurry and getting excited.

"2. Since I invariably have more things to do than time in which to do them, and this prospect preoccupies me and gets me all worked up, I will cease to think about all that I have to do, and only consider the time I have at my disposal. I will make use of that time, without losing a moment of it, beginning with the most important duties; and as regards those that may or may not get done, I shall not worry about them."

A jeweler will prefer the smallest fragment of diamond to several sapphires; and so, in the order established by God, our intimacy with Him gives Him more glory than all possible good, procured by us, for a great number of souls, but to the detriment of our own progress. Our Heavenly Father, "who devotes Himself more to the direction of a soul in which He reigns, than to the natural government of the whole universe and to the civil government of all empires,"[48] looks for this harmony in our zeal.

He prefers sometimes to let an enterprise go by the board, if He sees it becoming an obstacle to the charity of the soul engaged in it.

_____

48. P. Lallamant, *Doct. Spirit.*

But as for Satan, he, on the contrary, does not hesitate to encourage a purely superficial success, if he can by this success prevent the apostle from making progress in the interior life: so clearly does his rage guess what it is Our Lord values most highly. To get rid of a diamond, he is quite willing to allow us a few sapphires.

PART TWO

UNION OF THE ACTIVE LIFE AND THE INTERIOR LIFE

1. THE PRIORITY OF THE INTERIOR OVER THE ACTIVE LIFE IN THE EYES OF GOD

In God is life, all life. He is life itself. Yet it is not by exterior works, by the creation, for instance, that the infinite Being manifests this life in its most intense form, but rather by what theology calls *operationes ad intra*, by that ineffable activity of which the term is the perpetual generation of the Son and the unceasing procession of the Holy Spirit. Here, preeminently, is His eternal, His essential work.

Let us consider the mortal life of Our Lord, a perfect realization of the divine plan. Thirty years of recollection and solitude, then forty days of retreat and penance are the prelude to His brief evangelical career. How often, too, during His apostolic journeys, we see Him retiring to the mountains or the desert to pray: "He retired into the desert and prayed,"[1] or

---

1. *Secedebat in desertum et orabat* (*Luc.* 5:16).

passing the night in prayer: "He passed the whole night in the prayer of God."[2]

Still more striking is the example of Our Lord's reply to Martha who, desiring Jesus to condemn the supposed laziness of her sister, meant that He should proclaim the superiority of the active life. But Jesus said: "Mary hath chosen the better part,"[3] a reply which definitely establishes the pre-eminence of the interior life. What is to be concluded from this, if not that it was His express intention to show us, in this way, the superiority of the life of prayer over the life of action?

After the Master, the Apostles, faithful to His example, take upon themselves, first of all the duty of prayer; and then, after that, in order to devote themselves to their preaching ministry, they leave to the deacons all other, more external, duties. "We will give ourselves continually to prayer and to the ministry of the word."[4]

In their turn, Popes, holy doctors of the Church, and theologians affirm that the interior life is, of itself, superior to the active life.

Not many years ago a woman of faith, of virtue, and of great character, superior general of one of the most important teaching congregations in the Aveyron district of central France, was invited by her superiors to consent to the secularization of her nuns.

What should they do: sacrifice the religious life in order to continue teaching, or abandon their active work in order to keep their status as religious? Perplexed, and not knowing how to find out what was God's will in the matter, she left secretly for Rome, was granted an audience with Leo XIII,

---

2. *Pernoctans oratione Dei* (*Luc.* 6:12).

3. *Maria optimam partem clegit* (*Luc.* 10:42).

4. *Nos vero orationi et ministerio verbi instantes erimus* (*Acts* 6:4).

and placed before him her doubts, explaining what great pressure was being put upon her, in favor of active works.

The venerable pontiff, after a few moments of recollection, gave her this categorical reply: "Before everything else, before any kind of work, keep the religious life for those of your daughters who really possess the spirit of their holy state, and who really love the life of prayer. And if you cannot keep both your life of prayer and your active work, God will find a way to raise up other workers, in France, if they are necessary. As for you, by your interior life, above all by your prayers and sacrifices, you will be more useful to France by remaining true religious, although exiled from her, than you would by staying in your native land, though deprived of the treasure of your consecration to God."

In a letter addressed to a great religious institute, exclusively devoted to teaching, Pius X flatly declared his views on this subject in the following words:

"We learn that an opinion is current to the effect that you ought to put in the front rank the education of the young, and leave your religious profession in the second place, on the grounds that the spirit and the needs of the time make this necessary. *It is altogether against our wish* that such an opinion should receive any weight with you, or with any other religious institute which, like yours, has education as its object. Let it be taken as a firmly established truth, as far as you are concerned, that the religious life is vastly superior to the common life, and that even if you have grave obligations to your neighbor, in your duty to teach, far more grave still are the obligations that bind you to God."[5] But is not the

---

5. *Omnino nolumus aped vos caeterosque vestri similes, quorum religiosum munus est erudire adolescentulos, ea, quam pervulgari audimus, quidquam valeat institutioni puerili primas vobis dandas esse*

whole reason for the religious life, and its principal object, the acquiring of an inner life?

Vita contemplativa, says the Angelic Doctor, *simpliciter melior est . . . et potior quam activa*. "The contemplative life is by its very nature better and more effective than the active life."[6]

St. Bonaventure accumulates comparatives to demonstrate the excellence of this inner life: *Vita sublimior, securior, opulentior, suavior, stabilior*. "A life that is more sublime, more secure, richer, pleasanter, and more stable."

Vita sublimior

The active life is concerned with men, the contemplative introduces us into the realm of the highest truth, and never turns aside its gaze from the very principle of all life. *Principium, quod Deus est, quaeritur*. Being more sublime, it has a much more extensive horizon and field of action. "Martha, in one place, was busy in bodily work, with a few things. Mary, by her charity in many places, accomplished many things. For she, in the contemplation and love of God, beholds everything; her heart goes out to everything, comprehends and embraces

---

religiosae professioni secundas, idque aetatis hujus et ingenio necessitatibus postulari . . . Itaque in causa vestra illud maneat religiosae vitae genus longe communi vitae praestare: atque si magno obstricti estis erga proximos officio docendi, multo majora esse vincula quibus Deo obligamini (H. H. Pius X). However, to give up temporarily, the religious habit in order to keep a work going is not here blamed by Pius X, provided that every means is taken to preserve, in all things, the religious spirit.

6.   *Summa Theol.* 2 2ae, q. 182. a. 1.

In this article St. Thomas gives nine cogent reasons why the contemplative life is simply better than the active.

all, so that, by comparison with her, it can be said that Martha is troubled over only a *few things.*"[7]

Vita securior

There is less danger. In a life that is almost exclusively active, the soul is excited, worked up, scatters its energies and, by that very fact, weakens itself. It has a threefold defect: *sollicita es*[8] (thou art careful), it is worried with mental problems, *sollicitudines in cogitatu; turbaris* (thou art troubled), and here are the troubles that stir up the passions, *turbationes in affectu*; finally, *erga plurima* (about many things), occupations are multiplied, and so our energy and our action is divided: *divisiones in actu.* But for the interior life one thing alone is necessary: union with God. *Porro unum est necessarium.* All the rest can only be secondary, something accomplished solely by virtue of this union and in order to strengthen it more and more.

Vita opulentior

Contemplation brings with it all the other good things. "All good things came to me together with her."[9] It is the better part,[10] above all others. Contemplation overflows with much greater merits. Why? Because at the same time it increases the

---

7. *Martha in uno loco corpore laborabat circa aliqua, Maria in multis locis caritate circa multa. In Dei enim contemplatione et amore videt comprehendit et complectitur omnia, ita ut ejus comparatione. Martha sollicita dici potest circa pauca* (Richard of St. Victor. in *Cant.* 8).
8. *Martha, Martha, sollicita es et turbaris erga plurima, porro unum est necessarium* (*Luc.* 10:41, 42)
9. *Venerunt mihi omnia bona pariter cum illa* (*Sap.* 7:11).
10. *Optimam partem elegit quae non auferetur ab ea* (*Luc.* 10:42).

zest of the will and the degree of sanctifying grace in the soul, and makes the soul act with love as its motive power.

Vita suavior

The truly interior soul abandons itself to the good pleasure of God, and accepts with the same patience and evenness of heart both what is pleasing and what brings pain: indeed, it goes so far as to be joyful under affliction, and happy to carry the Cross.

Vita stabilior

No matter how intense it may be, the active life has its limit here below. Preaching, teaching, works of every sort all come to an end at the threshold of eternity. But the interior life will never cease: "Which shall not be taken away from her." Through this life, our stay here below becomes a continual ascent towards the world of light, an ascent which death only makes incomparably more radiant and more rapid.

One may sum up the perfections of the interior life by applying to it St. Bernard's words: "In this life man lives more purely, falls more rarely, recovers more promptly, advances more surely, receives more graces, dies more calmly, is more quickly cleansed, and gains a greater recompense."[11]

---

11. *Haec* (vita) *sancta, pura et immaculata, in qua homo vivit purius, cadit rarius, surgit velocius, incedit cautius, irrogatur frequentius, quiescit securius, moritur fiducius, purgatur citius, praemiatur copiosius* (St. Bernard. *Hom. Simile es . . . homini neg.*).

2. GOOD WORKS SHOULD BE NOTHING BUT AN OVERFLOW FROM THE INNER LIFE

"Be ye therefore perfect as your heavenly Father is perfect" (*Matt.* 5:48). With all due proportion, the way that God acts ought to be the criterion and the rule both of our interior and exterior life.

However, as we already know, it is God's nature to give, and experience teaches us that here below He spreads His benefits in profusion over all creatures and, especially, upon human beings. And so, for thousands and perhaps millions of centuries, the entire universe has been the object of this never failing prodigality, which pours it out in ceaseless gifts. And yet God is nothing the poorer, and this inexhaustible munificence cannot, in any way whatever, diminish His infinite resources.

To man, God does more than grant exterior gifts: He sends him also His Word. But here again, in this act of supreme generosity which is nothing else but the gift of Himself, God abandons and can abandon none of the integrity of His nature. In giving us His Son, He keeps Him, nevertheless, ever in Himself. "Take, as an example, the All-Highest Father of all, sending us His Word, and at the same time keeping Him for Himself."[12]

By the Sacraments, and especially by the Eucharist, Jesus Christ comes down to enrich us with His grace. He pours it out upon us without measure, for He also is a limitless ocean whose fullness overflows upon us without ever being exhausted. "Of His fullness we have all received."[13]

---

12. *Sume exemplum de summo omnium Parente Verbum suum emittente et retinente* (St. Bernard, *De Consideratione*, II, c. 3).

13. *De plenitudine ejus nos omnes accepimus* (*Joan.* 1:16).

And so we ought to be, in some manner, apostolic men who take upon ourselves the noble task of sanctifying others: " Your 'word' is your consideration. If it go forth from you let it still remain."[14] Yes, our "word" is the interior spirit formed, by grace, in our souls. Let this spirit, then, give life to all the manifestations of our zeal, but, though poured out unceasingly for the benefit of our neighbors, let it be renewed likewise without ceasing, by the means which Jesus offers us for this purpose. Our interior life ought to be the stem, filled with vigorous sap, of which our works are the flowers.

The soul of an apostle—it should be flooded first of all with light, and inflamed with love, so that, reflecting that light and that heat, it may enlighten and give warmth to other souls as well. That which they have heard, which they have seen with their eyes, which they have looked upon, and their hands have almost handled, this will they teach to men."[15]

Their lips will pour forth into souls the abundance of celestial joys, says St. Gregory.

Now, therefore, we can deduce the following principle:

The life of action ought to flow from the contemplative life, to interpret and extend it, outside oneself, though at the same time being detached from it as little as possible.

The Fathers and Doctors of the Church vie with one another in proclaiming this doctrine.

"Before allowing his tongue to speak," says St. Augustine, "the apostle should lift up his thirsting soul to God, in order

---

14. *Verbum tuum consideratio tua, quae si procedit, non recedat* (St. Bernard, *De Consideratione*, II, 3).
15. *1 Joan.* 1:1.

to give forth what he has drunk in, and pour forth that with which he is filled."[16]

Before giving, says the Pseudo-Denys,[17] one must first receive, and the higher angels only transmit to the lower the lights of which they have received the fullness. The Creator has established this universal order with respect to divine things: the one whose mission it is to distribute these things must first share them and fill himself abundantly with the graces that God wishes to give to souls through his intermediary. Then, and then only, will it be permitted him to share them with others.

Is there anyone who does not know St. Bernard's saying, to apostles: "If you are wise, you will be reservoirs and not channels." *Si sapis, concham te exhibebis et non canalem*? (Serm. xviii in *Cant.*) The channels let the water flow away, and do not retain a drop. But the reservoir is first filled, and then, without emptying itself, pours out its overflow, which is ever renewed, over the fields which it waters. How many there are devoted to works, who are never anything but channels, and retain nothing for themselves, but remain dry while trying to pass on life-giving grace to souls! "We have many channels in the Church today," St. Bernard added, sadly, "but very few reservoirs."[18]

---

16. *Priusquan exerat proferentem linguam ad Deum levet animam sitientem ut eructet quod biberit, vel quod impleverit fundat* (St. Augustine. *De Doctrina Christiana*, Book IV).
17. *De Coel. Hier.*, c. iii.
18. *Canales multas hodie habemus in Ecclesia, conchas vero perpaucas* (St. Bernard, Serm. xviii in *Cantica*).

Every cause is superior to its effect, and therefore more perfection is needed to make others perfect, than simply to perfect oneself.[19]

As a mother cannot suckle her child except in so far as she feeds herself, so confessor, spiritual directors, preachers, catechists, professors must first of all *assimilate* the substance with which they are later to feed the children of the Church.[20] Divine truth and love are the elements of this substance. But the interior life alone can transform divine truth and charity in us, to a truly life-giving nourishment for others.

3. ACTIVE WORKS MUST BEGIN
AND END IN THE INTERIOR LIFE,
AND, IN IT, FIND THEIR MEANS

Of course, we speak only of active works that are worthy of the name of "works." In our day, there are not a few that do not deserve this title at all. They are a species of enterprise, organized under a pious front, but with the real aim of acquiring, for their initiators, the applause of the public, and a reputation for an extraordinary ability. And these men are determined to achieve the success of such enterprises at any cost, even that of using the least justifiable of means.

Other works there are which, it is true, deserve a little more respect. Their intention, at least, is good. Their end and their

---

19. *Manifestum est autem majorem perfectionem requiri ad hoc quod aliquis perfectionem aliis tribuat quam ad hoc ut aliquis in se ipso perfectus sit, sicut majus est posse facere aliquem talem quam esse talem et omnis causa potior est suo effectu* (St. Thomas Aquinas, *Opusc. de Perfec. Vitae Spir.*).

20. *Oportet quod praedicator sit imbutus et dulcoratus in se. et post aliis proponat* (St. Bonaventure, *Illus. Eccl.*, Serm. xvii).

means are beyond reproach. And yet, because their organizers have little more than a wavering faith in the power of the
supernatural life to act upon souls, their results, in spite of
great efforts, are either totally, or at any rate almost totally,
futile.

To give a precise idea of what a good work ought to be,
let us quote a man whose apostolic work is the pride of his
district, and recall the lessons he gave to us at the beginning
of our priestly ministry. We were interested in the formation
of a club for young men. Having visited the Catholic clubs
of Paris and a few other French cities, the work going on at
Val-des-Bois, and so on, we went to Marseilles to study the
work done for Catholic youth by the saintly Father Allemand
and the venerable Canon Timon-David. We rejoice to recall
the emotions in our hearts (as a young priest) on hearing the
latter speak as follows: "Bands, theatricals, lantern-lectures,
movies—I do not condemn all that. When I started out, I
too thought no one could do without them. And yet they are
nothing but crutches, to be used when there is no alternative
left. However, the further I advance, the more my end and
my means become supernatural because I see more and more
clearly that every work built upon a merely human foundation is bound to collapse, and that only the work that aims at
bringing men closer to God by the interior life is blessed by
Providence."

"Our band-instruments have been relegated to the attic for a
long time, and our stage has become useless, and yet the work
is going on better than ever before. Why? Because, thanks be
to God, my priests and I see much clearer and straighter than
before, and our faith in the action of Christ and of grace has
increased a hundred percent."

"Take my advice, do not be afraid to aim as high as you

possibly can, and you will be astonished at the results. Let me explain: do not merely have, as your ideal, to give the youth a selection of clean amusements that will turn them aside from illicit pleasures and dangerous associations, nor simply to give them a Christian varnish, through routine attendance at Mass, or the reception of the Sacraments at long intervals and with questionable dispositions. "Launch out into the deep.[21] Let your ambition be, first of all, the noble one of making a certain number of them, at any cost, take the firm resolution of living as fervent Christians; that is, of making their mental prayer every morning, going to Mass every day, if they can, and doing a little spiritual reading, besides going frequently to Communion, and fervently too. Put all your efforts into giving this select group a great love for Jesus Christ, the spirit of self-denial, prayer, vigilance over themselves; in a word, solid virtues. And take no less trouble to develop in their souls a hunger for the Holy Eucharist. And then stir up these young men to act upon their companions. Train them as frank, devoted apostles, kind, ardent, manly, not narrow-minded in their piety, but full of tact, and never making the sad mistake of spying on their comrades under pretext of zeal. Before two years have gone by, come and tell me whether you still need a lot of brass or stage sets to catch your fish."

"I understand," I replied, "this minority will be the leaven. But what about the others that you will never be able to bring up to that level—what about the group as a whole, the youths of all ages and even the married men who will join the club we are planning: what are we going to do with them?"

"You are going to build up a strong faith in them, by a series of well prepared talks, which will take up many of their

---

21. *Duc in altum* (*Luc.* 5:4).

winter evenings. Your Christians will go out, after these talks, well enough armed not only to give complete and effective answers to their fellows in the various plants and offices, but also to resist the more treacherous action of newspapers and books. If you can give men unshakable convictions which they will know how to affirm if they have to, without regard to human respect, you will (already) have achieved a result that is not to be despised. But still, you will have to take them further yet, and give them piety, genuine and ardent piety, based on conviction and full of understanding."

"Shall I open the doors to all comers right from the start?" I asked him.

"Numbers will be no use to you unless every one is hand-picked. Let the growth of your club depend, most of all, on the influence exercised by the nucleus of apostles, the center of which will be Jesus and Mary, with you as their instrument."

"The premises won't be very impressive. Should I wait until we can raise the money for something better?"

"Well, when someone is starting out, spacious, comfortable rooms may serve as a big drum to advertise your new enterprise, and draw attention to it. But, I repeat, if you know how to build your club on the foundation of an ardent, complete, and apostolic Christian life, the barest minimum, in the way of premises, will always be enough to accommodate all the accessories demanded by the normal functioning of the club. Don't worry! You will soon find out that noise does not do much good—and that what is good doesn't make much noise. And you will see that a good clear understanding of the Gospel will cut down your expenses and, far from hurting your success, it will promote it! But above all, you will have to *pay the price yourself*, not so much by wearing yourself out rehearsing plays or getting up football games, as by *storing up in yourself the life of prayer*. For you can be sure that the extent to which you yourself are able to live on the love of Our Lord will be the *exact measure* of your ability to stir it up in other people."

"What it all comes to, then, is that you base everything on the inner life."

"Yes, absolutely. That way, you don't merely get an alloy, but pure gold. Besides, speaking from long experience, I know you can apply what I have just said about youth-clubs to any kind of work—parishes, seminaries, catechism classes, schools, soldiers' and sailors' groups, and so on. How much good a Christian society, really living on the supernatural level, can do in a city! It works there like a strong leaven, and only the angels can tell you how many souls are saved because of it."

"Ah," he concluded, "if only the majority of priests and religious and workers in Catholic action knew what a powerful lever they have in their hands, once that lever takes advantage of the Heart of Jesus as a fulcrum. Living in union with that Divine Heart they would soon transform our country! Yes indeed, they would bring our land to life, in spite of all the efforts of Satan and his slaves."[22]

---

22. *The zealous canon who thus spoke to me and of whose conversation I retain so precious a memory has developed these thoughts in several fine books: Méthode de Direction des Oeuvres de Jeunesse; 2nd, Traité de la Confession des Enfants et Jeunes Gens; 3rd, Souvenirs de l'oeuvre, ou vie et mort de quelques Congréganistes* (Paris, Mignar Frères).

4. THE ACTIVE AND INTERIOR LIVES ARE COMPLETELY INTERDEPENDENT

Just as the love of God is shown by acts of the interior life, so the love of our neighbor manifests itself by the works of the exterior life, and consequently the love of God and of our neighbor cannot be separated, and it follows that these two forms of life cannot exist without one another.[23]

And so, as Suarez points out, there cannot be any state that is properly and normally ordered to bring us to perfection, that does not at the same time share to some extent in both action and contemplation.[24]

The great Jesuit is simply commenting on the teaching of St. Thomas on this subject. The Angelic Doctor says that those who are called to the works of the active life would be mistaken if they thought that this duty dispensed them from the contemplative life.[25] This duty is *merely added to that of*

---

23. *Sicut per contemplationem amandus est Deus, ita per actualem vitam diligendus est proximus, ac per hoc, sic non possumus sine utraque esse vita, sicut et sine utraque dilectione nequaquam esse possumus* (St. Isidore, *Different*, ii:34, n. 135).

    Just as God is to be loved in contemplation, we must also love our neighbor through the active life, and follows that we cannot be without both these kinds of life, just as it is absolutely necessary for us to practice both kinds of love.

24. *Concedendum est nullum esse posse vitae studium recte institutum ad perfectionem obtinendam quod non aliquid de actione et de contemplatione participet* (Suarez, I, De Relig. Tract., I, c. 5, n. 5).

25. It may be necessary to point out that here, as everywhere else, Dom Chautard uses the terms active and contemplative life not in the sense of the active or contemplative states, such as are explicitly intended as the aim of the various active or contemplative religious orders, but merely in the sense of exterior works of virtue and of mercy on one hand, and interior union with God by prayer on the other. Every

contemplation without diminishing its necessity. And so these two lives, far from excluding one another, depend on one another, presuppose one another, mingle together and complete one another. And if there is a question of giving greater importance to one than to the other, it is the contemplative life that merits our preference, as being the more perfect and the more necessary.[26]

Action relies upon contemplation for its fruitfulness; and contemplation, in its turn, as soon as it has reached a certain degree of intensity, pours out upon our active works some of its overflow. And it is by contemplation that the soul goes to draw directly upon the Heart of God for the graces which it is the duty of the active life to distribute.

And so, in the soul of a saint, action and contemplation merge together in perfect harmony to give perfect unity to his life. Take St. Bernard, for example, the most contemplative and yet at the same time the most active man of his age. One of his contemporaries has left us this admirable portrait of him: Contemplation and action so agreed together in him that the saint appeared to be at the same time entirely devoted to external works, and yet completely absorbed in the presence and the love of his God.[27] Commenting on the text of sacred Scripture: "Put me as a seal upon thine heart and as a seal

---

Christian is bound to practice both of these, and without them there is no Christian life.

26. *Cum aliquis a contemplativa vita ad activam vocatur, non fit per modum substractionis, sed per modum additionis* (St. Thomas, 2a 2ae, q. 182, a1, ad 3).

When a man is called from the contemplative to the active life, he does not subtract anything from, but adds to his obligations.

27. *Interiori quadam, quam ubique ipse circumferebat, solitudine fruebatur, totus quodammodo exterius laborabat, et totus interius Deo vacabat* (Geoffrey of Auxerre, *Vita Bernardi.* I. 5; also III).

upon thine arm,"[28] Father Saint-Jure gives us a fine description of the relations of these two lives with each other. Let us, briefly, outline his thought:

The heart stands for the interior, or contemplative life: the arm for the active, or exterior life.

The sacred text speaks of them as the heart and the arm, to show how the two lives can be joined together and harmonize perfectly in the same person.

The heart is mentioned first, because as an organ it is far more noble and more necessary than the arm. In the same way contemplation is much more excellent and perfect, and deserves far greater esteem than action.

The heart goes on beating day and night. Let this all-important organ stop, even for a moment, and immediate death would result. The arm, however, merely an integral part of the human body, only moves from time to time. And thus, we ought sometimes to seek a little respite from our outward works, but never on the other hand, relax our attention to spiritual things.

The heart gives life and strength to the arm by means of the blood which it sends forth; otherwise, that member would wither up. And in the same way, the contemplative life, a life of union with God, thanks to the light and the constant assistance the soul receives from this closeness to Him, gives life to our external occupations, and it alone is able to impart to them at the same time a supernatural character and a real usefulness. But without contemplation, everything is sick and barren and full of imperfections.

---

28. *Pone me ut signaculum super cor tuum, ut signaculum super brachium tuum* (*Cant.* 8:6).

Man, unfortunately, too often separates what has been united by God, and consequently this perfect union is rarely found. Besides, it depends for its realization upon a number of precautions that are too often neglected. We must not undertake anything that is beyond our strength. We must habitually, but simply, see the will of God in everything. We must never get mixed up in works that are not willed for us by God, but only when, and to the extent that, He wants to see us engaged in them, and only out of the desire to practice charity. From the very start, we must offer our work to Him, and during the course of our labors, we must often make use of holy thoughts and ardent aspiratory prayers to stir up our resolution to act only for and by Him. For the rest, no matter how much attention our work may require, we must keep ourselves always at peace, and always remain completely masters of ourselves. We must leave the successful outcome of the work entirely in the hands of God, and desire to see ourselves delivered from all care only in order that we may be, once again, alone with Jesus Christ. Such are the extremely wise counsels of the masters of the spiritual life, to those who want to reach this union.

This perseverance in the interior life which, in St. Bernard of Clairvaux, was united to a very active apostolate, made a great impression on St. Francis de Sales. "St. Bernard," he said, "lost not a whit of the progress he desired to make in holy love. . . . He moved from place to place, but did not move in his heart nor did his heart's love change, nor did his love change in its object . . . he did not take upon himself the color of every business or of every conversation like a chameleon, taking the color of every place where it happens to be. But he remained ever united to God, ever white in his purity, ever crimson in his charity, and ever full of humility."[29]

At times, our duties will accumulate to such an extent that they will exhaust all our strength, not allowing us to get rid of our burden, nor even to make it any lighter. The result may possibly be that we will be deprived, for a more or less prolonged period, of the *sense of our union with God*, but the union itself will only suffer if we actually permit it to do so. If this condition should be prolonged, *we must feel suffering on account of it, we must lament it, and we must, above all, fear that we may become used to it.*

Man is weak and without constancy. If he neglects his spiritual life, he soon loses the taste for it. Absorbed in material duties, he gets to take satisfaction in them. But on the other hand, if the interior spirit gives signs of its latent vitality by pain and repugnance, the ceaseless complaints that issue from a *wound that refuses to close, even in the midst of intense activity*, these sufferings will themselves make up all the merit of our sacrificed contemplation. Rather, it is in this that the soul realizes the admirable and fruitful union of the interior and active lives. Maddened by the thirst for the interior life, a thirst which there is no time to quench, the soul returns as soon as possible to the life of prayer. Our Lord will *never fail* to make room for a few moments' colloquy. But he demands that we be faithful to these opportunities, and gives us grace to *make up*, by our *fervor*, for the brevity of these happy moments.

St. Thomas admirably sums up this doctrine in a passage of which every word deserves to be carefully pondered: "The contemplative life is, in itself, more meritorious than the active life. Nevertheless, a man may happen to gain more merit by

---

29. *Spirit of St. Francis de Sales*, Part xvii, ch. 2.

performing some exterior act; if, for instance, he endures, for a time, to be deprived of the sweetness of divine contemplation, in order, on account of the abundance of the love of God and for His glory, to fulfill God's will."[30]

We note what a great number of conditions the holy doctor lays down, to be fulfilled before active life can become more meritorious than contemplation.

The inmost cause that moves the soul to active works is nothing else but the overflow of its charity: *proper abundantiam divini amoris*. Therefore, it is not a matter of excitement, or caprice, nor of the craving to get out of ourself. Indeed, it is a source of suffering for the soul. *Sustinet*, it "endures" the privation of the sweetness of the life of prayer;[31] "*a dulcedine divinae contemplationis . . . separari*. Furthermore, the sacrifice is only temporary: *accidere—interdum—ad tempus*, and it is only for a purely supernatural end—the fulfilling of

---

30. *Ex suo genere contemplativa vita majoris est meriti quam activa. . . . Potest tamen contingere quod aliquis in operibus vitae activae plus mereatur quam alius in operibus vitae contemplativae; puta si propter abundantiam divini amoris, ut ejus voluntas impleatur, propter ipsius gloriam, interdum sustinet a dulcedine divinae contemplationis ad tempus separari* (2a 2ae, q. 182, a. 2).

   St. Thomas goes on to quote St. Chrysostom, who interpreted St. Paul's desire to be "an anathema from Christ for his brethren" in the above sense.

31. Since this "sweetness" resides principally in the "summit" of the soul, it is quite compatible with dryness: *exsuperat omnem sensum*. It transcends all feelings. The logic of pure faith, cold and dry in itself, is enough to allow the will to enflame the heart with supernatural fire, always with the help of grace.

   Saint Jane Chantal, who was one of the souls who had most to suffer in mental prayer, left to her daughters a spiritual legacy when she was on her deathbed at Moulins. It was the principle that had led her to base her life on this argument of faith: "The greatest happiness here below is to be able to converse with God."

God's will, and giving Him glory. Finally, what is sacrificed is only a part of the time to be given to prayer.

How full of wisdom and goodness God's ways are! How wonderfully He directs souls, by means of the interior life! This deep sorrow at having to devote so much time to the works of God and so little to the God of works, this sorrow which persists in the midst of action and which, nevertheless, we generously offer up to Him, has its compensations. Thanks to this pain, we are freed from all dangers of dissipation, self-love, natural feelings of pride, etc. Far from hurting our freedom of spirit or our activity, this disposition in our souls imparts to them a more deliberate character. It is the practical way to keep in the presence of God, because now the soul, *in the grace of the present moment*, is able to find the living Christ, giving Himself to us, concealed in the work that we have to perform. Jesus works with us and sustains us. How many persons in responsible positions owe to this salutary suffering once it has been well understood, to this desire, persistent though sacrificed, to visit the Blessed Sacrament, to these almost incessant spiritual communions—how many owe to all this not only the splendid results of their work, but even the safety of their souls and their progress in virtue?

5. THE EXCELLENCE OF THIS UNION

The union of the two lives, contemplative and active, constitutes the true apostolate, the chief work of Christianity: *principalissimum officium*, as St. Thomas says.[32]

The apostolate implies souls capable of being carried away

---

32. III, a. 67, a. 2, ad i.

with enthusiasm for an idea, of consecrating themselves to the triumph of a principle. When the realization of this ideal is supernaturalized by the interior spirit, and when our zeal, in its end, its center, and its means is quickened by the spirit of Christ, we shall have the life which is in itself *the most perfect of all*, the *highest possible life*, since the theologians prefer it even to simple contemplation: *praefertur simplici contemplatione.*[33]

The apostolate of a man of prayer is the word of the Gospel, conquering with the mandate of God; it is the zeal for souls, the ripening of conversions for the harvest: *missio a Deo, zelus animarum, fructificatio auditorum.*[34]

It is a vapor rising from faith, breathing forth health-giving exhalations: *zelus, id est vapor fidei.*[35]

The apostolate of the saints sows seed all over the world. The apostle casts into souls the wheat of God.[36] It is a blazing fire of love that devours the earth, the great fire of Pentecost, spreading unchecked across the nations of the world. "I am come to cast fire on the earth."[37]

The sublimity of this ministry lies in the fact that is provides for the salvation of others, without danger to the apostle himself: *sublimatur ad hoc ut aliis provideat.* To transmit divine truths to the intellects of men! Is not this ministry worthy of angels?

It is a good thing to contemplate the truth, and better still to pass it on to others. To reflect the light is something more than simply to receive it. It is better to give light, than to shine

---

33. St. Thomas.
34. St. Bonaventure.
35. St. Ambrose.
36. Fr. Léon, passim, op. cit.
37. *Ignem veni mittere in terram* (*Luc.* 12:49).

under a bushel. By contemplation the soul is fed: by the apostolate, it gives itself away. *Sicut majus est illuminare quam lucere solum, ita majus est contemplata aliis tradere quamsolum contemplare.*[38]

Contemplata aliis tradere: prayer remains at the source of this ideal of the apostolate. Such is the unmistaking meaning of St. Thomas.

This passage, like the words of the holy doctor that were quoted at the end of the preceding chapter, are an open condemnation of so-called "Americanism," the partisans of which envisage a mixed life in which contemplation is strangled by activity.

Two things are implied by this text.   1) That the soul is already *habitually* living a life of prayer, and doing so with sufficient intensity not to need to draw upon anything but its *surplus*, for others.   2) That action must not supersede the life of prayer, and that the soul, while spending itself, must be so well trained in keeping watch over its heart that it runs no risk of withdrawing its actions from the influence of Christ.

The beautiful words of Fr. Matheo, apostle of the enthroning of the Sacred Heart in the home, exactly express the thought of St. Thomas in their own way: "*The apostle is a chalice full to the brim with the life of Jesus, and his overflow pours itself out upon souls.*"

It is this mixture of action, with all its outpouring of zeal, and of contemplation with its lofty flights, that produced the greatest of the saints: St. Denis, St. Martin, St. Bernard, St. Dominic, St. Francis of Assisi, St. Francis Xavier, St. Philip Neri, St. Alphonsus—all of them just as ardent contemplatives as they were mighty apostles.

---

38. St. Thomas, 2a 2ae, q. 188, a. 6.

Interior life and active life! Holiness within works! A powerful union, and a fruitful one. What miracles of conversion it can work! O God, send many apostles to Thy Church, but stir up in their hearts, already consumed with the desire to give themselves, a desperate sense of their need for the life of prayer. Grant to Thy workers this contemplative activity, and active contemplation. Then Thy work will be done, and the workers of Thy Gospel will win those victories which Thou didst foretell to them before Thy glorious Ascension.

PART THREE

WITHOUT THE INTERIOR LIFE THE ACTIVE LIFE IS FULL OF DANGER: WITH IT, IT WILL GUARANTEE PROGRESS IN VIRTUE

1. ACTIVE WORKS, A MEANS OF SANCTIFICATION FOR INTERIOR SOULS, BECOME, FOR OTHERS, A MENACE TO THEIR SALVATION

A. MEANS OF SANCTIFICATION. Our Lord categorically demands that those whom He associates with His apostolate should not only *persevere* in their virtue, but *make progress* in it. Proof will be found on any page of St. Paul's epistles to Titus and Timothy, and the words addressed in the Apocalypse to the Bishops of Asia.

At the same time, as we proved at the outset, God wants active works.

Consequently, if we were to view works, considered in themselves, as an obstacle to sanctification, and assert that, *although springing from the Divine Will*, they *necessarily* slow down our advance towards perfection, it would be an insult, a blasphemy against the Wisdom and Goodness and Providence of God.

Hence, the following dilemma is inescapable: either the apostolate, no matter what form it takes, if it is *God's will*, not only does not bring about in itself as its effect any alteration in the atmosphere of solid virtue which ought to surround a soul that has a care for salvation and for spiritual progress, but it must also, and always, provide the apostle with a *means of sanctification*, so long as his apostolic work keeps within the *due conditions*.

Or else the person whom God has chosen to work with Him, and who is therefore obliged to answer the divine call, will have every right to offer the activity, the troubles and cares undergone for the sake of the work commanded by Him, as legitimate excuses for his failure to sanctify himself.

Now it is a consequence of the economy of the divine plan that God *owes it to Himself* to provide His chosen apostle with graces necessary to make distracting business compatible not only with the assurance of salvation but even with the acquisition of virtues which can lead as high as sanctity itself.

God *owes* the kind of help He gave to His St. Bernards and St. Francis Xaviers to the humblest of his preachers of the Gospel, to the lowest teaching brother, to the most obscure nursing sister, in the measure required by each of them. Such aid is a real *Debt of the Sacred Heart*, owed by Him to His chosen instruments. Let us not fear to repeat it over and over again. And every apostle, provided he fulfills the due conditions, should have an *absolute confidence in his inviolable right* to the graces demanded by a work whose very nature gives him a mortgage on the infinite treasure of divine aid.

"A man who devotes himself to works of charity," says

Alvarez de Paz, "must not imagine that they will close the door of contemplation in his face, nor make him any less capable of practicing it. On the contrary, he must hold it as certain that they will even serve as an excellent preparation for it. This truth is vouched for not only by reason and the authority of the Fathers, but also by daily experience, for we may see certain souls engaged in works of charity for their neighbor, like hearing confessions, preaching, teaching catechism, visiting the sick, and so on, raised by God to so high a degree of contemplation that one may fairly compare them with the anchorites of old."[1]

By the use of his term "degree of contemplation" the eminent Jesuit, like all the other masters of the spiritual life, is talking of the gift of the spirit of prayer which is a sign of the superabundance of charity in a soul.

The sacrifices exacted from us by active works draw so much supernatural value from the glory they give to God and from their effects in the sanctification of souls, and acquire from these sources such great wealth of merits, that a man vowed to the active life can, if he wills, rise himself each day a further degree in charity and union with God, that is to say, in sanctity.

Of course, in certain cases, where there is a grave and proximate danger of formal sin, particularly against faith and the angelic virtue, *God absolutely wills* that a man give up works of charity. But apart from such a case, He gives to all His workers, the interior life as a means of becoming immune to danger and of making progress in virtue. However, let us clearly define in what this progress consists. A paradox of the prudent and spiritual St. Theresa will help us to make our

---

1. Vol. III, bk. 4.

meaning clear: "Since I have been prioress, burdened with many duties and obliged to travel a great deal, I commit very many more faults. And yet, as I struggle generously and spend myself for God alone, I feel that I am getting closer and closer to Him." Her weakness shows itself much more than it did in the peace and quiet of the cloister. The saint is aware of this, but does not let it cause her any worry. The completely supernatural generosity of her devotion to duty and her greatly increased efforts in the spiritual combat make up for everything by providing an opportunity for victories which largely outweigh the surprise faults of a weakness that was always there, but formerly only in a latent state. Our union with God, says St. John of the Cross, resides in the union of our will with His, and is measured entirely by that union. Instead of taking the mistaken view of spirituality which would see no possibility of progress in divine union except in tranquility and solitude, St. Theresa judges that it is rather an activity truly imposed on us by God and carried out under the conditions laid down by His will, which, by nourishing her spirit of sacrifice, her humility, her abnegation, her ardor and devotion for the Kingdom of God, serves to increase the intimate union of her soul with Our Lord, who lives in her and gives life to her work; and it is thus that she advances on the road to sanctity.

Sanctity, as a matter of fact, consists above all in charity, and any apostolic work that is worthy of the name is simply charity in action. *Probatio amoris*, says St. Gregory, *exhibitio est operis*. The proof of love is in works of self-denial, and this proof of devotion is something God demands of all His workers.

"Feed my lambs, feed my sheep," is the form of charity which Our Lord demands of the apostle as a proof of the sincerity of his repeated protestations of love.

St. Francis of Assisi did not believe he could be a friend of Christ unless his charity devoted itself to the salvation of souls. *Non se amicum Christi reputabat nisi animas foveret quas ille redemit.*[2]

And if Our Lord looks upon all works of mercy, even corporal, as done to Himself, it is because He sees in each one of them the radiated light of the very same charity[3] which animates the missionary or sustains the hermit in the privations, the struggles, and the prayers of the desert.

The active life is concerned with the care of others. It treads the path of sacrifice, following Jesus, the worker and pastor, the missionary and wonderworker, the healer and physician of all, the tireless and tender provider for all the needy here below.

The active life remembers and is sustained by this word of the Master: "I am in the midst of you as he that serveth."[4] "The Son of Man did not come to be ministered unto, but to minister."[5]

It goes out into the byways of human misery, speaking the word that enlightens, and sowing all about it a harvest of graces that will grow up into benefits of every sort.

Thanks to the clear vision of its faith, thanks to the intuitions of its love, it discovers in the lowest of the wretched, in the most pitiful of sufferers, God, naked, sorrowful, despised by all, the great leper, the mysterious condemned criminal, pursued and beaten to the ground by the blows of eternal

---

2. He did not consider himself a friend of Christ unless he cared for the souls redeemed by Him (St. Bonaventure, *Life of St. Francis*, c. ix).
3. As long as you did it to one of these My least brethren, you did it to Me (*Matt.* 25:40).
4. *Ego autem in medio vestrum sum sicut qui ministrat* (*Luc.* 22:27).
5. *Filius hominis non venit ministrari sed ministrare* (*Matt.* 20:28).

justice, the Man of Sorrows whom Isaias saw rising up in the frightful wealth of His wounds, in the tragic purple of His Blood, so smashed and ravaged by the nails and by the whips of the scourging that He twisted like a worm under the heel that stamps out its life.

"Thus we have seen Him," cries the prophet, "and we have not recognized Him."[6]

Yes, but thou, O active life, dost recognize Him: and falling on thy knees, with eyes full of tears, thou servest Him in the poor.

The active life improves mankind. Enriching the world with its acts of generosity, with its work and with its toil and sacrifices, it sows merits for heaven.

It is a holy life, rewarded by God, for He gives Paradise in return for a cup of cold water given by one poor man to another, just as well as for the doctor's learned tomes or for the labors of the apostle. At the last day, He will canonize all the works of charity before the face of heaven and earth together.[7]

B. A MENACE TO SALVATION. How often, alas, in private retreats which we have directed, have we noticed that

---

6. *Et vidimus eum et non erat aspectus, et desideravimus eum, despectum et novissimum virorum, virum dolorum et scientem infirmitatem: et quasi absconditus vultus ejus et despectus, unde nec reputavimus eum* (*Is.* 53:2–3).

    And we have seen Him and there was no sightliness that we should be desirous of Him: despised and the most abject of men, a man of sorrows and acquainted with infirmity: and His look was, as it were, hidden and despised, whereupon we esteemed Him not.

7. *Lumiere et Flamme*, P. Léon, O.M.Cap. Notice that in this quotation the author is speaking of an active life full of the spirit of faith, made fruitful by charity, and, consequently. springing from an intense interior life.

active works, which ought to have been, for their organizers, a *means of progress* had turned into *forces that undermined* the whole edifice of their spiritual life.

A very active and energetic man, invited by us, at the beginning of a retreat, to look into his conscience and seek out the principal *cause* of his unhappiness, gave a perfect diagnosis in this answer which may seem at first sight incomprehensible:

"My self-sacrifice is what has ruined me! My nature and temperament make it a joy for me to spend myself, and a pleasure to serve. What with the apparent success of my enterprises, the devil has contrived, for long years, to make everything work together for my deception, stirring me up to furious activity, filling me with disgust for all interior life, and finally leading me over the edge of the abyss."

This abnormal, not to say monstrous state of mind can be explained in one word. The worker for God, carried away by the pleasure of giving free rein to his natural energy, had let the divine life fade out, and thus lost the supernatural heat which had been stored up in him to make his apostolate effective and which would have helped his soul to resist the encroachments of the numbing ice of natural motives. He had worked, indeed, but far from the rays of the lifegiving sun. *Magnae vires et cursus celerrimus, sed praeter viam.*[8] At the same time, his works, in themselves very holy, had turned against the apostle like a weapon dangerous to wield, a two-edged sword which wounds the man who does not know how to use it.

St. Bernard was warning Pope Bl. Eugenius III against just such a danger as this when he wrote: "I fear, lest in the midst

---

8. Much strength and great speed, but all off the track (St. Augustine, *In Psalm* 31).

of your occupations without number, you may lose hope of ever getting through with them, and allow your heart to harden. It would be very prudent of you to *withdraw from such occupations*, even if it be only for a little while, rather than let them get the better of you, and, little by little, lead you where you do not want to go. And where, you will ask, is that? To *indifference*.

"Such is the end to which these *accursed tasks* (*hae occupationes maledictae*) will lead you; that is, if you keep on as you have begun, giving yourself entirely to them, keeping nothing of yourself, for yourself."[9]

Is there anything more lofty and more sacred than the government of the Church? Is there anything more useful for the glory of God and for the good of souls? And yet "accursed task," St. Bernard calls them, if they are going to stand in the way of the interior life of the one who gives himself to them.

What an expression, *"accursed tasks!"* It calls for a whole book, so terrifying is it, and so powerfully does it force one to think! It might arouse protest did it not flow from the pen of one so precise as a Doctor of the Church, a St. Bernard.

2. THE ACTIVE WORKER WHO HAS NO INTERIOR LIFE

To sum such a one up in a word; perhaps he is not yet tepid, but he is bound to become so. However, when a man is tepid, with a tepidity that is not merely in the feelings, or due to weakness, but residing *in the will, that man has resigned himself to consent habitually to levity and neglect, or at any rate*

---

9. *En quo trahere te possunt hae occupationes maledictae, si tamen pergis ut coepisti, ita dare te totum illis nil tui tibi relinquens* (St. Bernard, *De Consideratione*, II, 2).

to cease fighting them. He has come to terms with deliberate venial sin, and by that very fact, *he has robbed his soul of its assurance of eternal salvation.* Indeed, he is disposing and even leading it on to mortal sin.[10]

Such also is St. Alphonsus' teaching on tepidity, so well expounded by his disciple, Fr. Desurmont.[11]

Now how is it that, without an interior life, the active worker inevitably slides into tepidity? Inevitably, we say; and the only proof we need for this is the statement of a missionary bishop to his priests, a statement all the more terrifying by its truth, since it comes straight from a heart consumed with zeal for good works and filled with a spirit that goes clean contrary to anything that smacks of quietism. "There is one thing," said Cardinal Lavigerie, "one thing of which you

---

10. It follows from St. Thomas' teaching on habits (1a 2ae, qq. 1iii) that when a soul in the state of grace places an act that is good in itself, but below the degree of fervor which God has a right to expect from it in its present state, that act, in a sense, tends to diminish its degree of charity. The texts, "Cursed be he who does the work of God with negligence" and "Because thou art luke-warm I will commence to vomit thee from my mouth," are explained in this sense.

   Furthermore, every venial sin, although it does not diminish the state of grace, does, as a matter of fact, diminish its fervor. And it is thus that is disposes us to mortal sin.

   But where there is not an intense interior life, deliberate venial sin will abound, and there will be many venial sins that are not even recognized as such, although they will be imputed to the lax and careless soul which has ceased to "watch and pray."

   Thus we may find in St. Thomas an explanation for the phrase "accursed occupations" used above, and of all that is to he developed in the present chapter.

   Cf. 1a 2ae, q. 1ii, a. 3: *Si vero intensio actus proportionaliter deficiat ab intensione habitus, talis actus non disponit ad augmentum habitus sed magis ad diminutionem ipsius.*

11. See note on tepidity, Part I, No. 3, "sixth truth," page 15. Cf. *"Le Retour Continuel à Dieu."*

must be fully persuaded, and it is that for an apostle there is no halfway between total sanctity, at least faithfully and courageously desired and sought after, and absolute perversion."

First let us go back to the seed of corruption fostered in our nature by concupiscence, and the fight to the death that is ever waged against us by your enemies, within as well as without. Let us go back to the dangers that threaten us on every side.

With this in mind, let us consider what happens to a soul that enters upon the apostolate without being sufficiently forewarned and forearmed against its dangers.

Fr. (or Mr.) So-and-So feels within himself a growing desire to consecrate himself to good works. He has no experience whatever. But his liking for the apostolate gives us the right to suppose that he has a certain amount of fire, some impetuosity of character, is fond of action, and also perhaps, inclined to relish a bit of a fight. Let us imagine him to be correct in his conduct, a man of piety and even to devotion; but his piety is more in the feelings than in the will, and his devotion is not the light reflected by a soul resolute in seeking nothing but the good pleasure of God, but a pious routine, the result of praiseworthy habits. Mental prayer, if indeed he practices it at all, is for him a species of day-dreaming, and his spiritual reading is governed by curiosity, without any real influence on his conduct. Perhaps the devil even eggs him on by reason of an illusory artistic sense, which the poor soul mistakes for an "inner life," to dabble in treatises on the lofty and extraordinary paths of union with God, and these fill him with admiration and enthusiasm. All in all, there is little genuine inner life, if any at all, in this soul which still has, we grant, a certain number of good habits, many natural assets and a certain loyal desire to be faithful to God; but that desire is altogether too vague.

There you have our apostle, filled with his desire to throw himself into active works, and on the point of entering upon this ministry which is so completely new to him. It is not long before circumstances that inevitably arise from these works (as will readily be understood by anyone who has led the active life) produce a thousand-and-one occasions to draw him more and more out of himself; there are countless appeals to his naive curiosity, unnumbered occasions of falling into sin from which we may suppose he has hitherto been protected by the peaceful atmosphere of his home, his seminary, his community, or his novitiate—or at least by the guidance of an experienced director.

Not only is there an increasing dissipation, or the ever growing danger of a curiosity that has to find out all about everything; not only more and more displays of impatience or injured feelings, of vanity or jealousy, presumption or dejection, partiality or detraction, but there is also a progressive development of the weaknesses of his soul and of all the more or less subtle forms of sensuality. And all these foes are preparing to force an unrelenting battle upon this soul so ill-prepared for such violent and unceasing attacks. And it therefore falls victim to frequent wounds!

Indeed, it is a wonder when there is any resistance at all on the part of a soul whose piety is so superficial—a soul already *captivated by the too natural satisfaction it takes in pouring out its energies and exercising all its talents upon a worthy cause!* Besides, the devil is wide awake, on the look-out for his anticipated prey. And far from disturbing this sense of satisfaction, he does all in his power to encourage it.

Yet a day comes when the soul scents danger. The guardian-angel has had something to say: conscience has registered a protest. Now would be the time to *take hold of himself,* to examine himself in the calm atmosphere of a retreat, to resolve to draw up a schedule and follow it rigorously, even at the cost of neglecting the occasions of trouble to which he has become so attached.

Alas! It is already late in the day! He has already tasted the pleasure of seeing his efforts crowned with the most encouraging success. "Tomorrow! tomorrow!" he mumbles. "Today, it is out of the question. There simply is no time. I have got to go on with this series of sermons, write this article, organize this committee, or that 'charity,' put on this play, go on that trip—or catch up with my mail." *How happy he is to reassure himself with all these pretexts!* For the mere thought of being left alone, face to face with his own conscience, has become unbearable to him. The time has come when the devil can have a free hand to encompass the ruin of a soul that has shown itself disposed to be such a willing accomplice. The ground is prepared. *Since activity has become a passion in his victim, he now fans it into a raging fever.* Since it has become intolerable for him to even think of forgetting his urgent affairs and recollecting himself, the demon increases that loathing into sheer horror, and takes care at the same time to intoxicate the soul with fresh enterprises, skillfully colored with the attractive motives of God's glory and the greater good of souls.

And now our friend, up to so recently a man of virtuous habits, is going from weakness to ever greater weakness, and will soon place his foot upon an incline so slippery that he will be utterly unable to keep himself from falling. Deep in his heart he is miserable, and vaguely realizes that all this agitation is not according to the Heart of God, but the only result is that *he hurls himself even more blindly into the whirlpool in order to drown his remorse.* His faults are piled up to a fatal degree. Things that used to trouble the upright conscience of this man are now despised as vain scruples. He is fond of proclaiming that a man ought to live with the times, meet the enemy on equal terms, and so he praises the *active* virtues to the skies, expressing nothing but scorn for what he disdainfully calls "the piety of a bygone day." Anyway, his enterprises prosper more than ever. Everybody is talking about them. Each day witnesses some new success. "God is blessing our work," exclaims the deluded man, over whom, tomorrow, perhaps the angels will be weeping for a mortal sin.

How did this soul fall into so lamentable a state? *Inexperience, presumption, vanity, carelessness, and cowardice* are the answer. Haphazardly, without stopping to reflect on his inadequate spiritual resources, he threw himself into the midst of dangers. When his reserves of the interior life ran out, he found himself in the position of an uncautious swimmer who has no longer the strength to fight against the current, and is being swept away to the abyss.

Let us pause a moment to look back over the road that has been traveled, and to estimate the depth of the fall.

FIRST STAGE. The soul began by progressively losing the *clarity* and *power* (if ever it had any at all) of its *convictions* about the supernatural life, the supernatural world, and the economy of the plan and of the action of Our Lord with regard to the relation between the inner life of the apostle and his works. He ceases to see these works except through a delusive mirage. In a subtle way, vanity comes to act as a pedestal to his supposed good intentions. "What else can I do? God has given me the gift of oratory, and I thank Him for it," was the reply made by a certain preacher, puffed up with vain complacency, and totally extroverted, to those who are flattering him. The soul seeks itself more than it seeks God.

The foreground is completely taken up by reputation, glory, and personal interests. The text, "If I pleased men, I should not be the servant of Christ,"[12] becomes, to him, something altogether without meaning.

Besides ignorance of principles, the *lack of supernatural foundations* which characterizes this stage has sometimes as its cause and sometimes as its immediate result, dissipation, forgetfulness of God's presence, giving up ejaculatory prayers and custody of the heart, want of delicacy of conscience and of regularity of life. Tepidity is close at hand, if it has not already begun.

SECOND STAGE. If the worker were a supernatural soul, being a slave of duty he would be greedy of his time, and regulate its use, living by a schedule. He would well realize that otherwise he would be living purely from morning to night.

But if he has no supernatural basis, he will soon find out about it. Since there is no spirit of faith governing his use of his time, he gives up his spiritual reading. Or else, if he still reads anything at all, he makes no studies. It was all right for the Fathers of the Church to spend the whole week preparing their Sunday sermons! For him, unless his vanity is at stake, he prefers to improvise. Yet his improvisations always hit it off with singular aptness—at least that is what *he* thinks! He likes to read magazines rather than books. He has no method. He flutters about from one thing to another like a butterfly. The law of work, that great law of preservation, of morality and of penance, is something he manages to escape by wasting his free time, and by the extreme pains he takes to provide himself with amusements.

Anything that would interfere with his free and easy ways,

---

12. *Si adhuc hominibus placerem, Christi servus non essem* (*Gal.* 1:10).

he considers tiresome, and a mere matter of theory—nothing practical. He does not have nearly enough time for all his works and social obligations, or even for what he deems the necessary care of his health, or his recreations. "Really," says the devil to him, "you are giving too much time to pious exercises: meditation, office, Mass, work of the ministry. Something has to be cut out!" Invariably he begins by shortening the *meditation*, by making it only irregularly, or perhaps he even gets to the point where, bit by bit, he drops it altogether. The one indispensable requisite for remaining faithful to his meditation—namely, getting up at the right time—is all the more logically abandoned since he has so many good reasons for having gone to bed late the night before.

Now for a man in the active life to give up his meditation is tantamount to throwing down his arms at the feet of the enemy. "Short of a miracle," says St. Alphonsus, "a man who does not practice mental prayer will end up in mortal sin." And St. Vincent de Paul tells us: "A man without mental prayer is not good for anything; he cannot even renounce the slightest thing. 'It is merely the life of an animal.'" Some authors quote St. Theresa as having said: "Without mental prayer a person soon becomes either a brute or a devil. If you do not practice mental prayer, you don't need any devil to throw you into hell, you throw yourself in there of your own accord. On the contrary, give me the greatest of all sinners; if he practices mental prayer, be it only for fifteen minutes every day, he will be converted. If he perseveres in it, his eternal salvation is assured." The experience of priests and religious vowed to active works is enough to establish that an apostolic worker who, under pretext of being too busy or too tired, or else out of repugnance, or laziness, or some illusion, is *too easily brought* to cut down his meditation to ten or fifteen minutes instead of binding himself to half an hour's serious mental prayer from which he might draw plenty of energy and drive for his day's work, will inevitably fall into tepidity of the will.

In this stage, it is no longer a matter of avoiding imperfections. His soul is crawling with venial sins. The ever growing impossibility of vigilance over his heart makes most of these faults pass unnoticed by his conscience. *The soul has disposed itself in such a manner that it cannot and will not see.* How will such a one fight against things which he no longer regards as defects? His lingering disease is already far advanced. Such is the consequence of the second stage, which is characterized by *the giving up of mental prayer and of daily schedule.*

Everything is now ripe for the—

THIRD STAGE, of which the symptom is *neglect in the recitation of the* BREVIARY. The prayer of the Church, which ought to give the soldier of Christ joy and strength to lift himself up, from time to time, and let God carry him in a flight high above the visible world, has now become a very tiring duty to be borne with patience. The liturgical life, source of light, joy, strength, merit and grace for himself and for the faithful, is now nothing more than the occasion of a distasteful task, grudgingly discharged. The interior virtue of religion is more than affected by the disease. The fever for active works is beginning to dry it up altogether. The soul no longer sees the worship of God except insofar as it can be tied up with striking exterior display. The obscure and personal but heartfelt sacrifice of praise, of supplication, of thanksgiving, of reparation, no longer means anything to such a man. In the old days, when he was reciting his vocal prayers, he used to say with legitimate pride, as though to enter into rivalry with a choir of monks: I too "shall sing to Thee in the sight of angels." *In conspectu angelorum psallam tibi.*[13]

The sanctuary of this soul, once fragrant with the liturgical life, has become a public thoroughfare where noise and disorder reign. Exaggerated worry over business and habitual dissipation are enough to multiply his distractions tenfold. And, for the rest, he fights these distractions with less and less vigor. "The Lord is not in noise."[14] Genuine prayer is no longer to be found in this soul. He prays in a rush, with interruptions that have not the slightest justification; all is done neglectfully, sleepily, with many delays, putting it off until the last minute, at the risk of being finally overcome by sleep. And, perhaps, now and again, he skips parts of the office and leaves them out. All of this transforms what should be a medicine into a poison. The sacrifice of praise becomes a long litany of sins, and sins which may end up by being more than venial.

FOURTH STAGE. Everything links up. Deep calls to deep. Now it is the SACRAMENTS. They are received and administered, no doubt, as something worthy of respect; but there is no longer any sense of the vital energy contained in them. The presence of Jesus in the tabernacle or in the holy tribunal of Penance is no longer able to make the springs of faith shudder even to the depths of his soul. *Even the Mass*, the Sacrifice of Calvary, has become a closed garden. Of course, the soul is still far from sacrilege—let us at least believe that much! But there is no longer any reaction to the warmth of the Precious Blood. His Consecrations are cold; his Communions tepid, distracted, superficial. A familiarity without respect, routine, maybe even repugnance, are lying in wait for him now.

---

13. *Ps.* 137:2.
14. *Non in commotione Dominus* (*3 Reg.* 19:11).

Thus deformed, the apostle lives outside of Christ, and as for the confidential words spoken by Jesus to His true friends: they are no longer for him.

And yet, at long intervals, the heavenly Friend manages to reach him with a movement of remorse, a light, an appeal. He waits. He knocks. He ask to be let in. "Come to Me, poor wounded soul, won't you come to Me? I will heal you." *Venite ad me omnes . . . et ego reficiam vos.*[15] For I am your salvation: *salus tua ego sum.*[16] I came to save that which was lost: *Venit Filius hominis quaerere et salvum facere quod perierat.*"[17] So gentle, so kind, so discreet, so urgent, this voice brings moments of emotion, and sentimental, evanescent urges to do better. But the door of the heart is only slightly ajar. *Jesus cannot get in.* These good movements in the tepid soul come to nothing at all. Grace goes by in vain, and will turn against the soul. Perhaps Jesus, in His mercy, to avoid piling up a huge store of wrath, will even cease His appeals. "Fear Jesus passing by, and never returning."[18]

Now, let us go further and penetrate even into the depths of this soul whose features we are sketching.

Thoughts play a most important part in the Supernatural, as well as in the moral and intellectual life. Now what are the thoughts that occupy this man, and what direction do they take? Human, earthly, vain, superficial, and egotistical, they converge more and more upon *self* or upon creatures, and that, sometimes, with every appearance of devotion to duty and of sacrifice.

This disorder in the mind brings with it a corresponding

---

15. *Matt.* 11:28.
16. *Psalm* 34:3.
17. *Luc.* 19:10.
18. *Time Jesum transeuntem et non revertentem.*

unruliness in the *imagination*. Of all our powers, this one is the most in need of being repressed at this stage. And yet it never even occurs to him to put on the brakes! Therefore, having free rein, it runs wild. No exaggeration, no madness, is too much for it. And the progressive suppression of all mortification of the eyes soon gives this crazy tenant of his soul opportunities to forage wherever it wills, in lush pastures!

The disorder pursues its course. From the mind and the imagination it gets down into the *affections*. The heart is filled with nothing but will-o'-the-wisps. What is going to become of this dissipated heart, scarcely concerned any more with the Kingdom of God within itself? It has become insensible to the joys of intimacy with Christ, to the marvelous poetry of the Mysteries, to the severe beauty of the Liturgy, to the appeals and attractions of God in the Blessed Eucharist. It is, in a word, insensible to the influences of the supernatural world. What will become of it? Shall it concentrate upon itself? Suicide! No. It must have affection. No longer finding happiness in God, it will love creatures. It is at the mercy of the first occasion for such love. It flings itself without prudence or control into the breach, without a care perhaps even for the most sacred of vows, nor for the highest interests of the Church, nor even for its own reputation. Let us suppose that such a heart would still be upset by the thought of apostasy—and profoundly so. But still, it feels far less fear at the thought of scandalizing souls.

Thanks be to God, it is doubtless the exception for anyone to follow this course to the very limit. But is there anyone incapable of seeing that this getting tired of God, and accepting forbidden pleasures, can drag the heart down to the worst of disasters? Starting from the fact that "the sensual man perceiveth not the things that are of the Spirit of God,"[19] we must necessarily end up with: "He who was reared in the purple has embraced dung."[20] Obstinate clinging to illusion, blindness of mind, hardness of heart all follow one another in progressive stages. We can expect anything.

To crown his misfortunes, the *will* is now found to be, though not destroyed, reduced to such a state of weakness and flabbiness that it is practically impotent. Do not ask him to fight back with vigor; that would make a simple effort, and all you will get will be the despairing answer, "*I can't.*" Now a man who is no longer capable of making any effort, at this stage, is on the way to dreadful calamities.

A well-known enemy of the Church dared to say that he was unable to believe in the fidelity of certain persons to their vows and obligations, since they were forced by their works to mix freely in the life of the world. "They are walking a tightrope," he said, "they are bound to fall." We must answer this insult to God and His Church by replying, without hesitation, *these falls can be MOST CERTAINLY avoided when one knows how to use the precious balancing pole of the interior life. It is only the abandonment of this INFALLIBLE instrument that brings dizziness and the fatal false step into space.*

That admirable Jesuit, Fr. Lallemant, takes us right back to the first cause of these disasters when he says: "There are many apostolic workers who never do anything purely for God. In all things, they seek themselves, and they are always secretly mingling their own interests with the glory of God in the best of their work. And so they spend their life in this intermingling of nature and grace. Finally death comes along,

---

19. *Animalis homo non intelligit quae sunt Spiritus Dei* (*1 Cor.* 2:14).
20. *Qui nutriebantur in croceis amplexati sunt stercora* (*Lam. Jerem.* 4:5).

and *then alone do they open their eyes*, behold their deception, and tremble at the approach of the formidable judgment of God."[21]

Far be it from us, of course, to include among these self-preaching apostles so zealous and powerful a missionary as was the famous Fr. Combalot. But surely it is not out of place at this point to quote what he said at the approach of death. The priest who had just administered the last Sacraments said to him: "Have confidence, dear friend. You have preserved all your priestly integrity, and your thousands of sermons will argue in your behalf before God, to excuse this lack of inner life of which you speak." "My sermons!" cried the dying man, "Oh what a light I see them in now! My sermons! If Our Lord is not the first in bringing up the subject of them, you can be sure that I won't mention it!" In the light of eternity, this venerable priest saw, in the very best of his good works, imperfections that filled his conscience with alarm, and which he attributed to a lack of interior life.

Cardinal du Perron, at the hour of his death, expressed his sorrow at having been more devoted, during his life, to perfecting his intellect by science than his will by the exercises of the interior life.

O Jesus, Thou Apostle above all others, did anyone ever spend himself as much as Thou, when Thou didst live among us? Today Thou dost give Thyself more generously still by Thy Eucharistic life, without, for all that, ever leaving the bosom of Thy Father. Would we were unable to forget that Thou dost not want to know our works unless they be animated by a truly Supernatural principle; unless they be rooted deep in Thy adorable Heart.

---

21. P. Lallemant, *Doct. Spirit.*

3. THE INTERIOR LIFE: BASIS OF THE HOLINESS OF THE APOSTOLIC WORKER

Since holiness is nothing but the interior life carried to such a point that the will is in close union with the will of God, ordinarily, and short of a miracle of grace, the soul will not arrive at this point without traveling through all the stages of the purgative and illuminative lives—and that with many and grueling efforts. Let us take note of a law of the spiritual life, that all through the course of the sanctification of a soul, the activity of God and that of the soul are in inverse proportion to one another. From day to day God does more and more of the work, and the soul does less and less.

The activity of God in the souls of the perfect is something quite different from His activity in the souls of beginners. In the latter, being less obvious, it consists mostly in inciting and sustaining vigilance and suppliant prayer, thus offering them a means of obtaining grace for new efforts. But, in the perfect God acts in a much more complete fashion, and sometimes all He asks is a simple consent, that will unite the soul to His supreme action.

Beginners, even the tepid soul and the sinner, whom the Lord wants to draw close to Himself, feel themselves first of all moved to seek God, then to prove to Him more and more their desire of pleasing Him, and finally to rejoice in all providential opportunities that permit them to dislodge self-love from its throne and set up, in its place, the reign of Christ alone. In such cases, the action of God is confined to stimulation and to help.

In the *saint* this action is far more powerful and far more entire. In the midst of weariness and suffering, satiated with humiliations or crushed by illness, the saint has nothing to do but abandon himself to the divine action; otherwise he would be unable to bear the torments which, according to the designs of God, are intended to bring his perfection to full maturity. In him is fully realized the text: "God put all things under Him that God may be all in all."[22] He depends so completely upon Christ for all things that he seems no longer to live by himself. Such was the testimony of the apostle, with regard to himself: "I live, now not I, but Christ liveth in me."[23] It is the spirit of Christ alone that does the thinking and the acting, and makes all the decisions. No doubt this divinization is far from achieving the intensity that it will have in glory, and yet this state already reflects the characteristics of the beatific union.

Is there any need to point out that all this is far from being the case with a *beginner*, or a *tepid* soul, or with one that is merely *fervent?* There exists a whole series of means adapted to their states, means which, as a matter of fact, can serve one of these types just as well as the other. But the beginner, like an apprentice, will have much trouble, will advance slowly; and, in short, will not accomplish very much. The fervent man, already a skilled workman, will do his job fast and well, and, with little difficulty, will gain much more profit.

But no matter what class of apostles we may be discussing, the intentions of Providence in regard to them are always the same. God desires that always, and in all these souls, active work should be a means of sanctification. But whereas for the soul that has arrived at sanctity the apostolate offers no serious danger, does not exhaust his strength and provides him with abundant opportunities to grow in virtue and in merit, we have seen how rapidly it brings on spiritual anemia, and

---

22. *Deus subjicit sibi omnia ut sit Deus omnia in omnibus.* (*1 Cor.* 15:28).
23. *Vivo autem jam non ego, vivit vero in me Christus* (*Gal.* 2:20).

consequently regression on the road to perfection, in souls only feebly united with God—souls in whom the love of prayer, the spirit of sacrifice, and above all habitual watchfulness over the heart are but poorly developed.

This habit of vigilance will never be refused by God when He sees insistent prayer and repeated proofs of fidelity. He pours it without measure upon a generous soul who, by unceasing new-beginnings, has managed to transform its power and make them supple in responding to the inspirations from above, and capable of joyfully accepting contradiction and failure, loss and deception.

Let us consider six main features of the way the interior life filters into a soul to establish it in genuine virtue.

a. It Protects the Soul against the Dangers of the Exterior Ministry

"It is more difficult to live well, when one has care of souls, on account of the dangers from without," says St. Thomas.[24] We have spoken of these dangers in the preceding chapter.

While the active worker who has no interior spirit is unaware of the dangers arising from his work, and thus resembles an unarmed traveler passing through a forest infested with brigands, the *genuine apostle*, for his part, *dreads them* and each day he takes precautions against them by a serious examination of conscience which reveals to him his weak points.

If the interior life did nothing more than procure for us the advantage of *realizing* our incessant danger, it would already be contributing very much to our protection against surprises

---

24. *Difficilius est bene conversari cum cura animarum propter exteriora pericula* (2a 2ae, q. 184. a.8).

along our way; for to foresee a danger is half the battle in avoiding it. And yet the inner life has an even greater utility than merely this. It becomes, for the man engaged in the ministry, a complete set of armor. "Put you on the armor of God, that you may be able to stand against the deceits of the devil."[25] It is a divine armor which permits him not only to *resist the temptations* and avoid the snares set before him by the devil (that you may be able to resist in the evil day), but also to sanctify his every act (and stand in all things perfect).

It girds him with *purity of intention*, which concentrates all his thoughts, desires, and affections upon God and keeps him from going astray and seeking his own comfort, pleasures, and distractions: "having your loins girt about with truth."

It puts on him the breastplate of *charity*, which gives him a manly heart and defends him against the seductions of creatures and of the spirit of the world, as well as against the assaults of the demon: "having on the breastplate of justice."

He is shod with *discretion* and *reserve* in order that in all that he does he may know how to combine the simplicity of the dove and the prudence of the serpent: "And your feet shod with the preparation of the Gospel of peace."

Satan and the world will try to deceive his intellect with the sophisms of false doctrine, and to sap his energies with the enticements of lax principles. But the interior life faces all

---

25. Put you on the armor of God that you may be able to stand against the deceits of the devil . . . that you may be able to resist in the evil day and to stand in all things perfect. Stand therefore, having your loins girt about with truth, and having on the breastplate of justice. And your feet shod with the preparation of the Gospel of peace in all things taking the shield of faith, wherewith you may be able to extinguish all the fiery darts of the most wicked one. And take unto you the helmet of salvation, and the sword of the spirit, which is the word of God (*Eph.* 6:11–17).

these lies with the shield of *faith*, which keeps ever before our eyes the splendor of the divine ideal: "In all things taking the shield of faith, wherewith you may be able to extinguish all the fiery darts of the most wicked one."

The soul will find, in the knowledge of its own nothingness, in care for its own salvation, in the conviction that we can do absolutely nothing without grace, and consequently need at all times insistent, suppliant, and frequent prayer (all the more efficacious in proportion to its confidence)—in all this the soul will find a brazen helmet against which all the blows of *pride* are dulled: "take unto you the helmet of salvation."

Thus armed from head to foot, the apostle can give himself without fear to good works, and his zeal, enkindled by meditation on the Gospel and fortified by the Bread of the Eucharist, will become a sword that will serve him both *in combat* against the enemies of his own soul and *in conquest* of a host of souls for Christ: "the sword of the spirit, which is the word of God."

b. It Renews the Strength of the Apostle

Only a saint, as we have said, is able to keep intact the interior spirit and always direct all his thoughts and intentions to God alone, in the midst of a welter of occupations, and in habitual contact with the world. In such a one, every outlay of external activity is so supernaturalized and enflamed with charity that, far from diminishing his strength, it brings with it, necessarily, an increase of grace.

In other people, even fervent souls, the supernatural life seems to suffer loss after more or less time spent in exterior occupations. Their less perfect hearts, too preoccupied with the good to be done to their neighbor, too absorbed with a compassion (for the woes to be alleviated) that is not nearly Supernatural enough, seem to send up to God flames less pure, darkened with the smoke of numerous imperfections.

God does not punish this weakness by a decrease of His grace, and does not demand a strict account of these failings, *provided there is a serious attempt* at vigilance and prayer in the midst of action, and that the soul is ready, when its work is done, to return to Him and rest and regain its strength. This habit of constantly *beginning over again*, which is necessitated by the combination of the active with the interior life, gives joy to His paternal Heart.

Besides, in those who really put up a fight, these imperfections become less and less serious and frequent in proportion as the soul learns to return, tirelessly, to Christ, whom we will always find ready to say to us: "Come back to Me, poor panting heart, athirst with the length of the course. Come and find in these living waters the secret of new energy for other journeys. Withdraw thyself a little from the crowd that is unable to offer thee the nourishment required by thy exhausted strength. *Come apart and rest a little.*[26] In the peace and quiet thou shalt enjoy being with Me, not only wilt thou soon recapture thy first vigor, but also wilt thou learn how to do more work with less expense of strength. Elias, disheartened, discouraged, found his strength renewed in an instant by a certain mysterious bread. Even so, My apostle, in this enviable task of co-redeemer that it has pleased Me to impose upon thee, I offer thee the chance, both by My word, which is all life, and by My grace, that is, by My Blood, to direct thy spirit once again towards the horizons of eternity and to renew the pact of friendship between thy heart and Mine. Come, I will console

---

26. *Venite in locum desertum seorsum et requiescite pusillum* (*Marc.* 6:31).

thee for the sorrows and deceptions of the journey. And thou shalt temper once again the steel of thy resolutions in the furnace of My love." "Come to Me all you that labor and are heavily burdened and I will refresh you."[27]

c. *It Multiplies His Energies and His Merits*

"Thou therefore, my son, be strong in the grace which is Christ Jesus."[28] Grace is a participation in the life of the man-God. The creature possesses a certain measure of strength and can, in a certain sense, be qualified and defined as a force. But Christ is power in its very essence. In Him dwells in all its fullness the power of the Father, the omnipotence of divine action, and His Spirit is called the Spirit of Power.

"O Jesus," cries St. Gregory Nazianzen, "in Thee alone dwells all my strength." "Outside of Christ," says St. Jerome, in his turn, "I am powerlessness itself."

The Seraphic Doctor, in the fourth book of his *Compendium Theologiae*, enumerates the five chief characteristics which the power of Christ takes on in us. The first is that it undertakes difficult things and confronts obstacles with courage: "Have courage and let your heart be strong."[29]

The second is contempt for the things of this earth: "I have suffered the loss of all things and counted them but as dung that I may gain Christ."[30]

---

27. *Venite ad me omnes qui laboratis et onerati estis, et ego reficiam vos* (*Matt.* 9:28). In connection with these appeals of our Lord to souls of good will we call their attention in a special manner to what is said further on page XXX about learning custody of the heart.
28. *Tu ergo, fili mi, confortare in gratia* (*2 Tim.* 2:1).
29. *Viriliter agite et confortetur cor vestrum* (*Ps.* 30:25).
30. *Omnia detrimentum feci et arbitror ut stercora ut lucrifaciam Christum* (*Philipp.* 3:8).

The third is patience under trial: "Love is strong as death."[31]

The fourth is resistance to temptation: "As a roaring lion he goeth about . . . whom resist ye, strong in faith."[32]

The fifth is interior martyrdom, that, is, the testimony not of blood but of one's very life, crying out to Christ: "I want to belong to Thee alone." It consists in fighting the concupiscences, in overcoming vice and in working manfully for the acquisition of virtues: "I have fought a good fight."[33]

While the exterior man counts on his own natural powers, the man of interior life, on the other hand, sees them as nothing but helps; useful helps, no doubt, but far from being everything that he needs. The sense of his weakness and his faith in the power of God give him, as they did to St. Paul, the exact limit of his strength. When he sees the obstacles that rise up one after another before him, he cries out in humble pride: "When *I am weak, then am I powerful*."[34]

"Without interior life," says Pius X, "we will never have strength to persevere in sustaining all the difficulties inseparable from any apostolate, the coldness and lack of co-operation even on the part of virtuous men, the calumnies of our adversaries, and at times even the jealousy of friends and comrades in arms . . . Only a patient virtue, unshakably based upon the good, and at the same time smooth and tactful, is able to move these difficulties to one side and diminish their power."[35]

By the life of prayer, comparable to the sap flowing from the vine into the branches, the divine power comes down

---

31. *Fortis ut mors dilectio* (*Cant.* 8:6).
32. *Tamquam leo rugiens circuit . . . cui resistite fortes in fide* (*1 Pet.* 5:8–9).
33. *Bonum certamen certavi* (*2 Tim.* 4:7).
34. *Cum enim infirmor, tunc potens sum* (*2 Cor.* 12:10).
35. Encyclical of Pius X, June 11, 1905, to the Priests of Italy.

upon the apostle to strengthen the *understanding* by giving it a firmer footing in faith. The apostle makes progress because this virtue lights his path with its clear brilliance. He goes forward with resolution because he knows where he wants to go, and how to arrive at his goal.

This enlightenment is accompanied by *such great supernatural energy in the will* that even a weak and vacillating character becomes capable of heroic acts.

Thus it is that the principle, "abide in Me,"[36] union with the Immutable, with Him who is the Lion of Juda and the Bread of the strong, explains the miracle of invincible constancy and perfect firmness, which were united, in so marvelous an apostle as was St. Francis de Sales, with a humility and tact beyond compare. The mind and the will are strengthened by the interior life, because love is strengthened. Christ purifies our love and directs and increases it as we go on. He allows us to share in the movements of compassion, devotion, abnegation, and selflessness of His adorable Heart. If this love increases until it becomes a passion, then Jesus takes all the natural and supernatural powers of man, and exalts them to the limit, and uses them for Himself.

Thus it is easy to judge what an increase of merit will flow from the multiplication of energies given by the interior life, when one remembers that merit depends less upon the difficulty that may be entailed by an action, than upon the *intensity of charity* with which it is carried out.

---

36. *Manete in me* (*Joan.* 15:4).

d. It Gives Him Joy and Consolation

Only a burning and unchangeable love is capable of filling a whole life with sunlight, for it is love that possesses the secret of gladdening the heart even in the midst of great sorrows and crushing fatigue.

The life of an apostolic worker is a tissue of sufferings and hard work. What hours of sadness, anxiety, and gloom await the apostle who has not the conviction that he is loved by Christ—no matter how buoyant his character may be—unless perhaps the demon fowlers make the mirror of human consolations and of apparent success glitter before this simple bird, to draw him into their inextricable nets. Only the man-God can draw from a soul this superhuman cry: "I exceedingly abound with joy in all our tribulation."[37] In the midst of my inmost trials, the Apostle is saying, the summit of my being, like that of Jesus at Gethsemani, tastes a joy that, though it has nothing sensible about it, is so real that, in spite of the agony suffered by my interior self, I would not exchange it for all the joys of the world.

When trials come, or contradiction, humiliation, suffering, the loss of possessions, even the loss of those we love, the soul will accept all these crosses in a far different manner than would have been the case at the beginning of his conversion.

From day to day he grows in charity. His love has nothing spectacular about it, perhaps; the Master may give him the treatment accorded to strong souls and lead him through the ways of an ever more and more profound annihilation or by the path of expiation for himself and for the world. It matters little. Protected by his recollection, nourished by the Holy Eucharist, his love grows without ceasing, and the proof of

---

37. *Superabundo gaudio in omni tribulatione nostra* (*2 Cor. 7:4*).

this growth is to be found in the generosity with which he sacrifices and abandons himself; in the devotedness which urges
him to press forward, careless of the difficulty, to find those
souls upon whom he is to exercise his apostolate with such
patience, prudence, tact, compassion, and ardor as can only be
explained by the penetration of the life of Christ in him. *Vivit
vero in me Christus.*

The Sacrament of love must be the *Sacrament of Joy.* There
is no interior soul that is not at the same time a Eucharistic
soul, and consequently, one who enjoys inwardly the gift of
God, delights in His presence, and tastes the sweetness of the
Beloved possessed within the soul and there adored.

The life of the apostolic man is a life of prayer. And the
Saint of Ars says: "The life of prayer is the *one big happiness*
on this earth. O marvelous life! The wonder of the union of a
soul with God! Eternity will not be long enough to understand
this happiness . . . . The interior life is a bath of love, into
which the soul may plunge entirely. . . . And there the soul is,
as it were, drowned in love. . . . God holds the interior soul the
way a mother holds her baby's head in her hand, to cover him
with kisses and caresses."

Further, our *joy is nourished* when we contribute to cause
the object of our love to be served and honored. The apostle
will know all these joys.

Using active works to increase his love, he feels, at the same
time, an increase of joy and consolation. A "hunter of souls"—
venator animarum—he has the joy of contributing to the salvation of beings that would have been damned, and thus he
has the joy of consoling God by giving His souls from whom
He would have been separated for eternity. And finally he has
the joy of knowing that he thus obtains for himself one of the
firmest guarantees of progress in virtue and of eternal glory.

e. It Refines His Purity of Intention

The man of faith judges active works by quite a different light from the man who lives in outward things. What he looks at is not so much the outward appearance of things, as their place in the divine plan and their supernatural results.

And so, considering himself as a simple instrument, his soul is all the more filled with horror at any self-satisfaction in his own endowments, because he places his sole hope of success in the conviction of his own helplessness and confidence in God alone.

Thus he is confirmed in a state of abandonment. And as he passes through his various difficulties, how different is his attitude from that of the apostle who knows nothing of intimacy with Christ!

Furthermore, this abandonment does not in the least diminish his zeal for action. He acts as though success depended entirely on his own activity, but in point of fact he expects it from God alone.[38] He has no trouble subordinating all his projects and hopes to the unfathomable designs of a God who often uses failure even better than success to bring about the good of souls.

Consequently this soul will remain in a state of holy indifference with respect to success or failure. He is always ready to say: "O my God, Thou dost not will that the work I have begun should be completed. It pleases Thee that I confine myself acting valiantly yet ever peacefully, to making efforts to achieve results, but that I leave to Thee alone the task of deciding whether Thou wilt receive more glory from my success, or from the act of virtue that failure will give me the opportunity to perform. Blessed a thousand times be Thy holy

---

38. St. Ignatius Loyola.

and adorable Will, and may I, with the help of Thy grace, know just as well how to repel the slightest symptoms of vain complacency, if Thou shouldst bless my work, as to humble myself and adore Thee if Thy Providence sees fit to wipe out everything that my labors have produced."

The heart of the apostle bleeds, in very truth, when he beholds the sufferings of the Church, but his manner of suffering has nothing in common with that of the man animated by no supernatural spirit. This is easily seen when we consider the behavior and the feverish activity of the latter as soon as difficulties arise, and when we look at his fits of impatience and of dejection, his despair sometimes, his complete collapse in the presence of ruins beyond repair. The genuine apostle makes use of everything, success as well as failure, to increase his hope and expand his soul in confident abandonment to Providence. There is not the slightest detail of his apostolate that does not serve as the occasion for an act of faith. There is not a moment of his persevering toil that does not give him a chance to prove his love, for by practicing custody of the heart he manages to do everything with more and more perfect purity of heart, and by his abandonment he makes his ministry day by day more selfless.

Thus, every one of his acts takes on ever more and more of the character of sanctity, and his love of souls, which at the outset was mixed with many imperfections, gets purer and purer all the time; he ends up by only seeing these souls in Christ and loving them only in Christ, and thus, through Christ, he brings them forth to God. "My children of whom I am in labor again, until Christ be formed in you."[39]

---

39. *Filioli mei quos iterum parturio. donec formetur Christus in vobis* (*Gal.* 4:19).

f. It Is a Firm Defense against Discouragement

Bossuet has a sentence which is beyond the comprehension of an apostle who does not realize what must be the soul of his apostolate. It runs: *"When God desires a work to be wholly from His hand, he reduces all to impotence and nothingness, and then He acts."*

Nothing wounds God so much as pride. And yet when we go out for success, we can get to such a point, by our lack of purity of intention, that we set ourselves up as a sort of divinity, the principle and end of our own works. This idolatry is an abomination in the sight of God. And so when He sees that the activities of the apostle lack that selflessness which His glory demands from a creature, he sometimes leaves the field clear for secondary causes to go to work, and the building soon comes crashing down.

The workman faces his task with all the fire of his nature—active, intelligent, loyal. Perhaps he realizes brilliant success. He even rejoices in them. He takes complacency in them. It is his work. All his! *Veni, vidi, vici.* He has just about appropriated this famous saying to himself. But wait a little. Something happens, with the permission of God; a direct attack by Satan or the world is inflicted upon the work or even the person of the apostle; result, total ruin. But far more tragic is the interior upheaval in this ex-champion—the product of his sorrow and discouragement. The greater was his joy, the more profound his present state of dejection.

Something happens, with the permission of God; direct attack by Satan or the world is inflicted upon the work or even the person of the apostle; result, total ruin. But far more tragic is the interior upheaval in this ex-champion—the product of his sorrow and discouragement. The greater was his joy, the more profound his present state of dejection.

Only Our Lord is capable of raising up this wreck. "Get up," He says to the discouraged apostle, "and instead of acting alone, take to your work again, but with Me, in Me, and by Me." But the miserable man no longer hears this voice. He has become so lost in externals that it would take a real miracle of grace for him to hear it—a miracle upon which his repeated infidelities give him no right to count. Only a vague conviction of the Power of God and of His Providence hovers over the desolation of this benighted failure, and it is not enough to drive away the clouds of sadness which continue to envelop him.

What a different sight is the real priest, whose ideal it is to reproduce Our Lord! For him, prayer and holiness of life remain the two chief ways of acting upon the Heart of God and on the hearts of men. Yes, he has spent himself, and generously too. But the mirage of success seemed to him to be something unworthy of the undivided attention of a real apostle. Let storms come if they will, the secondary cause that produced them is of no importance. In the midst of a heap of ruins, since he has worked only with Our Lord, he hears clearly in the depths of his heart the "Fear not"—*noli timere*—which gave back to the disciples, in the storm, their peace and confidence.

He runs to renew his love of the Blessed Sacrament, his deep, personal devotion to the Sorrows of Our Lady; and that is the first result of the trial.

His soul, instead of being crushed by failure, comes out of the wine press with its youth renewed. His youth will be renewed like an eagle.[40] Where does he get this attitude of humble triumph in the midst of defeat? Seek the secret of it

---

40. *Sicut aquilae juventus renovabitur* (*Psalm* 102).

nowhere else but in that union with Christ and in that unshakable confidence in His omnipotence which made St. Ignatius say: "If the Company were to be suppressed, without any fault on my part, a quarter of an hour alone with God would be enough to give me back my calm and peace." "The heart of an interior soul," says the Curé d'Ars, "stands in the middle of humiliations and sufferings like a rock in the midst of the sea."

We wonder if most active workers are capable of applying to their own lives the idea expressed by General de Sonis in this wonderful daily prayer related by the author of his life?

"My God, here I am before You, poor, little, stripped of everything.

"Here I am at Your feet, sunk in the depths of my own nothingness.

"I wish I had something to offer You, but I am nothing but wretchedness! You, You are everything. You are my wealth.

"My God, I thank You for having willed that I should be nothing in Your sight. I love my humiliation and my nothingness. I thank You for having taken away from me a few satisfactions of self-love, a few consolations of the heart. I thank You for every deception that has befallen me, every ingratitude, every humiliation. I see that they were necessary: the goods of which they deprived me might have kept me far from You.

"O my God, I bless You when You give me trials. I love to be used up, broken to pieces, destroyed by You. Crush me more and more. Let me be in the building not as a stone worked and polished by the hand of the mason, but like an insignificant grain of sand, gathered from the dust of the road.

"My God, I thank You for having let me catch a glimpse of the sweetness of Your consolations, and I thank You for having taken that glimpse away. Everything that You do is just and good. I bless You in my abject poverty, I regret nothing except that I have not loved You enough. I desire nothing but that Your will be done.

"You are my Owner, I am Your property. Turn me this way or that way. Break me up, work on me however You like. I want to be reduced to nothing for love of You.

"O Jesus, how good is Your hand, even at the most terrible intensity of my trial. Let me be crucified, but crucified by You. Amen."

The apostle does indeed suffer. Perhaps the event that has just frustrated his efforts and ruined his work will result in the loss of several of his flock. A bitter sorrow for this true pastor—but it will not be able to dampen the ardor that will make him start over again. He knows that all redemption, be it merely that of a single soul, is a great work, accomplished above all by suffering. He is certain that generosity in supporting trial increases his progress in virtue, and procures greater glory for God; and this certainty is enough to sustain him.

Besides, he knows that often God wants from him nothing more than the seeds of success. Others will come, who will reap rich harvests, and perhaps they will think themselves entitled to all the credit. But heaven will be able to see the cause of it all in the thankless and seemingly sterile work that went before "I have sent you to reap that which you did not labor; others have labored and you have entered into their labors."[41]

Our Lord, Author of the success of the Apostles after Pentecost, willed that, in the course of His public life, He should

---

41. *Misi vos metere quod vos non laborastis; alii laboraverunt et vos in labores eorum introistis* (*Joan.* 4:38).

only sow the seed of that success by teaching and example, and He predicted to His apostles that it would be given them to do works greater than His own: "The works I do, he also shall do, and greater than these shall he do."[42]

What! A true apostle lose courage! He allow himself to be shaken by the words of cowards! He condemn himself to go into retirement just because of some failure! To say such a thing is to lack all understanding either of his interior life or his faith in Christ. A tireless bee, he sets about joyfully building up new honeycombs in his plundered hive.

---

42. *Opera quae ego facio, et ipse faciet, et majora horum faciet* (*Joan.* 14:12).

PART FOUR

ACTION MADE FRUITFUL BY THE INTERIOR LIFE

THE INTERIOR LIFE IS THE CONDITION ON WHICH THE FRUITFULNESS OF ACTIVE WORKS DEPENDS

Let us leave to one side the cause of fruitfulness called by theologians *ex opere operato*. Considering only what is produced *ex opere operantis*, we recall that if the apostle carries out the principle of "He who abideth in Me and I in him," the fecundity of his work, willed by God, is guaranteed: "the same beareth much fruit."[1] Such is the plain logic of this text. After such an authority, there is no need to prove this thesis. Let us simply confirm it by facts.

For more than thirty years we have been able to observe, from afar, the progress of two orphanages for little girls, maintained by two separate congregations. Each one had to go through a period of evident decline. To be frank: out of sixteen orphans, all of whom had entered under the same

---

1. *Qui manet in me et ego in eo, hic fert fructum multum* (*Joan.* 15:5).

conditions and had left upon coming of age, three from the first house and two from the second had passed, in from eight to fifteen months, from the practice of frequent Communion to the most degraded level of the social scale. Of the eleven others, one alone remained deeply Christian. And yet every one of them had been placed, on leaving, in a good situation.

In one of these orphanages, eleven years ago, there was a single change: a new Mother Superior was installed. Six months afterwards a radical transformation was apparent in the spirit of the house.

The same transformation was observed three years later in the other orphanage because, while the same superior and the same sisters remained, the chaplain had been changed.

Now since that time, not a single one of the poor girls who left, at the age of twenty-one, has been dragged down by Satan into the gutter. Every one, every single one of them without exception, has remained a good Christian.

The reason for these results is very simple. At the head of the house, or in the confessional, the spiritual direction previously given had not been really supernatural. And this was enough to paralyze, or at least to cripple, the action of grace. The former superior in one case and the former chaplain in the other, although sincerely pious people, had had no deep interior life and, consequently, exercised *no deep or lasting influence.* Theirs was a piety of the feelings, produced by their upbringing and environment, made up exclusively of pious practices and habits, and giving them nothing but vague beliefs, a love without strength, and virtues without deep root. It was a flabby piety, all in the show-window, mawkish, mechanical. It was a fake piety, capable of forming good little girls who would not make a nuisance of themselves, affected little creatures, full of pretty curtsies but with no force of character, dragged this way and that by their feelings and imaginations. A piety powerless to open up the wide horizons of Christian life, and form valiant women, ready to face a struggle; all it was good for was to keep these wretched little girls locked up in their cages, sighing for the day when they would be let out.

That was the poor excuse for a Christian life produced by Gospel-workers who knew almost nothing of the interior life. In the midst of these two communities, a superior, a chaplain, are replaced. Right away the face of things is altered. What a new meaning prayer begins to take on; what a new fruitfulness in the Sacraments. How different are the postures and bearing in chapel, even at work, at recreation. Analysis shows up a deep transformation which also manifests itself in a serene joy, a new enthusiasm, the acquisition of virtues, and in some souls an intense desire for a religious vocation. To what is such a transformation to be ascribed? The new superior, the new chaplain, led lives of prayer.

No doubt an attentive observer will have connected up similar effects to the same kind of causes in any number of boarding schools, day schools, hospitals, clubs, even parishes, communities, and seminaries.

Listen to St. John of the Cross: "Let the men eaten up with activity," he says, "and who imagine they are able to shake the world with their preaching and other outward works, stop and reflect a moment. It will not be difficult for them to understand that they would be *much more useful* to the Church and more pleasing to the Lord, not to mention the good example they would give to those around them, if they devoted more time to prayer and to the exercises of the interior life.

"Under these conditions, by *one single work* of theirs they would do *far more good*, and with much less trouble, than they do by a *thousand others* on which they exhaust their lives. Prayer would merit them this grace, and would obtain for them the spiritual energies they need to bring forth such fruits. But without prayer, all they do amounts to nothing more than noise and uproar; it is like a hammer banging on an anvil and echoing all over the neighborhood. They accomplish a *little more than nothing, sometimes absolutely nothing at all, and sometimes downright evil.* God save us from such a soul as this, if it should happen to swell up with pride! It would be vain for appearances to be in his favor: the truth is that he would be doing nothing, because no good work can be done without the power of God. Oh, how much could be written on this subject, for the information of those who give up practicing the interior life, and aspire to brilliant works which will put them up on a pedestal and make them the admiration of all. Such people know nothing at all about the source of living water, and of the mysterious fountain which makes all fruit to grow."[2]

Some of the expressions this saint uses are just as strong as the "accursed occupations" quoted above from St. Bernard. Nor is it possible to accuse him of exaggerating when we remember that the qualities which Bossuet admired in St. John of the Cross were his perfect good sense and the zeal he had for warning souls against the desire of extraordinary ways of arriving at sanctity, as well as the most precise exactness in expressing his thoughts, which are, themselves, of remarkable depth.

Let us attempt a study of a few of the causes of the fruitfulness of the interior life.

----

2.   *Spiritual Canticle*, Stanza 29.

a. The Interior Life Draws Down the Blessings of God

I will inebriate the souls of the priests with satiety and my people will be filled with my blessings.[3]

Notice the close connection between the two parts of this text. God does not say: "I will give My priests more zeal and more talent," but: "I will inebriate their souls." What does that signify if not: "I will give them very special graces, and *for that reason my people will be filled with My blessings.*"

God might have given His grace according to His good pleasure, without taking any account of the holiness of the minister nor of the dispositions of the faithful. That is the way He acts in the Baptism of infants. But it is the ordinary law of His Providence that these two factors are the measure of His heavenly gifts.

Without Me you can do nothing.[4] This is the principle. The Blood that redeemed us was shed on Calvary. How was God going to insure its fruitfulness at the very start? By a miracle of the diffusion of interior life. There was nothing more paltry than the ideals and the zeal of the apostles before Pentecost. But once the Holy Spirit had transformed them into men of prayer, their preaching began at once to work wonders.

But God does not, in the ordinary course of things, repeat the miracle of the Upper Room. His way is to leave the graces for our sanctification to fight it out with the free and arduous correspondence of His creature. But in making Pentecost the official birthday of the Church, did He not give us a clear enough indication that his ministers would have to make the

---

3. *Inebriabo animam sacerdotum pinguedine et populus meus bonis meis adimplebitur (Jer. 31:14).*
4. *Sine me nihil potestis facere (Joan. 15:5).*

first step, in their work as co-redeemers, the sanctification of their own souls?

Therefore, all true apostolic workers expect much more from their sacrifices and prayers than from their active work. Father Lacordaire spent a long time in prayer before ascending the steps of the pulpit, and on his return he had himself scourged. Father Monsabré, before speaking at Notre Dame, used to say all fifteen decades of the Rosary on his knees. "I am taking my last dose of tonic," he said with a smile to a friend who questioned him about this practice. Both these religious lived according to St. Bonaventure's principle, that the secret of a fruitful apostolate is to be found much more at the foot of the Cross than in the display of brilliance. "These three remain: word, example, prayer; but the greatest of these is prayer,"[5] cries St. Bernard. A very strong statement, but it is simply a commentary on the resolution taken by the Apostles to leave certain works alone in order to give themselves first of all to prayer, *orationi;* and only after that to preaching, *ministerio verbi.*[6]

Have we not often enough pointed out, in this connection, what a fundamental importance the Savior gave to this spirit of prayer? Looking out upon the world and upon the ages that were to come, He cried out in sorrow: "The harvest indeed is great, but the laborers are few."[7] What would He propose as the quickest way to spread His teaching? Would He ask his apostles to go to school in Athens, or to study, at Rome, under the Caesars, how to conquer and govern empires? You

---

5. *Manent tria haec, verbum, exemplum, oratio: major autem his est oratio.*

6. *Acts* 6:4.

7. *Messis quidem multa, operarii autem pauci. Rogate ergo Dominum messis ut mittat operarios in messem suam* (*Matt.* 9:37–38).

men of active zeal listen to the Master. He reveals a program and a principle full of light: "Pray ye therefore the Lord of the harvest that He send forth laborers into the harvest." No mention of techniques of organization, of raising funds, building churches or putting up schools. Only *"pray ye"—Rogate.* This one fundamental truth of prayer, and the spirit of prayer, is something the Master constantly repeated. Everything else, without exception, flows from it.

Pray ye therefore! If the faint murmur of supplication from a holy soul has more power to raise up legions of apostles than the eloquent voice of a recruiter of vocations, who has less of the spirit of God, what are we to conclude? Simply that the spirit of prayer, which goes hand in hand, in the true apostle, with zeal, will be the chief reason for the fruitfulness of his work.

Pray ye therefore! First of all, pray. Only after that, does Our Lord add "going, teach . . . preach."[8] Of course, God will make use of this other means; but the blessings that make a ministry fruitful are reserved for the prayers of a man of interior life. Such prayer will have the power to bring forth from the bosom of God the strength for an apostolate that souls cannot resist.

The voice of one so great as Pius X throws the following highlight upon the theme of this our book: "To restore all things in Christ by the apostolate of good works, we need divine grace, and the apostle will only receive it if he is united to Christ. Not until we have formed Christ within ourselves will we find it easy to give Him to families and to societies. And therefore all those who take part in the apostolate must develop a solid piety."[9]

---

8. *Euntes docete . . . praedicate* (*Matt.* 10:7).
9. Encyclical of H. H. Pius X to the Bishops of Italy, June 11, 1905.

What has been said of prayer should be equally applied to that other element of the interior life, *suffering:* that is, everything, whether from the outside or from within us, that goes against natural feeling.

A man can suffer like a pagan, like the damned, or like a saint. If he wishes to suffer with Christ, he must try to suffer like a saint. For then, suffering is of benefit to our own souls, and applies the merits of the Passion to those of others: "I fill up those things that are wanting of the sufferings of Christ, in my flesh, for His Body, which is the Church."[10] And St. Augustine, commenting on this text, says: "The sufferings were filled up, but in the Head only, there was wanting still the sufferings of Christ in His members. Christ went before as the Head, and follows after in His body."[11] Christ has suffered as Head, now it is the turn of His Mystical Body to suffer. Every priest can say: I am that Body. I am a member of Christ, and it is up to me to complete what is wanting in the sufferings of Christ, for His Body, which is the Church.

Suffering, says Fr. Faber, is the greatest of the Sacraments. This acute theologian shows the necessity of suffering, and concludes what must be its glories. Every argument of the famous Oratorian can be applied to the fruitfulness of works by the union of the sacrifices of the apostle to the Sacrifice of Golgotha, and thus by their participation in the efficacy of the Precious Blood.

---

10. *Adimpleo ea quae desunt passionum Christi, in carne mea, pro corpore ejus, quod est Ecclesia (Coloss.* 1:24).

11. *Impletae erant omnes, sed in capite, restabant adhuc passiones Christi in membris. Christus praecessit in capite. sequitur in corpore.*

b. It Makes the Apostle Capable of Sanctifying Others by His Example

In the Sermon on the Mount, Our Lord called His apostles the *salt of the earth, the light of the world*.[12] We are the salt of the earth in proportion as we are saints. But if the salt has lost its savor, what use has it? "What shall be cleaned by the unclean?"[13] It is only good to be cast out and trampled under foot.

But on the other hand, a genuinely holy apostle, the true salt of the earth, will be a real agent of preservation in that sea of corruption which is human society. As a beacon shining in the night, "the light of the world," the brightness of his example, even more than the light of his words, will dispel the darkness piled up by the spirit of the world, and will cause to shine forth in splendor the ideal of true happiness which Jesus set forth in the eight beatitudes.

The one thing most likely to induce the faithful to lead a really Christian life is precisely the virtue of the one charged with teaching it. On the other hand, his imperfections are almost infallible in turning people away from God. "For the Name of God, through you, is blasphemed among the gentiles."[14]

That is why the apostle ought more often to have the torch of good example in his hands than fine words upon his lips, and should be the first to excel in the practice of the virtues he preaches. A man whose mission it is to preach great things, says St. Gregory, is, by that very fact, bound to perform them.[15]

---

12. *Matt.* 5:3.
13. *Ab immundo quid mundabitur?* (*Eccl.* 34:4).
14. *Nomen Dei per vos blasphematur inter gentes* (*Rom.* 2:24).
15. *Qui enim sui loci necessitate exigitur summa dicere, hac eadem necessitate compellitur summa monstrare* (St. Gregory the Great: Pastor., ii. c. 3).

It has been pointed out, and with truth, that a physician of the body can heal the sick without being well himself. But to heal souls, a man must himself have a healthy soul, because in order to heal them he has to give them something of himself. Men have every right to be exacting and to ask much of those who offer to teach how to lead a new life. And they are quick to discern if their works measure up to their words, or if the moral theories which they so willingly display are nothing more than a lying front. It is on the basis of their observations in this matter that they will give him their confidence or refuse it.

What power the priest will have, in talking about prayer, if his people see him often in intimate converse with Him who dwells in the Tabernacle, so often forgotten by so many! They will not fail to listen to him, when he preaches penance and hard work, if he is, himself, a hard worker and a man of mortification. When he exhorts them to love one another, he will find them ready to listen to him if he is himself careful to spread throughout his flock the good odor of Christ, and if the gentleness and humility of the divine Exemplar are reflected in his own conduct. "A pattern of the flock from the heart."[16]

The professor who has no interior life imagines he has done all that is required of him if he keeps within the limits of the program of his examination. But if he is a man of prayer some word will now and again slip out, not only from his lips but from his heart: some sentiment or other will show itself in his expression, some significant gesture will escape him, yes, the mere way he makes the Sign of the Cross, or says a prayer before or after class—even a class in mathematics!— may have a more profound influence on his students than a whole sermon.

---

16. *Forma gregis ex animo* (*1 Ptr.* 5:3).

A sister in a hospital or an orphanage has the power and the effective means to sow in souls a deep love of our Lord and His teachings, even while remaining prudently within the limits of her duties. But if she has no interior life, she will not even suspect the presence of such a power, or it will not occur to her to do anything more than encourage acts of exterior piety.

Long and frequent discussions did far less to spread Christianity than the sight of Christian conduct, so opposed to the egotism, injustice, and corruption of the pagans. Cardinal Wiseman, in his masterpiece, *Fabiola*, brings out what a powerful effect the example of the early Christians had upon the souls even of those pagans who were most prejudiced against the new religion. The story shows us the progressive and almost irresistible advance of a soul towards the light. The noble sentiments, the virtues, whether modest or heroic, which the daughter of Fabius found in various persons of all classes and conditions, excited her admiration. But what a change took place in her, what a revelation it was for her soul, when she found out, one by one, that all those whose charity, devotion, modesty, gentleness, moderation, love of justice and chastity she admired, all belonged to that sect which had always been represented to her as worthy of execration. From that time forth she was a Christian.

Is there anyone who can keep himself from exclaiming, on finishing this book: "Oh! If only present-day Catholics, or at least their active workers, had something of this splendid Christian life which the great Cardinal here portrays and which, nevertheless, is nothing but the Gospel put into practice! How irresistible would then be their apostolate among the modern pagans, who are too frequently prejudiced against Catholicism by the calumnies of heretical sects, or repelled by the bitterness of our own answers to our opponents, and by a certain way we sometimes have of asserting our rights in a tone that suggests wounded pride far more than the desire to maintain the interests of Christ!"

What tremendous power there is in the influence radiated by a soul united to God! It was the way Fr. Passerat celebrated Mass that convinced the young Desurmont that he should enter the Congregation of the Most Holy Redeemer—in which he himself was later to achieve such holiness and importance.

The public has a sort of intuition that cannot be fooled. When a real man of God preaches, people come in crowds to hear him. But as soon as the conduct of an apostle ceases to measure up to what is expected of him, no matter how ably his enterprise is run, it will be much harmed, and perhaps ruined beyond recovery.

"Let them see your good works, and glorify your Father who is in heaven."[17] said Our Lord. Good example is something St. Paul stressed over and over again in writing to his two disciples, Titus and Timothy. "In all things show thyself an example of good works."[18] "Be thou an example of the faithful in word, in conversion, in charity, in faith, in chastity."[19] He himself says: "The thing which you have seen in me, these do you."[20] "Be ye followers of me, as I also am of Christ."[21] And these words full of truth sprang from a confidence and a zeal that far from excluded humility, and were of the same kind as those which prompted Our Lord's own challenge:

---

17. *Videant opera vestra bona et glorificent Patrem vestrum qui in coelis est* (*Matt.* 5:16).

18. *In omnibus teipsum praebe exemplum bonorum operum* (*Titus* 2:7).

19. *Exemplum esto fidelium in verbo, in conversatione, in caritate, in fide, in castitate* (*1 Tim.* 4:12).

20. *Quae vidistis in me haec agite* (*Phil.* 4:9).

21. *Imitatores mei estote sicut et ego Christi* (*1 Cor.* 11:1).

"Which of you shall convince me of sin?"[22]

Under these conditions the apostle, following in the footsteps of Him of whom it is written: "He began to do and to teach"[23] will soon become *operarium inconfusibilem*—"a workman that need not to be ashamed."[24]

"Above all, my dear sons," said Leo XIII, "remember that the indispensable condition of true zeal, and the surest pledge of success is purity and holiness of life."[25]

"A holy, perfect and virtuous man," said St. Theresa, "actually does far more good to souls than a great many others who are merely better educated or more talented."

Pius X declared that: "If our own spirit does not submit to the control of a truly Christian and holy way of life, it will be difficult to make others lead a good life." And he adds, "All those called to a life of Catholic Works ought to be men of a life so spotless that they may give everybody else an effective example."[26]

c. *It Makes the Apostle Radiate the Supernatural: the Efficacy of This Radiation*

One of the most formidable obstacles to the conversion of a soul is the fact that God is a hidden God: *Deus absconditus*.[27]

But God, in His goodness, reveals Himself, in a certain manner, through His saints, and even through fervent souls.

---

22. *Quis ex vobis arguet me de peccato?* (*Joan.* 8:46).
23. *Coepit facere et docere* (*Acts* 1:1).
24. *2 Tim.* 2:15.
25. Encyclical of H. H. Leo XIII, September 8, 1899.
26. Encyclical of H. H. Pius X to the Bishops of Italy, June 11, 1905.
27. *Is.* 45:15.

In this way, the supernatural filters through and becomes vis-
ible to the faithful, who are thus able to apprehend something
of the mystery of God.

How does this diffusion of the supernatural come about?
It is the visible brilliance of sanctity, the shining-forth of that
divine influx which theology commonly calls sanctifying
grace; or, better still perhaps, we may say it is the result of
the unutterable presence of the Divine Persons within those
whom They sanctify.

St. Basil gave it precisely this explanation. When the Holy
Spirit, he said, unites Himself to the souls purified by His
grace, He does so in order to make them still more spiritual.
Just as the sunlight makes the crystal upon which it falls, and
which it penetrates, more sparkling and bright, so too the
sanctifying Spirit fills the souls in which He dwells with light,
and, as a result of His presence, they become blazing fires,
spreading all around them grace and charity.[28]

The *manifestation of the Divine* which showed itself in
every movement, and even in the repose of the Man-God, can
also be perceived in certain souls gifted with an intense interior life. The amazing conversions which some saints were
able to effect merely by the fame of their virtues, and the
groups of aspirants to perfection that attached themselves to
them, proclaim loudly enough the secret of their silent apostolate. St. Anthony caused the deserts of Egypt to become filled
with men. St. Benedict was the reason why an unnumbered
army of holy monks rose up to civilize Europe. St. Bernard's
influence, throughout the Church, both upon rulers and their
people, was something unparalleled. St. Vincent Ferrer was
greeted, wherever he went, by the wild enthusiasm of huge

---

28. *De Spiritu Sancto*, ix, 23.

crowds of people; and what is more, he converted them. There rose up such an army of valiant saints in the wake of St. Ignatius Loyola that one of them, all by himself, St. Xavier, was enough to save the souls of an incredible number of pagans. The only thing that can explain these wonders is the power of God Himself, radiated through His human instruments.

It is a terrible misfortune when there is not to be found one really interior soul among all those at the head of important Catholic projects. Then it seems as though the supernatural had undergone an eclipse, and the power of God were in chains. And the saints teach us that, when this happens, a whole nation may fall into a decline, and Providence will seem to have given evil men a free hand to do all the harm they desire.

Make no mistake, there is a sort of instinct by which souls, without clearly defining what it is they sense, are aware of this *radiation of the supernatural.*

What else would bring the sinner, of his own accord, to cast himself at the feet of the priest and ask pardon, recognizing God Himself in His representative? On the other hand, it was when the full conception of sanctity ceased to be the necessary ideal of a minister of a certain Christian sect, that this sect found itself, infallibly, abolishing confession.

"John, indeed, did no sign."[29] Without working a single miracle, John the Baptist attracted great crowds. St. John Vianney had a voice so weak that it could not reach most of those in the crowd that surged around him. But if people could hardly hear him, they saw him; they saw a living monstrance of God, and the mere sight of him overwhelmed those who were there, and converted them.

---

29. *Joannes quidem signum fecit nullum* (*Joan.* 10:41).

A lawyer had just returned from Ars. Someone asked him what it was that had impressed him. He said: "*I have seen God in a man.*"

Perhaps we may be permitted to sum all this up in a rather commonplace comparison. It is a familiar experiment with electricity. Put a man on an insulating stool, and then establish contact between him and an electric machine. His body becomes charged with electricity, and as soon as anyone else touches him, he gives off a spark and shocks the one who has contacted him. It is the same with a man of prayer. Once he is detached from creatures, a continous flow is established between him and Christ, an uninterrupted current. The apostle becomes an *accumulator of supernatural life*, and condenses, in himself, a divine current which is diversified and adapted to the conditions and all the needs of the sphere in which he is working. "Virtue went out from Him and healed all."[30] His words and acts become mere emanations of this latent power: but the power itself is supremely efficient in overcoming every obstacle, obtaining conversions, and increasing fervor.

The more a man's soul is filled with the theological virtues, the more such emanations will bring these same virtues to life in other souls.

THE INTERIOR LIFE MAKES THE APOSTLE RADI-ATE FAITH. Those who hear him realize that God is present within him.

He follows the example of St. Bernard, of whom it was said: "Taking with him, wherever he went, the solitude of his own heart, he was everywhere alone."[31] And so he keeps apart from others, and in order to do so he creates a hermitage within

---

30. *Virtus de illo exibat et sanabat omnes* (*Luc.* 6:19).
31. *Solitudinem cordis circumferens, ubique solus erat.*

himself, but it is easy to see that he is not all by himself in this retreat and that he has, in his heart, a mysterious and familiar Guest, and that he goes within, at every moment, to commune with Him, and that he does not talk until he has received. His directions, His advice, His orders. We are made to feel that he is sustained and guided by Him and that the words uttered by his lips are simply a faithful echo of those of this interior Word: "as the Words of God."[32] And thus what is made manifest by his speech is not so much the logic and conviction of his arguments as the interior Word, the *Verbum docens*, speaking through His creature. "The words that I speak to you, I speak not of myself. But the Father Who abideth in me, He doth the work."[33] The effects of such speech will be deep and enduring indeed, far deeper than the superficial admiration or passing burst of devotion that can be aroused in others by a man without the interior spirit. Such a one can move his hearer to declare that what he says is true and interesting. But that only indicates a state of mind in itself powerless to lead to supernatural faith, or to make that faith live in the soul.

Brother Gabriel, the Trappist lay brother, did much more to revive the faith of numerous visitors to his monastery merely by carrying out his duties as assistant to the guest master,[34] than could have been done by a learned priest whose words

---

32. *Quasi Sermones Dei (1 Ptr.* 4:11).
33. *Verba quae ego loquor vobis, a meipso non loquor. Pater autem in me manens ipse facit opera (Joan.* 14:10).
34. His life is published under the title: "Du Champ de Bataille à la Trappe." Bro. Gabriel had been a captain of dragoons in the Franco-Prussian war. In 1870, at the battle of Gravelotte, he made a vow to enter the Trappists, as a lay brother. The duties of assistant to the guest master are the simple ones of washing dishes, waiting on table, making beds, and so on: but those in this position are allowed to speak with the guests.

might appeal more to the mind than to the heart. General Miribel frequently came to converse with the humble brother, and used to say: "I came here to revive my faith."

Never has there been so much preaching, and arguing, or such a spate of learned works of apologetics as in our day, and yet never, at least as far as the bulk of the faithful is concerned, has the faith been so dead. Those whose job it is to teach too often seem to see nothing in the act of faith but an act of the intellect; but as a matter of fact the will also has a large part in it. They forget that belief is a supernatural gift, and that there is a deep gulf between merely seeing the motives of credibility and making a definite act of faith. This gulf can be bridged by God alone, together with the will of the one who is being instructed: but the divine light reflected by the sanctity of the instructor is of immense assistance in accomplishing this task.

HE RADIATES HOPE. It would be impossible for a man of prayer not to radiate hope. By his faith, he is unshakably fixed in the conviction that happiness is to be found in God, and in Him alone. And so, with what persuasive accents does he speak of heaven, and what power he has to console the sorrowful! The best way to get men to listen to you is to hold out to them the secret of carrying the Cross, which is the lot of every mortal, with joy. This secret lies in the Eucharist and in the hope of Heaven.

What life there is in the words of consolation uttered by a man who can say, in all truth, that his "conversation is in Heaven."[35] Someone else may, perhaps, display finer phrases and more fancy rhetoric in talking about the joys of our heavenly home: all his speeches will fall flat. But the interior soul, with a few convincing words that reveal the state of mind of

---

35. *Nostra conversatio in coelis est* (*Phil.* 3:20).

him who utters them, will be able to calm the grief, soothe the sorrow felt by our souls, and help us to accept the keenest suffering with resignation.

And thus the virtue of hope goes forth from this man of prayer and communicates itself irresistibly to a soul who had perhaps never felt its warmth before, and who was about to sink into the depths of despair.

HE RADIATES CHARITY. The chief ambition of a soul that aspires to sanctity is to possess charity. The interpenetration of Jesus and the soul, the state expressed in the words: "he that abideth in Me and I in him," is the end that every man of interior life has in view.

Experienced preachers are unanimous in declaring that although the introductory sermons on death, judgment, and hell are indispensable and always salutary in a retreat or mission, the sermon on the love of Our Lord generally does more good. When it is preached by a true missionary, who is able to make his hearers share in the sentiments with which he is filled, it is a guarantee of success and leads to many conversions.

When there is question of detaching a soul from sin or of leading one from fervor to perfection, the love of Christ is always the best means of all. A Christian who has sunk deep into the mire, yet who is able to *sense, in another, the presence of a burning love enkindled by invisible realities*, and who, on the other hand, considers the deception and hollowness of earthly loves, begins to feel intense disgust at sin. He has understood something of God, something of Christ's immense love for His creatures. He feels within himself the stirrings of the latent grace of his Baptism and first Communion. Christ has appeared to him, living and real, for the love of His Heart has shown itself through His minister's countenance and voice. The sinner has caught a glimpse of another kind of love, one that is pure, ardent, and noble, and he has said to himself: "So it *is* possible, after all, to love, on this earth, with a love that transcends the love of creatures!"

Yet a few more intimate manifestations of the God of Love through His herald, and the soul will emerge from the mire in which it was held fast, and will no longer fear the sacrifices that must be made to acquire the love of God, which, up until that time, had been something almost unknown in its life.

Though this is not the place to develop this idea further, one may easily see what great increase of love, and therefore what progress, a true pastor will be able to effect in souls that have already emerged from sin, or have become fervent. Even those workers in Catholic Action who are not ordained priests will be able, by their ardent charity, to cause this, the highest of theological virtues, to spring to life all around them.

HE RADIATES KINDNESS. "A zeal that is not charitable," says St. Francis de Sales, "comes from a charity that is not genuine."[36] When a soul tastes, in prayer, the delights of One whom the Church calls an "ocean of kindness," *bonitatis oceanus*, it will soon undergo a great transformation. Even if a man is naturally disposed to egotism and unkindness, all these defects will vanish little by little. If he nourishes his soul upon Him in whom appeared the "goodness and kindness of God our Savior,"[37] to the world, upon Him who is the Image and adequate expression of the divine Goodness (*imago bonitatis*

---

36. *Un zèle qui n'est pas charitable vient d'une charité qui n'est pas véritable.*
37. *Benignitas et humanitas apparuit Salvatoris nostri Dei (Titus 3:4).*

illius),[38] the apostle will share in the bounty of God and will feel the need to be, like God, "*diffusivus*," spreading kindness.

The more a soul is united to Christ, the more it shares in the dominant quality of the Divine and Human Heart of the Redeemer—His kindness. In such a soul forbearance, benevolence, compassion are all multiplied beyond belief and his generosity and self-sacrifice may be carried to the limits of joyful and magnanimous immolation.

Transfigured by divine love, the apostle will have no trouble in winning the sympathy of souls. "In the goodness and readiness of his soul he was pleasing."[39] His words and acts will be full of kindness, a kindness that is completely disinterested and has nothing in common with that which is inspired by a desire for popularity or by subtle egoism.

"God," wrote Lacordaire, "has willed that no good should be done to man except by loving him, and that insensibility should be forever incapable either of giving him light, or inspiring him to virtue." And the fact is that men take glory in resisting those who try to impose anything on them by force; they make it a point of honor to raise countless objections against the wisdom that aims at arguing everybody, all the time, around to its own point of view. But because there is no humiliation involved in allowing oneself to be disarmed by kindness, men are quite willing to yield to the attraction of its advances.

The Little Sister of the Poor, the Little Sister of the Assumption, the Sister of Charity would be able to tell us of a host of conversions brought about without any arguing, merely by the power of a tireless and often heroic kindness.

---

38. *Sap.* 7:26.
39. *In bonitate et alacritate animae suae placuit* (*Eccl.* 45:29).

The unbeliever, in the presence of such self-sacrifice, exclaims: "God is there. I can see Him, and see that He is what He is called: 'the good God.' He would have to be good, if living with Him were to be enough to make so frail a creature as man trample his own self-love under his feet and silence his most legitimate repugnances."

These angels of this earth fulfill the definition of Fr. Faber: "Kindness is the overflow of self on others. To be kind is to put others in one's place. Kindness has convinced more sinners than zeal, eloquence, or learning, and these three things have never converted anybody without kindness having something to do with it. In a word, kindness makes us as gods towards one another. It is the manifestation of this feeling in apostolic men which draws sinners to them and brings them thus to their conversion."[40]

And he adds: "Everywhere kindness shows itself the best pioneer of the Precious Blood. . . . Without doubt the fear of the Lord is frequently the beginning of that wisdom which we call conversion: but we must frighten men kindly, for otherwise fear will only make infidels."

"Have the heart of a mother," says St. Vincent Ferrer, "whether you have to encourage souls or scare them, show to them a heart full of tender charity, and let the sinner feel that your language is inspired by it. If you want to be useful to souls, begin by appealing to God with all your heart, asking Him to fill you with charity which is the compendium of all the virtues, in order that by its means you may efficaciously attain the end you have in view."[41]

It is as far a call from natural kindness, which is nothing

---

40. *Spiritual Conferences.*
41. *Traité de la Vie Spirituelle*, p. II, Ch. 10.

but the result of our temperament, to supernatural kindness, in the soul of an apostle, as it is from man to God. The former may arouse a certain respect, even sympathy for the minister of Christ, and sometimes it can even divert an affection that belongs to God alone and direct it to His creature. But it will never induce any soul to stir itself up, with a pure intention of pleasing God, to make the sacrifice that is necessary if it is to return to its Creator. Only the kindness that flows from a close friendship with Christ can achieve this result.

An ardent love of Christ and a true flair for saving souls will give an apostle all the daring compatible with tact and prudence. Here is a story that was told us directly by an eminent layman. On the occasion of a conversation with Pius X he chanced to let fall a few biting words against an enemy of the Church. "My son," said the Pope, "I do not approve of the way you talk. For your penance, listen to this story. A priest I used to know very well had just arrived in his first parish. He thought it his duty to visit every family, including Jews, Protestants, and even Freemasons. Then he announced from the pulpit that he would repeat the visits every year. His confreres got very excited at this, and complained to the Bishop, and the Bishop, in turn, sent for the culprit and reprimanded him severely. 'My Lord,' answered the priest modestly, 'Jesus orders his pastors, in the Gospel, to bring all His sheep into the fold, *oportet illas adducere.* How are we going to do that without going out after them? Besides, I never compromise on principles, and I confine myself to expressing my interest and my charity towards all the souls entrusted to me by God, even the ones that have gone furthest astray. I have announced from the pulpit that I would make these visits; if you formally desire me to give them up, please be good enough to give me this prohibition in writing, so that everybody may know that I am simply obeying your orders.' Moved by the justice of this appeal, the Bishop did not insist. And in any case, the future proved that the priest was right, because he had the happiness to convert a few of these strays, and inspired all the others with a great respect for our holy religion. This humble parish priest, by the will of God, eventually became the Pope who is now giving you this lesson in charity, my son! Therefore, cling firmly to principles through thick and thin, but let your charity go out to all men, even the worst enemies of the Church."

HE RADIATES HUMILITY. It is easy to understand how the goodness and kindness of Christ attracted people to Him in crowds. Nor is there any doubt that they were just as powerfully drawn to Him by His humility.

"Without Me, you can do nothing."[42] The apostle, raised up by his Creator to the exalted position of collaborator, is destined to become an instrument in the performance of supernatural works, but only on the condition that *Christ alone be seen as the One who does these works*. The better the apostle knows how to keep out of the picture, and remain impersonal, the more surely will Christ show Himself. But without this impersonal quality, which is the fruit of the interior life, the apostle will plant and water his garden in vain, nothing will grow.

True humility has a special charm that comes directly from Christ. It has something of the *divine* in it. In proportion to the apostle's zeal to efface himself and let Christ alone be seen as performing the work ("He must increase, but I must decrease"[43]), Our Lord will give him a greater and greater power over the hearts of men.

---

42. *Sine me nihil potestis facere* (*Joan.* 15:5).
43. *Illum oportet crescere, me autem minui* (*Joan.* 3:30).

That is how humility becomes one of the chief means of converting souls. "Believe me," St. Vincent de Paul said to his priests, "we will never be any use in doing God's work until we become thoroughly convinced that, of ourselves, we are better fitted to ruin everything than to make a success of it."

The reader may perhaps be surprised to see us returning so often to the same ideas. But it seems to us that the only way to drive them home and firmly establish their importance in your minds is to keep on repeating them.

Is it not true that failure very often comes, largely, from a high-handed way of doing things, and airs of superiority?

The so-called "modern" Christian wants to preserve his independence. He will consent to obey God, all right: *but God alone.* And therefore he is only going to take orders, or direction, or even advice, from a minister of God when he is quite sure that the orders do come from God.

Consequently, the apostle has got to cultivate humility (and only the interior life will show him how) to the point of effacing himself and disappearing from view until those who look at him *see right through him to God*, so to speak. And thus he will carry out the Master's words: "He that is the greatest among you shall be your servant. Be you not called Rabbi . . . neither be you called masters."[44]

The mere outward appearance of a man of prayer can teach men the *science of living*, that is, the *science of prayer*.[45] Why? Because his humility breathes the sweet fragrance of dependence on God. This dependence, which is the unvarying disposition of such a soul, manifests itself by a habit of recourse to God under every possible circumstance, either in

---

44. *Qui major est vestrum erit minister vester. Vos autem nolite vocari Rabbi . . . nec vocemini magistri* (*Matt.* 23:8, 11).
45. St. Augustine.

order to come to some decision, or to seek consolation in all troubles, or else to obtain the strength to overcome them.

In the Common of Confessors not Pontiffs, in the Breviary, the priest reads St. Bede's wonderful comment upon the words of the Gospel, "Fear not, little flock."[46] "The Savior," he says, "calls the flock of the elect *little* either by comparison with the multitude of the reprobate, or, better still, because of their *great zeal for humility*, for no matter how great and extensive His Church may have become, He wills that she should ever *grow in humility* right up to the end of the world, and thus arrive at the *Kingdom promised to the humble*."[47]

This text draws its inspiration from the powerful lessons of Our Lord to His Apostles when, for instance, they wanted to turn their apostolic vocations to their own personal profit, and showed themselves so full of ambition and jealousy in their expressions of that desire! "You know," He said, "that the princes of the gentiles lord it over them; and they that are the greater exercise power upon them. It shall not be so among you, but whosoever will be the greater among you, let him be your master, and he that will be the first among you, shall be your servant."[48]

"But," asks Bourdaloue, "would not that take away the power of authority? There will always be enough authority among you, if there is enough humility, and *if humility is lost*, authority will become an *intolerable burden*."

If the apostle has not humility, he will go to one of two extremes. It will be either a matter of careless and excessive familiarity, with all its free-and-easy licenses, or else of

---

46. *Luke* 12:32.
47. *Comm. Conf. non Pont., Alterae lectiones, III Noct.* (From St. Bede's *Homilies on St. Luke's Gospel*, Bk. iv, Ch. 54).
48. *Matt.* 20:25–27.

domineering over everybody else. The latter case is the more likely.

Leaving questions of doctrine to one side, let us suppose that the apostle has enough sense to protect his mind from an unlimited tolerance on one hand and, on the other, from a harsh and bitter zeal of which the excesses would be very displeasing to God. Let us credit him with good, sane principles and correct knowledge. When all this has been granted, we still affirm that without humility, the apostle will not be able to hold a middle course between the two extremes, and that his behavior will either betray weakness or, more likely, overweening pride.

On the one hand, he will yield to a false humility and become timid, allowing the spirit of charity to degenerate into weakness. He will be ready to make any exaggerated concession, to seek conciliation at any price, and a thousand pretexts will serve to overcome his zeal for maintaining his principles. He will be prepared to sacrifice them for any motive of human prudence, or any immediate material gain, without a thought for the ultimate consequences.

Or else, on the other hand, his purely natural way of doing things, and the misdirection of his will, will bring into play his pride, his touchiness, his *Ego*. There will follow any number of personal dislikes, attempts to lay down the law, bitterness, spite, rivalries, antipathies, jealousies, a purely human desire to get ahead of everybody else, calumnies, backbiting, sarcastic talk, a worldly spirit of partisanship, great harshness in defending his principles, and so on.

The glory of God, instead of remaining the true *end* in the pursuit of which our passions can be sublimated, will be reduced, by such an apostle as we are describing, to the level of a *pretext and a means* of supporting and encouraging and excusing his passions in all that is weakest and most human about them. The slightest attack upon the glory of God, or upon the Church, will be the signal for an outburst of anger in which the psychologist will be able to see that the apostle is rushing to the defense of his own personality or of the privileges of his religious caste in society, insofar as it is a *human group*, and not showing devotion to God's cause, which is the sole reason for the existence of the Church insofar as it is a *perfect Society instituted by Our Lord*.

Correct doctrine and good judgment will not be enough to preserve him from these aberrations, because the apostle without interior life, and, therefore without humility, will be at the mercy of his passions. Humility alone, by keeping him to the path of right judgment and preventing him from acting on impulse, will maintain a more perfect balance and stability in his life. It will unite him to God, and so make him participate, in a sense, in the changelessness of God. In the same way, the frail strands of ivy become strong and stable with all the unshakable strength of the oak when, with all its fibers, it clings to the sturdy trunk of this forest king.

Let us therefore not hesitate to recognize that, without humility, if we do not fall into the first error, our nature will carry us into the second; or else we will float in and out with the tide, according to circumstances or to the impulsion of our passions, now towards one extreme and again towards the other. We will bear out St. Thomas' words that man is a changing being, constant only in his inconstancy.

The logical result of such an imperfect apostolate will be either that men despise an authority that has no strength, or mistrust, and even detest, an authority which does not give forth any reflection of God.

HE RADIATES FIRMNESS AND GENTLENESS. The saints have often been extremely outspoken against error, the contagion of loose living, and hypocrisy. Take St. Bernard, for example. This oracle of his own time was one of those saints who showed most firmness in his zeal for God. But the attentive reader of his life will be able to see to what an extent the interior life had made this man-of-God selfless. He only fell back on strong measures when he had clear evidence that all other means were useless. Often, too, he varied between gentleness and strength. After having shown his great love for souls by avenging some principle with holy indignation and stern demands for remedies, reparation, guarantees, and promises, he would at once display the tenderness of a mother in the conversion of those whom his conscience had forced him to fight. Pitiless towards the errors of Abelard, he speedily became the friend of the one whom his victory had reduced to silence.

When it was a matter of choosing means, if he saw that no principle was necessarily involved, he always stood before the hierarchy of the Church as a champion of non-violent procedure. Learning that there was a movement on foot to ruin and massacre the Jews of Germany, he left his cloister without a moment's delay and hurried to their rescue, preaching a crusade of peace. Fr. Ratisbonne quotes a document of great significance in his *Life of St. Bernard*. It is a statement of the most exalted Rabbi of that land, expressing his admiration for the monk of Clairvaux, "without whom," he says, "there would not be one of us alive in Germany." And he urges future generations of Jews never to forget the debt of gratitude they owe to the holy abbot. On this occasion St. Bernard uttered the following words: "We are the soldiers of peace, we are the army of the peacemakers, fighting for God and peace: *Deo et paci militantibus.* Persuasion, good example, loyalty to God are the only arms worthy of the children of the Gospel."

There is no substitute for the interior life as a means of obtaining this spirit of selflessness which characterizes the zeal of every saint.

In the Chablais district of the Alps, every effort of orthodox Christianity fell through, until the appearrance of St. Francis de Sales upon the scene. On his arrival, the Protestant leaders made ready for a fight to the death. They desired nothing less than the life of the Bishop of Geneva. But he appeared among them full of gentleness and humility. He showed himself to be a man whose *Ego* had become so subdued and effaced that the love of God and of other men possessed him almost entirely. History teaches us the almost incredibly rapid results of his apostolate.

But even the gentle Francis de Sales knew when to be inexorably firm. He did not hesitate to call upon the power of human laws to confirm the results obtained by kind words and the example of virtue. Hence the saint advised the Duke of Savoy to take severe measures against any heretics who went back on their agreements.

All that the saints ever did was copy their Master. We see our Savior, in the Gospel, welcoming sinners with great mercy. He was the friend of Zacchaeus and the publicans, full of goodness towards the sick, the suffering, and the little ones. And yet He who was gentleness and meekness incarnate did not hesitate to take a whip to chase the money-changers out of the temple. And what severe and powerful words He uses when He speaks of Herod, or castigates the vices of the scribes and hypocrite pharisees!

But it is only in certain very rare cases, after all other means have failed us, or when it is obvious that they would be of no use, that one may, against his will, so to speak, have recourse to a seemingly more drastic procedure, out of charity and to prevent the spread of evil.

Apart from such exceptional cases, and when some principle is not actually at stake, it is meekness that must direct the conduct of the Gospel worker. "You catch more flies," said St. Francis de Sales, "with a little honey than with a barrel of vinegar."

Remember how Our Lord reproved His Apostles when they were hurt and ruffled in their human dignity and allowed themselves to be led by a zeal that was by no means either disinterested or pure, to seek violent means, demanding fire from heaven to consume the little Samaritan town that had refused to receive them. "You *know not of what spirit you are*," He said to them.[49]

One of our Bishops, who is often pointed out as an example of unshakable firmness in his defense of principles, went through his episcopal city visiting stricken families during the First World War. Making himself all things to all men, he went to say a few words of consolation to a Calvinist who was mourning a son fallen on the field of honor—words that came straight from the heart, and were full of a sincere tenderness. Touched by this act of humble charity, the Protestant afterwards declared: "Is it possible that this Bishop, a man so nobly born, should have condescended to enter my poor little home, in spite of the difference of our religion? What he has done and said goes straight to my heart." The manufacturer in whose employment the Protestant was added, as he told us of this event, "As far as I can see, this Protestant is already halfway to conversion. And in any case the Bishop has done

---

49. *Luc.* 9:55.

more, by his kindness, to promote his conversion than he would have done by any number of heated arguments." This pastor of souls gave evidence of the meekness of Our Lord. The Protestant saw the Savior before him, in a manner of speaking, and was forced to conclude that a church with Bishops who so truly reflect him whom he admired in the Gospels must be the true Church.

The interior spirit will keep both mind and will working in the service of the Gospel. A soul that sees all things and acts always according to the Heart of Jesus will never be thrown off balance by indolence on one hand or unjustified violence on the other. Its prudence and its ardor alike come only from that adorable Heart. That is the secret of its success.

On the other hand, it is lack of interior life, and, consequently, the manifestation of human passions, that is the reason why we are so often defeated.

HE RADIATES MORTIFICATION. The spirit of mortification is another principle of fruitfulness in good works. Everything is summed up in the Cross. *And as long as we have not made the mystery of the Cross sink deeply into the souls of men, we have, as yet, barely touched their surface.* But who will ever be able to get people to accept this mystery which so repels that horror of suffering which is so natural to mankind? Only the man who can say, with the great Apostle: "With Christ I am nailed to the Cross."[50] The only ones capable of such a task are those who carry in themselves Jesus crucified: "Always bearing about in our body the mortification of Jesus, that the life of Jesus may be made manifest in our bodies."[51]

---

50. *Christo confixus sum Cruci (Gal. 2:19).*
51. *Semper mortificationem Jesu in corpore nostro circumferentes ut vita Jesu manifestetur in corporibus nostris (2 Cor. 4:10).*

To mortify oneself is to reproduce the "Christ who did not please Himself."[52] That is, to renounce ourselves under all circumstances, to get to love everything that displeases our nature and, finally, to tend to the ideal of being a victim that is immolated without ceasing every moment of the day.

Now, without the interior life, it is simply impossible to uproot all our most stubborn instincts in this way.

The *Poverello* of Assisi could walk in silence through the streets of the old hill-town preaching the mystery of the Cross by his mere appearance: but an apostle who knows no mortification wastes his time preaching Calvary even if he is able to borrow the finests flights of Bossuet to do so. The world is so firmly entrenched in the spirit of pleasure that ordinary arguments, and even the most brilliant analyses and intuitions will be incapable of destroying its citadel. What is needed is for some minister of God to make the *Passion a vivid, living reality* by his own mortification and detachment.

They are "enemies of the Cross of Christ,"[53] St. Paul would say of those numerous Christians who only see in Christianity a form of social conformity: men for whom our religion is nothing but a habit of certain external practices, handed down by tradition and carried out from time to time with respect, of course, but without any relation to the amendment of life, the combat against the passions, or the introduction of the Gospel spirit into our practical living. The Lord might well say of such as this: the people appear to honor Me; "They honor Me with their lips, but their heart is far from Me."[54]

"Enemies of the Cross of Christ," those weakkneed

---

52. *Christus sibi no placuit* (*Rom.* 15:3).
53. *Inimicos Crucis Christi* (*Phil.* 3:18).
54. *Populus hic labiis me honorat, cor autem eorum longe est a me* (*Matt.* 15:8).

Christians who think it is indispensable that they should surround themselves with every comfort, and give in to all the
demands made by the world, to seek its inordinate pleasures,
and to follow with passionate interest all its changing fash-
ions. Such people are shocked by these words of Our Lord,
which they can no longer understand; and yet it is something
He said for the benefit of every man:

"*Except you do penance, you shall all likewise perish.*"[55]
As St. Paul says, the Cross has become to them a "stumbling
block."[56]

And yet how is the apostle going to produce other Christians if he himself has no interior life?

Any true priest will naturally feel great satisfaction when
he sees large crowds at his various services: and yet he will
have no real enthusiasm over all this if he knows that they
have all come as a matter of routine, merely out of fidelity to
certain respectable family customs, to certain habits which do
nothing to influence the course of their lives in general. Nor
will he draw any joy from this big attendance if he finds that
its only cause is the pleasure the people take in hearing good
music, in seeing nice decorations, or listening to a rhetorical
exercise which they have come to enjoy for its form and style
alone.

One might think that this enthusiasm would be quite legitimate when there was question of many people making frequent Communions. But at this point, a memory of my trip to
America[57] comes to my mind. As I visited certain parishes,

---

55. *Luc.* 13:5.
56. *1 Cor.* 1:23.
57. The previous translator of the *Soul of the Apostolate* into English, writ-
     ing in English, saw fit to omit this passage from his translation, perhaps
     with an undue regard for the sensitiveness of American readers. But

I was delighted to find out that a good number of men there were faithful to the Communion of the First Friday of the month. But a holy New York priest commented on my delight with: "*homo videt in facie, Deus autem in corde*"—Man sees the face, but God sees the heart! "Do not forget," he went on, "that you are in a country where nobody is held back by human respect, and where bluff is fairly universal. Restrain your admiration until you come to a parish where a reliable observer can testify that frequent Communion is a genuine indication, if not of a complete amendment of life, at least of sincere efforts to lead a Christian life, and a loyal desire not to compromise with heavy drinking and the ruthless ambition to make a lot of money."

Far be it from us to underrate the slightest traces of Christian life, however paltry. But the real burden of these pages is to deplore our lamentable incapacity, without interior life, to produce any effects except these trivial, though not altogether negligible, results.

All that Jesus wants is our heart. The reason why He came to reveal to men the sublime truths of faith was to conquer their hearts, possess their wills, and inspire them to follow Him in the path of renunciation.

An apostle who is accustomed to an interior life based on Our Lord's words, "Let him deny himself,"[58] will be fully capable of producing in others this selfdenial, which is the foundation of all moral perfection. But one who only lags far behind Our Lord, in carrying the Cross, will be incapable of

---

such solicitude is no compliment to us! Did the good Father think that we would listen complacently to Dom Chautard pointing out faults in his own country, and yet fall into despair if he suggested that there might be a few imperfections over here too?

58. *Abneget semetipsum* (*Matt.* 16:24).

such a result: *Nemo dat quod non habet.*[59] Since he himself is such a coward, when it comes to imitating Christ crucified, how will he ever preach to his people the holy war against the passions—the war in which Our Lord sounded the rallying cry for us all?

Only an apostle who is disinterested, humble, and chaste can lead souls on into the battle against the ever-growing forces of greed, ambition, and impurity. Only an apostle who has learned the science of the Crucifix will be able to check that everlasting search for comfort and ease, that worship of pleasure that threatens to sweep the whole world and undermine families and whole nations to their eventual destruction.

St. Paul summed up his apostolate as "preaching Christ crucified." Because he lived in Christ, and in Christ crucified, he was able to give souls a taste for the mystery of the Cross, and teach them to live it.

Too many apostles in our own day no longer have enough interior life to fathom this life-giving mystery, to steep themselves through and through with it, until it shines forth from everything they do. They look at religion too much from the point of view of philosophy, sociology, or even of esthetics. They see in it only those elements which appeal to the mind and excite the sensibilities and imagination. They give free scope to their inclination to regard religion as a sublime school of poetry and of incomparable art. It is quite true that religion possesses all these qualities; but to consider it only under these secondary aspects would be to subject the economy of the Gospel to a grievous distortion, making an end of something that is nothing but a means. But it is a species of sacrilege to take the Christ of Gethsemani, of the Pretorium,

---

59. Nobody gives what he does not possess.

of Calvary, merely as a good subject for a holy picture. Ever since man sinned, penance, reparation, and spiritual war have become necessary conditions of our life. At every turn, the Cross of Christ is there to remind us of the fact. The Incarnate Word's zeal for His Father's glory will not be satisfied with mere admiration: He wants imitation.

Benedict XV invited all true apostles, in his Encyclical of November 1, 1914, to put their hand to the plow with greater determination than ever, in their labor of getting souls away from their love of comfort, their egotism, their flippant tastes, and their forgetfulness of eternal values. That amounted to an appeal to all ministers of our crucified God to lead an interior life.

God, who has given us so much, asks of the Christian, as soon as he has reached the age of reason, to unite something of himself to the bitter bloodshedding of Christ's passion: to unite what we might call our *soul's* blood, that is, all the sacrifices that are required in the observance of the law of God. How will the faithful be inspired to generosity in sacrificing wealth, pleasure, and honor? Only by the example of a director of souls who has made himself familiar with the spirit of sacrifice.

When we see the repeated victories of our infernal foes, we may well wonder, in our anxiety, where to look for the salvation of our society. When will it be the Church's turn to win a few battles? The answer is easy: we can say with Our Lord, "This kind is not cast out but by prayer and fasting."[60] It will be our turn when the ranks of the clergy and of the religious orders will have begun to produce a body of mortified

---

60. *Hoc autem genus non ejicitur nisi per orationem et jejunium* (*Matt.* 17:20).

men who *will make the great splendor of the mystery of the Cross blaze in the eyes of all peoples:* and the nations of the earth, seeing, in mortified priests and religious, how reparation is made for the sins of the world, will also understand the Redemption of the world by the Precious Blood of Jesus Christ. Only then will the army of the devil begin to retreat, and the ages of human history will no longer echo with the terrible anguished cry of our outraged Lord— that cry that will at last have found some to make reparation: "And I sought among them for a man that might set up a hedge, and stand in the gap before Me in favor of the land, that I might not destroy it, and I found none."[61]

Someone has tried to find out why a single Sign of the Cross from Fr. de Ravignan was enough to electrify indifferent Catholics and even unbelievers who had come to hear him out of mere curiosity. The conclusion to which he was led after questioning many of those who had heard the holy Jesuit, was that it was the *preacher's austerity of life* which was given a most striking manifestation by this Sign of the Cross, uniting him with the mystery of Calvary.

d. It Makes the Gospel Worker Truly Eloquent

What we are talking about is, of course, that eloquence which is effective enough as a *vehicle of grace* to bring about the conversion of souls and lead them to virtue. We have already treated of it in an incidental fashion. We will only add a few words to these considerations here.

---

61. *Et quaesivi de eis virum qui interponeret sepem et staret oppositus contra me pro terra, ne dissiparem eam, et non inveni (Ezech. 22:30).*

In the Office of St. John we read this responsory: "reclining on the breast of the Lord, he *drank in from the sacred fountain itself,* of the Heart of the Lord, the fluency of his Gospel, and he *spread the grace of the word of God over the whole world.*"[62]

What a profound lesson is to be found in these few words for all those whose duty it is as preachers, writers, or catechists to spread abroad the word of God! In these powerful words, the Church reveals to the priests the *source* of all true eloquence.

All the Evangelists were equally inspired. All had their providential purpose. And yet, nevertheless, each one has an eloquence all his own. St. John, more than all the others, has the power to reach our wills by filling our hearts with the grace of God's word, *verbi Dei gratiam.* His Gospel, together with the Epistles of St. Paul, is the favorite book of souls for whom life here below is meaningless without union with Jesus Christ.

Where did St. John get an eloquence of such power? In what mountain is the source of that great river whose life-giving waters spread their bounty over the whole earth? (*Fluenta in toto orbe terrarum diffudit.*)

The liturgical text tells us: he is one of the rivers of Paradise. *Quasi unus ex Paradisi fluminibus Evangelista Joanne.*

What is the use of so many high mountains and glaciers, in this earth? Some people who know nothing might perhaps

---

62. *Supra pectus Domini recumbens, Evangelii fluenta de ipso sacro Dominici pectoris Fonte potavit et verbi Dei gratiam in toto terrarum orbe diffudit* (*Monastic Breviary*, R. xi, Third Nocturn). The *Roman Breviary*, R. viii, Third Noct. of Matins has part of this quotation: *sc., Fluenta Evangelii de ipso sacro Dominici pectoris fonte potavit, but that is all.*

come to the conclusion that it would be much more profitable if all these vast mountainous areas were nice fertile plains. But they would be forgetting that without these high peaks, all the plains and valleys would be as barren as the Sahara. For it is the mountains that give the earth its fertility, by means of the rivers for which they serve as reservoirs.

This great peak of Paradise, where springs the fount by which is fed the Gospel of St. John, is nothing else but the Heart of Jesus: *Evangelii fluenta de ipso sacro Dominici pectoris fonte potavit.* It was because the Evangelist, by his interior life, was able to detect the beatings of the Heart of the Man-God, and the immensity of His love for men, that his word is the *vehicle of the grace* of the divine Word: *Verbi Dei gratiam diffudit.*

In the same way it can be said that all men of prayer are in a way rivers of Paradise. Not only do they draw down from heaven, upon the earth, by their prayers and sacrifices, the living waters of grace, and deflect or mitigate the chastisements which the world deserves, but ascending even to the height of heaven, they draw from the Heart of Him in Whom the inner life of God resides, the floods of that very life, and distribute it in great abundance upon souls. "You shall draw waters out of the Savior's fountains."[63] Called to give forth the word of God, they do so with an eloquence of which they alone possess the secret. They speak to the earth of heaven. They bring light, warmth, consolation, and strength. Without all these qualities together, no eloquence is quite complete. And the preacher will only be able to combine them all if he lives in and by Jesus Christ.

Am I really one of those who depend upon their mental

---

63. *Haurietis aquas de fontibus salvatoris* (*Is.* 12:3).

prayer, their visits to the Blessed Sacrament, above all upon their Mass or their Communion, to put real moving power into their preaching? If I am not, I may perhaps be a loudly "tinkling cymbal," or even give forth the more pompous din of "sounding brass," but I am not communicating to others any love, that love which makes the eloquence of the friends of God impossible to resist.

A preacher endowed with learning but of only mediocre piety may be able to paint a picture of Christian Truth that will stir souls, bring them a little closer to God, even increase their faith. But if one is to fill souls with the life-giving savor of virtue, he must first have tasted the true spirit of the Gospel and made it enter into the substance of his own life by means of mental prayer.

Let us repeat once more that only the Holy Spirit, the Principle of all spiritual fruitfulness, can make converts and impart the graces that determine men to flee vice and follow virtue. The preaching of the apostle, when it is filled with the unction of the sanctifying Spirit, becomes a living channel which holds back nothing of the divine action. Before Pentecost the apostles had preached almost with no result at all. After their ten-day retreat, given entirely to the interior life, they were overwhelmed by the Spirit of God, and transformed by Him. Their first attempts at preaching were miraculous draughts of fishes. It will be the same with the sowers of the Gospel. Their interior life will make them true Christ-bearers. They will plant and water their seedlings with great success and the Spirit of God will always give them increase. Their word will at the same time be the seed that is sown and the rain that waters. There will be no lack of the ripening sun, giver of growth.

"It is vain merely to give light," says St. Bernard, "and it is but little merely to burn; but to burn and give light together is perfection." Further on he adds: "It is in a particular manner to apostle and apostolic men that are addressed these words: Let your light shine before men. For such as these ought to be ardent, yea, very ardent."[64]

This eloquence in preaching is to be drawn, by the apostle, not only from a life of union with Jesus by prayer and custody of the heart but also from the Sacred Scriptures, which he will study with great zeal, and in which he will take a genuine delight. God's every word to men, every word fallen from the lips of Jesus, will be treasured by him as a diamond; and he will admire all its facets by the light of the gift of wisdom, which has reached a considerable per fection in him. But since he never opens the inspired book without first *having lifted his mind and heart to God in prayer*, he not only *admires* but *relishes* the teachings he finds in it, just as if they had been dictated by the Holy Spirit for him personally. With what unction, then, will he quote the word of God in the pulpit, and what a difference there will be between the light that he draws forth from it and the ingenious and learned applications worked out by a preacher with no other resources than reason and an abstract, half-dead faith. The former will show us truth as *living*, surrounding souls with a reality that desires not only to enlighten them, but to give them life. The latter is only able to talk of truth as of a sort of algebraic equation, possessing, of course, certitude, but cold and unrelated to the inmost realities

---

64. The Saint is commenting on the text. "He was a burning and a shining light," applied to St. John Baptist in a Sermon for the feast of the Great Precursor—a model for all apostles. "*Est tantum lucere vanum tantum ardere parum, ardere et lucere perfectum.—Singulariter apostolis et apostolicis viris dicitur: Luceat lux vestra coram hominibus, nimirum tamquam accensis, et vehementer accensis.*"

of our life. He leaves it in the abstract state, a simple record, or, at best, something that may touch our hearts by virtue of the so-called esthetic aspect of Christianity. "The majesty of the Scriptures fills me with astonishment; the simplicity of the Gospels goes straight to my heart," the sentimentalist, J. J. Rousseau, admitted. But what difference did these vague and sterile emotions make, to the glory of God?

The true apostle, on the other hand, knows how to bring out not only the truth of the Gospel but the actuality of that truth, and the fact that it is ever renewed, and (because divine) ever active in the soul that enters into contact with it. And without stopping to move the feelings, he goes on, by the word of divine life unil he reaches the will, where correspondence with the Life of all takes place. The convictions that he produces are of a kind to arouse love and determination. He alone knows how to preach the Gospel.

No interior life would be complete without devotion to Mary Immaculate, the most perfect of all channels of grace, above all of those special graces that make saints. The experienced apostle is always having recourse to Mary, a fact which St. Bernard could never conceive as being lacking in a true disciple of that incomparable Mother; and the apostle, when he sets forth the dogmas on the Mother of God, and of men, will find himself speaking with a warmth that not only interests his hearers and deeply moves them, but also excites in them a similar need to fly, in all their troubles, to this Mediatrix of all the Graces won for us by the Precious Blood. Such a one has only to let his experience and his heart do the talking, and he will win souls for the Queen of Heaven, and, through Her, cast them into the Heart of Jesus.

e. Because the Interior Life Begets Interior Life, Its Results Upon Souls Are Deep and Lasting

It might be a good idea to write this chapter in the form of a letter to the heart of each one of our confreres. Such a form would be very appropriate.

In any case, we have been looking at good works in their dependence above all on the interior life of the apostle. Prayer and reflection have led us to the analysis of the sterility of certain enterprises from another point of view, and it would seem to be quite reasonable and true to sum up our findings in this proposition:

No work takes deep root, or has real stability, or will per-petuate itself, unless the apostle has begotten the interior life in other souls. Naturally, he cannot do this unless he himself is strong in the inner life.

In the third chapter of Part II we quoted the words of Canon Timon-David concerning the importance of forming, in every work of Catholic Action, a nucleus of very fervent Christians who should in their turn carry on a regular apostolate among their companions. It is easy to see the great value of this leaven, and to what an extent these *co-workers* can multiply the active power of the apostle. He does not have to work *alone:* his resources for action are increased a hundred per cent.

Let us hasten to repeat that only a really interior man of works will *have enough life to produce other centers of fruit-ful life.* Any purely worldly and nonChristian enterprise is able to obtain eager proselytes who will spread propaganda, and make friends and influence others, in general, whether prompted by brotherly spirit or by rivalry. In such a case, fanaticism or a spirit of competition, sectarianism, or vain-glory, solidarity or rivalry are all that is needed to stir them up to activity. But when it comes to creating apostles after the Heart of Christ, apostles who share His gentleness and humil-ity, His disinterested goodness and His zeal for the glory of God His Father alone, is there any other force than can pre-tend to do this work than an intensive interior life?

As long as an enterprise has not been able to produce such a result as this, its survival is uncertain. It is almost a fore-gone conclusion that it will not outlive the one who started it. But there is no doubt whatever that the reason for the long life of certain other works is generally to be found in the single fact that interior life has begotten more interior life.

Consider this example.

Father Allemand, who died in the odor of sanctity, founded, before the Revolution, in Marseilles, a youth movement for students and workers. This movement still bears the name of its founder, and for more than a century it has continued to enjoy a remarkable success. And yet, from the natural stand-point, this priest had very few gifts. Half blind, shy, devoid of any talent as a speaker, he was, humanly speaking, incapable of the prodigious activity that his work called for.

A certain lack of proportion in his features should, ordi-narily, have aroused derision in young people, but the beauty of soul that was reflected in his looks and in all his bearing prevented it. Thanks to that beauty, the man of God gained a great ascendancy over these energetic youths, by which he dominated them and gained their esteem, respect, and love. Fr. Allemand wanted to build on no foundation but the interior life, and he was strong enough to form a nucleus of young men, at the center of his movement, men of whom he did not hesitate to ask, to the extreme limit permitted by their condition, a complete inner life, uncompromising custody of the heart, morning meditation, and so on. In a word, he asked the complete Christian life, in the sense in which it was understood and practiced by the Christians of the earliest times.

And these young apostles, succeeding one another, have continued to be the true center of this movement at Marseilles; and the movement has given to the Church several Bishops, and continues to give her many secular priests, missionaries, religious, as well as thousands of family men who are at all times the chief support of the parochial works in the great Mediterranean seaport, where they form a group that not only does honor to business and industry and the professions, but constitutes a real center for the apostolate.

We have mentioned "family men." That brings to mind the burden of the refrain that can be heard almost everywhere: "The apostolate is relatively easy in the case of young men and girls and especially married women, mothers. But when it comes to mature men, it is just about impossible. And yet so long as we have not made the fathers of families not only into Christians but also into apostles, the influence of Christian mothers, great as it is, will be obstructed or short-lived and we will never set the social kingdom of Christ on a firm basis. Now in such and such a parish, or district, or hospital, or factory, there is just no way of getting the men to become deeply Christian."

When we thus admit helplessness, do we not display our poverty in the exterior life, which alone can teach us the means of preventing so many men from getting away from the influence of the Church? Do we not prefer the easy sermons that are so successful with youths and women to the intensive labor of preparation demanded by sermons that have power to arouse convictions and love and lasting resolutions in the minds and hearts of men? Only the interior life can sustain us in the hidden, backbreaking labor of planting the seed that seems to go so long without fruit. Only the interior life can teach us how much active power there is to be derived from the labor of prayer and penance, and how great an increase in our efficacy in preaching to men would follow from progress in the imitation of all the virtues of Jesus Christ.

So surprising were the reports we received, concerning Catholic Action among the soldiers in a city of Normandy, that we hesitated to believe such success. For instance, how was it possible that the attendance of soldiers at the club should be much greater when there was a long evening of adoration in reparation for the blasphemy and debauchery of the barracks than when a concert or show was presented? And yet we had to give in before the evidence. But our surprise vanished when we were shown to what an extent the chaplain realized the Real Presence of Jesus in the Eucharist, and what apostles he had thus been able to form around him.

After that, what are we to think of those apostles for whom movies, plays, and athletics appear to constitute a fifth Gospel for the conversion of nations?

When all else is lacking, no doubt these means may obtain some result by attracting practicing Catholics, or keeping others away from occasions of sin; but how limited and short-lived such a result usually is! God preserves us from cooling the zeal of our beloved confreres who can neither *imagine* nor employ any other tactics, and who have already conjured up visions (as we did ourselves, in our youth and inexperience) of an empty clubhouse or parish hall, if they should happen to devote less time to putting on these modern amusements, which are, in their estimation, indispensable to success. Let us simply put them on their guard against the danger of giving these things too important a place, and wish them the grace to grasp the doctrine of Canon Timon-David, whose views we presented towards the beginning of this book.

One day—it was only two years after our ordination—this venerable priest was forced to close one of his conversations with us by saying fraternally, but not without a certain amount of pity: "*You cannot bear them now.*"[65] Wait a little, until you have made a little progress in the interior life, and you will understand better. At present, all things considered, you probably cannot do without such things. All right, then, go ahead, use them, if they are all you have. For my part I am well able to hold on to my young workers and clerks, and to get new recruits, even though in our place we don't have anything much but a few of those old-time games that are always new and which don't cost anything, and relax the soul because they are so completely simple. Listen," he added slyly, "you were up in the attic and saw the band instruments that I, too, thought indispensable when I started out. Well, in a moment the band we have today will be coming this way. You will be able to judge for yourself."

Sure enough, in a few minutes a group of youths between twelve and seventeen went marching by. There were forty or fifty of them. What an uproar! It was impossible to keep from bursting out laughing at this fantastic brigade upon which the old Canon gazed with such delight. "Look," he said, "you see that fellow marching backwards at the head of the gang waving his stick like an orchestra leader, and, now, putting it up to his lips and playing it like a clarinet? He is a non-commissioned officer on leave, and one of our most energetic workers. He does his best to get to Communion every day,

---

65. *Non potestis portare modo* (*Joan.* 16:12).

but, above all, he never misses his half-hour of mental prayer. This real saint is also a terrific joker, and he knows how to use all his talents to see that the games we use as our *means* don't get dull. He has no limit to his original ideas, and so he keeps all these little fellows happy all the time. But nothing escapes his adjutant's eyes, or his apostle's heart."

Really, it was extremely funny to see and hear this band of musicians "playing" all the old tunes. They would change as soon as the leader gave the signal by his example. Each member of the "band" imitated some instrument. Some had their hands in front of their mouths like a horn, others were humming into a sheet of tissue-paper, and one or two had mouth-organs. I forgot: in the front rank of the musicians there were a slide-trombonist and a big drummer.

The first had two sticks, and moved one of them back and forth while the other was beating on an old gasoline can. The shining faces of all these youngsters showed that they were really carried away by their game.

"Let's follow the band," said the Canon. At the end of the garden path was a statue of the Blessed Virgin. "On your knees, men," cried the leader, "let's sing an *Ave Maris Stella* to our dear Mother, and say a decade of the Rosary." All these little fellows were quiet for a minute, and then answered the *Aves* just as piously and slowly as if they were in the chapel. These little southerners, most of them with their eyes down, had been real rascals a few minutes ago, and now they were transformed into angels out of a picture by Fra Angelico!

"Don't forget," said the guide, "that is the thermometer of the movement. All our workers aim at this one end: to hold even our most mature youths, those of twenty or more, by simple games, and to get them to like to come here for their time of prayer and recreation, to become children again, and get fun out of any little thing, but above all to get them to pray, and really pray, even in the middle of their games." The whole group was on its feet again, and off to further musical exploits that echoed throughout the big yard. A moment later the place was in an uproar with "prisoner's base." Meanwhile we had noticed that the adjutant, when he got up after the *Ave Maris Stella*, had whispered a few words in the ear of two or three of the youngsters, who at once, gaily, and as though following a familiar practice, went to change into their street clothes and then were off to the chapel to spend a quarter of an hour with the Divine Prisoner in the Tabernacle.

"Our ambition," continued Canon Timon-David, speaking with profound conviction, "our ambition must be to form workers in whom the love of God is so strong that after they have married and left the club they should remain apostles, eager to share their charity with the greatest possible number of souls." And the holy priest continued: "If our apostolate were to aim only at forming good Christians, then our ideal would be feeble indeed! What we have to do is create legions of apostles so that the family, the fundamental social unit, may become in turn a center of the apostolate. Now this whole program cannot be realized unless we lead lives of sacrifice and of intimate friendship with Christ; otherwise we shall never be strong enough, nor discover the secret of success. On these conditions alone will our activity make itself felt in society, or the word of our Master be fulfilled: "I have come to cast fire upon the earth, and what will I but that it be kindled?"[66]

Not until long afterward, alas, did we understand the drift of the living lessons of the Canon, who was such a profound

---

66. *Ignem veni mittere in terram, et quid volo nisi ut accendatur?* (*Luc.* 12:49).

psychologist and tactician, and compare the results of the different means employed, under the eye of God, to whom merely apparent successes mean nothing at all.

According as the means employed are simple, like the Gospel, or complicated, after the fashion of all things that have too much that is merely human in them, we can evaluate both a movement and those who are running it.

The mighty men of Israel, armed from head to foot, had fought in vain against Goliath. But young David took the field against him with a sling, a stick, and five stones from the brook. That was all the boy needed. Yet his cry: "I come to thee in the name of the Lord of hosts"[67] sprang from a soul capable of *attaining sanctity.*

We hear a lot today about postgraduate training offered by secular groups. It will make little difference if these movements have at their disposal huge sums of money officially contributed by the state, luxurious quarters, and all that. The Church's postgraduate training groups, for all their poverty, will have nothing to fear from their competition, if they are built on the interior life, and the charm of their ideal, which is the thing that attracts youth before everything else, will win over the pick of the younger generation.

Finally, one more example. It will help us to analyze those active workers who appear to be drawing souls to God so effectively as to make apostles of them, but who, in actual fact, are only working up a certain amount of enthusiasm based on their own natural personal appeal, and on the magnetic influence they exercise on all who come in contact with them. Their following, delighted to be on friendly terms with so attractive and holy a man, and proud to see that he takes an interest in them,

---

67. *In nomine Domini exercituum* (*1 Reg.* 17:45).

form a sort of a court around him and vie with one another even in accepting the painful tasks and duties that appear to reflect true devotion; but they do so mostly to please him.

A Congregation of nuns, excellent catechists, was under the direction of a religious whose life has just been written. He was a man of prayer. One day he said to the local Superior, "Reverend Mother, I think it would be a good thing if Sister So-and-So were to give up teaching catechism for at least a year."

"Father! What are you saying! Why, she's the best we have! Children come from every part of town to be in her class, she has such a marvelous knack of teaching! If we take her off, it means most of these little boys will simply desert us!"

"I followed her class from the gallery," said Father, "and it is true that she sweeps them all off their feet, but it is in all too human a way. Give her another year in the novitiate, and let her get a better foundation in the interior life; then she will sanctify both her own soul and the souls of the children by her zeal and the use of her talents. But at the present time, without being aware of it, she is standing in the way of the direct action of Our Lord upon these souls that are being prepared for First Communion. Come now, Mother, I see that my insistence in this matter makes you unhappy. Very well, I will make a bargain with you! I know a certain Sister N__, a very interior soul, but without any special talent. Ask your Superior General to send her here for a while. The other Sister can come for the first fifteen minutes and start the class off, just to calm your fears of desertion; but little by little she will drop out of the picture. Then you will see that the children will pray better, and will sing their hymns with much more devotion. Their recollection and docility will reflect a more supernatural character. That will be your barometer."

A fortnight later the Superior was able to verify this fore-cast. Sister N__ was teaching all alone, and yet the number of children grew larger. It was really Christ that was teaching catechism through her. Her looks, her modesty, her gentle-ness, her kindness, her way of making the Sign of the Cross all *spoke* Our Lord. Sister X had been able to take the dryest topic, give it a clever exposition, and make it interesting. Sis-ter N__, did more than that. Of course, she did not neglect to prepare her explanations, and to express them in all clarity; but her secret, and the thing that was paramount in her class, was *unction*. And it is by this unction that souls really enter into contact with Jesus.

In Sister N__'s class there were far fewer bursts of noisy enthusiasm, or looks of astonishment, far less of that fascina-tion that could have been equally well produced by an inter-esting lecture by some explorer, or by the account of a battle.

On the other hand, there was an atmosphere of recollected attention. These little boys behaved in the catechism class as they would in Church. No human methods were brought into play to dispel boredom or prevent dissipation. What, then, was the mysterious influence that dominated this group? Make no mistake, it was Christ, working directly. For a soul of inte-rior life teaching a catechism lesson is like a harp that sounds under the fingers of the Divine Musician. And no human art-istry, no matter how wonderful, can be compared to the action of Jesus on the soul.

f. Importance of the Formation of "Shock Troops" and of Spiritual Direction

Returning once more to that striking conversation with Father Timon-David,[68] surely, the reader must have been struck by one of the words that fell from the lips of that experienced founder of good works. I refer to the vivid metaphor of "crutches," with which the Canon summed up his opinion on the use of various modern amusements (like plays, bands, movies, complicated and expensive games, and so on) to attract youths to their clubs and keep them there. These attractions more often than not serve only to wear everybody out, and leave all listless and depressed, instead of resting and expanding the soul. Or else they merely cater to physical health, or flatter vanity, or overstimulate the imagination and the emotions. For the rest, the term "crutches" in no way supplies to those refreshing though extremely simple games which relax the soul and strengthen the body, and which have been found sufficient by so many generations of Christians.[69]

---

68. 2nd Part, Chap. iii. page 52 ff.
69. Translating Dom Chautard's ideas into English and American terms, we see that he approves and heartily recommends all those games that form a part of the social heritage, and which appeal spontaneously to all the young people in a given environment. Hence, cricket and baseball, football and soccer and basketball, all receive his approval provided they are kept on a simile and spontaneous basis, and do not demand any outlay for special equipment, and involve no fanfare. When however it is a question of athletics on the scale reached by college and even high school football in America, Dom Chautard justly points out the futility of any pretense that such things serve the interests of Christ on this earth.

If one were to make a comparison between the advice of this extremely prudent Canon with that of other able leaders of Catholic Action, without quite seeing his correct meaning, one might well wonder if he was not too sweeping in his enumeration of the cases when "crutches" can be discarded.

Leaving to one side works that are founded chiefly for the relief of bodily ills, we may divide the others into two classes: those which take only carefully selected members, and those which exclude none but the scabby sheep.

But we also assume that even in the latter case, a nucleus of "shock troops" will be formed, youths who will be able, by their fervor, to bring home to the others what the principal aim of the movement is, and to bring all the other members to lead a life that is Christian not merely on the surface, but deep down in the soul. Otherwise, what have we got? "An ordinary social club, run by a priest," according to the ironical expression of a state-school teacher of great ability who was able to detect, behind the clerical front, just about as many weaknesses as he deplored in those establishments that were beyond the reach of the Church's influence.

Directors who do not hesitate to reject from their movements members that are clearly incapable of being incorporated into the shock troops, will find the term "crutches" exactly expresses to what an extent they consider as secondary those means that they can well do without, or which they only tolerate with unfeigned repugnance.

And as a matter of fact, they do not easily run short of arguments in favor of their viewpoint.

As far as they are concerned, the regeneration of society, and especially of France, can come only as a result of a more intense radiation of the holiness of the Church. It is by this means, they say, rather than by lectures and apologetics that

Christianity developed so rapidly in the first centuries of its history, in spite of the power of its enemies, of prejudices of all sorts, and of the general corruption.

They put an end to all argument by an answer like this: Can you quote any fact, just one fact, to show that during that time the Church needed to think up amusements to turn aside the souls she was going to conquer from the filth of pagan shows?

One of these directors of Catholic Action remarked, in allusion to the thirst for money and the infatuation for the films which keep the bulk of the population in our days in a fever of excited craving for enjoyment: "The *Panem et Circenses* (Bread and Circuses) of the decadent Romans might be translated into modern terms as 'Relief and Movies.'" Now look at St. Augustine, or St. Ambrose, for example: what a prodigious attraction they exercised over souls! And yet do we ever see them, at any time in their lives, organizing some movement to provide amusements that would make their flock forget the pleasures held out by paganism?

And when St. Philip Neri set out to convert Rome, lukewarm with the spirit of the Renaissance, do we read that he needed any of those "crutches" that so aroused the scorn of Canon Timon-David?

It is very certain that the primitive Church, as we have already hinted, knew how to organize magnificent and numerous shock troops, in the midst of the faithful, and their virtues both struck the pagans with astonishment and excited the admiration of honest souls, even those most prejudiced against Christianity by their principles, their traditions, and their social background. Conversions were the result, even in circles to which no priest had access.

In the presence of these lessons from the past, how can we avoid asking ourselves if, in our own century, we do not have an excessive confidence not only in certain garish forms of amusement, but even in various other means (like pilgrimages, ostentatious festivals, congresses, speeches, publications, syndicates, political action, and so on), which are lavished upon us with such abundance in our day and which are doubtless very *useful*, but which it would be a great mistake to put in the first place. *Preaching by example* will always be the foremost instrument of conversions. Only *exempla trahunt*. Lectures, good books, Christian newspapers and magazines, and even fine sermons must gravitate around this fundamental program: that we need to influence people by an *apostolate of good example*, the example of fervent Christians, who make Jesus Christ live again on this earth by spreading about them the good odor of His virtues.

Priests who allow themselves to be absorbed by all the other functions of their ministry and do not give themselves, except in an insufficient manner, to the chief of them, which is the *formation of perfect Christians who will do the great work of propaganda by good example*, have no right to be surprised when they see that three-quarters of the male population in France (and in many other nations the proportion is still greater) remain steeped in indifference and see nothing in the Church but a worthy institution with a certain social usefulness but do not see that it is the one true source of all personal strength, and the keystone of the whole structure of families and nations, and above all the great distributor of truth and of eternal life.

"*What is this religion that can give such light and strength and fire to the hearts of men?*" cried the pagans when they saw the wonderful effects of *the silent League of action by good example*.

The strength of this League which existed among the early

Christians was surely not derived solely from the practice of "Declining from evil."[70]

Merely to shun the acts forbidden by the Decalogue would not have been enough to arouse both admiration and a strong urge to imitate such men. The principle of *exempla trahunt* springs rather from the second half of the Psalmist's admonition, *fac bonum* (do good). What was needed, then, was the full *splendor of the Evangelical virtues* as they were proposed to the world in the Sermon on the Mount.

An eminent but unbelieving statesman once said to us: "If the Church could find a way to impress more deeply on the hearts of men the testament of her Founder, "*Love one another*," she would become the one great power *indispensable* to all nations." Might we not also apply the same thought to several other virtues?

With his deep understanding of the needs of the Church, Pius X often saw things with a most remarkable clarity. An interesting conversation of the Holy Pontiff with a group of Cardinals was reported in the French clerical publication, "*L'Ami du Clerge*."[71] The Pope asked them:

"What is the thing we most need, today, to save society?"

"Build Catholic schools," said one.

"No."

"More churches," said another. "Still no."

"Speed up the recruiting of priests," said a third. "No, no," said the Pope, "*the MOST necessary thing of all, at this time, is for every parish to possess a group of laymen who will be at the same time virtuous, enlightened, resolute, and truly*

---

70. *Declina a malo* (*Psalm* 36).
71. *Prédication*, January 20, 1921.

apostolic."[72] Further details enable us to assert that this holy Pope at the end of his life saw no hope for the salvation of the world, unless the clergy could use their zeal to form faithful Christians full of apostolic ardor, preaching by word and example, but *especially by example*. In the diocese where he served before being elevated to the Papacy, he attached less importance to the census of parishioners than to the list of Christians capable of radiating an apostolate. It was his opinion that shock troops could be formed in any environment. Furthermore, he *graded* his priests according to the results which their *zeal* and *ability* had produced in this regard.

The views of this saintly Pope give immense weight to the opinion of the directors of Catholic Action who fall into the first class mentioned above. The ones, that is, who believe that *if the only true strategy for action on the bulk of the population is to form shock troops of perfect Christian laymen, it follows that to retain in the movement members who arouse no hope that they will ever become fervent* is a real fault insofar as one thus exposes himself to lowering the level of the *elite* to such a point that it is only "select" in name, not in fact.

Other leaders, who confine themselves to discarding the positively noxious candidates, will still have much to say against

---

72. After comparing certain passages from Pius X's first Encyclical with various later statements made by him, it becomes evident that in the interview we quote here he is depending on the fervor of priests to produce the shock troops he mentions. But that it is on the latter, the select laymen, that he counts, more than on any other means, for the increase in numbers of the true faithful. Once this has been accomplished, the recruitment of priests and construction of new schools and churches will be assured.

But when quantity does not spring from quality we run a tremendous risk of producing nothing but a display of noisy empty, delusive pseudoreligion.

the expression of "crutches" as a name for certain of their methods which appear, in their own estimation, most effective.

They come forward with the argument that unless souls will be exposed to great danger, or that if one Catholic Action provides a shelter for them, such aimed only at forming select groups, one would have to be satisfied with a microscopic recruitment, or that those who are to be evangelized live in a plagueinfested atmosphere, and so on. It would be unjust and cruel, they say, to neglect the masses and to seek only to reach them through the operations of shock troops without attempting direct action upon the mediocre souls, were it only in order to keep them from falling lower—if not to produce among them some candidates for the select corps.

*   *   *

We have listened with great respect to these various opinions as expressed by both men and women engaged in Catholic Action, all of them persons of incontestable zeal and good faith. We will not make any attempt to reconcile the opposing factions. Writing, as we do, with our venerated confreres in the priesthood chiefly in mind, we prefer to ask ourselves what kind of an answer would have been given by the saintly Fr. Allemand, or Fr. Timon-David if they were asked to bring these two doctrines into harmony with one another in a just mean.

These two priests had the following plan:

1. To bring to light, from among the hundreds of young Christians in their movement, a minority, even though *infinitesimally small*, capable of really desiring and seriously practicing the interior life.

2. Then to enkindle their souls to white heat with love for Our Lord, inspiring them with the ideal of the evangelical virtues, and isolating them as much as possible from contact with other students, clerks, or workers, etc., as long as their interior life had not reached the point where it could truly make them immune to all contagion.

3. Finally, at the right time, to give these young men a zeal for souls, in order to use them to reach their comrades more effectively.

It would take too long to say precisely what was the minimum which these two priests demanded of non-fervent candidates, to keep them for a certain length of time in the movement. Let us, rather, draw attention to the *great importance they gave to spiritual direction* in carrying out their plan.

Fr. Allemand[73] *undertook the individual direction of each youth*, and excelled in arousing holy enthusiasm for perfection, and in convincing them that the best proof of devotion to the Sacred Heart is to imitate the virtues of our Divine Model.

As for Canon Timon-David, he was not only an excellent *confessor*, highly skilled in discovering and dressing wounds of the soul, but also a remarkable *spiritual director*. No one knew better than he did how to set hearts on fire with love of virtue, and he stirred up those who shared this work of direction with him not to be content, in their guidance of souls, with the principles of moral theology proper to the purgative life, but to make use of their directions to steer souls towards the illuminative life. His earnest desire to make his priestly collaborators true directors of souls was something hard to equal.

Both of these men considered that their short exhortations

---

73. *La Vie et l'Esprit do Jean-Joseph Allemand*, by Fr Gaduel, Paris, Lecoffre.

before the weekly absolution were not enough, nor were they content to stop at their talks to the youths as a group, their organization of the liturgical life, nor even their extremely interesting conferences for the select group. They considered that *personal direction, for each member, once a month, was indispensable.*

They were convinced that after prayer and sacrifice the most effective means of obtaining from God the grace to form these shock troops, which are to rebuild the world, is the activity of a real priest in all the branches of his ministry, but *especially in spiritual direction.*

Let us leave the limited area of youth movements and consider the whole field which the Church is to cultivate: works of every sort, parishes, seminaries, communities, even missions.

No man is capable of being his own guide. Everyone has weakness to overcome, attractions to keep in order, duties to fulfill, dangers to undergo, occasions of peril to be avoided, difficulties to overcome and doubts to resolve. If one *needs* help in all this, *a fortiori* he will require it in his struggle for perfection.

It would be an omission, and sometimes a grave omission, in a priest, bound by his duty as teacher and surgeon of souls, if he were to deprive them of this great supplement to confession, this indispensable source of energy for the spiritual life, which is spiritual direction.

It is too bad for those enterprises, or movements, or institutions whose confessors, *always in a hurry*, scarcely give their penitents anything before absolution except a pious but vague exhortation, often the same for everyone, instead of providing the specific remedy which an experienced and painstaking doctor would know how to select, according to the state of each patient. Even though he may have great faith in the efficacy of the Sacrament, is the penitent not exposed in such a case to view the confessor as a sort of "automatic dispenser," like those slot machines on station platforms which mechanically slip you a piece of candy?

How privileged, on the other hand, are those *clubs, schools, orphanages, etc.*, where the confessor knows the art of direction, and is convinced that he must, *before everything else*, make use of it if he wants to make all these souls, potentially attuned to a high ideal, throw themselves wholeheartedly into the practice of the interior life!

How many *fathers and mothers* have noticed that their influence on their children and their friends has greatly increased because they have found a real director!

What wealth there is to put into circulation *in a child's soul!* The tree is just about to lean one way or another—and stay that way. For lack of *spiritual direction* to fit their age and dispositions, from childhood on, many of them become adults whom we will no longer be able to number among the fairer flowers of Christ's garden. *How many priestly and religious vocations might have blossomed forth among them!*

Often a parish or a mission will go on for several generations showing the influence of some priest who was able to do something besides giving absolution. Besides Ars and Mesnil-Saint-Loup, we could cite other places which are true centers of the spiritual life in the midst of a general tepidity because they once had the happiness to possess a zealous, prudent and experienced director.

Some years ago when I was in Japan I was astonished and deeply moved when I had the happiness to come in contact with some members of the numerous Christian families which were discovered years ago near Nagasaki. I have never heard anything so amazing! Surrounded by pagans, forced to conceal their religion, deprived of priests for three centuries, these

Christians of staunch courage received from their parents not only faith but fervor. Where are we to find the moving power strong enough to explain the strength and duration of this extraordinary heritage? The answer is easy. Their ancestors had been trained by a superb director of "shock troops," St. Francis Xavier.

How can some of our *minor seminaries*, having no spiritual directors, serve as nurseries for future priests? When most of their students have not been put on *the path to perfection* at an early age, how will they be able to avoid mediocrity later on, in the exercise of their priesthood? Indeed, they will be fortunate enough, these souls who are groping to find their way, if they are not completely derailed from their desire to become priests by their admiration for the glitter of natural talents in certain of their teachers who manifest indifference for the interior life and disdain for consistent spiritual direction.

The proof of the fact that many subjects in *religious communities*, contemplative as well as active, merely vegetate, for lack of spiritual direction, is to be found in the radical change we have *frequently* observed in tepid souls who have returned to the fervor they had at profession as soon as they finally found a conscientious director.

Some confessors seem to forget that the consecrated souls in their charge are *obliged to tend to perfection* and have a *real need* of help and encouragement to achieve that continuous progress which may be applied the words of the psalm: "In his heart he hath disposed to ascend by steps . . . they shall go from virtue to virtue,"[74] and to become, after that, true apostles of the interior life.

---

74. *Ascensiones in corde suo disposuit . . . ibunt de virtute in virtutem* (*Psalm 83*).

How many priests, too, would be far more fervent and find all their happiness in the eucharistic and liturgical life, and in the progress of souls, if the confessor of their choice showed them a genuine friendship, tactfully drawing them, by persuasion, into monthly direction in view of obligation to strive for that perfection which is incumbent upon them even more than it is upon religious.

Have you ever noticed what a great importance the writers of the lives of saints give to the spiritual directors of those whose biographies they compose?

Do you not think that the Church would have *many more saints* if generous souls, especially priests and religious, received more serious direction?

If the priest had not given such intimate direction to the parents of St. Therese of the Child Jesus, and if, later on, the representatives of God had not exercised a direct influence upon this soul chosen by Our Lord, would the earth now be receiving from Heaven the showers of roses that cover it?

Father Desurmont often returns, in his writings, to the thought that *for certain souls* salvation is completely tied up with sanctity. All or nothing. Burning love of Christ, or adoration of the world and allegiance to the direction of Satan. Sanctity or damnation!

If this is the case, would it be rash for us to fear that many priests will receive a frightful shock at the Last Judgment when they find out that they are, to a certain extent, responsible for the mediocrity and even the loss of souls, because they neglected to study the art of spiritual direction and would not take the trouble to practice it? They may have been good administrators, wonderful preachers, full of solicitude for the sick and the poor, but they have nonetheless neglected this outstanding feature of Our Lord's own strategy: *the transformation of society by means of chosen souls.* The little flock of Disciples chosen and formed by Christ Himself, and afterwards set on fire by the Holy Spirit, was enough to begin the regeneration of the world.

We compliment those ever more numerous bishops who follow Pius X in believing that a course of ascetic and even mystical theology is much more valuable, in their major seminaries, than lectures on sociology.

To emphasize the importance of direction they demand above all that their seminarians be faithful to it for the sake of their own personal progress, and that all the professors hold it in high esteem and *prove that they do so by radiating the interior life.*

In addition to this, they also want all their candidates for the priesthood to learn everything that has anything to do with the direction of souls, *regimen animarum*, an art based on well established principles and on wise counsels which have been actually lived by those who learned the art by experience. Of this *art of arts* is it especially true that it is not enough to know merely *what* to do, one must also know *how to do it.*

Consult the authors whom the Church considers masters of the spiritual life, and you will find that there are *plenty of false ideas and prejudices* about spiritual direction, and we must get rid of them.

Just let the priest allow his zeal to wander off the course, without a compass, let him hold the tiller with too weak a grip, and he will find out that some people excel in leading spiritual direction away from its true object.

It soon becomes a session of sterile gossip or he has to coddle the penitent's feelings, or flatter his self love; or else things take a quietistic turn, and he begins minimizing personal responsibility for sin. Then it is a mere school of fake piety and sentimentality which encourages the growth of sensible emotions, or of a sham religion made up of purely external devotions. Perhaps it becomes a sort of attorney's office where the penitent comes, out of habit, to get advice about all the trifling incidents of his life, his temporal affairs and all the little material problems of the home. How many other wrong roads there are, for the director and those he directs to go astray!

Furthermore, the priest must take care that the character of his spiritual direction does not get warped. Everything ought to converge upon the object stated in this definition: *Spiritual direction consists in the sum total of methodical and continuous advice given by a person having grace of state, knowledge, and experience* (especially a priest) *to an upright and generous soul, in order to help that soul advance towards solid piety and even towards perfection.*

It is above all a *training of the will*, that queen of faculties, which St. Thomas calls *vis unitiva* and the only one, in the last analysis, in which we will achieve union with Our Lord and the imitation of His virtues.

A director worthy of the name will find out not only the inner cause of the faults a soul may have, but also its various attractions. He will analyze the difficulties and repugnances it meets with in the spiritual combat. He will show it the beauty of an ideal, and will try out, and select, and control ways of living that ideal; he will point out the pitfalls and illusions; he will give the torpid a good shaking, will encourage and reprimand and console as required, but only to freshen up the will and steel it against discouragement and despair.

Generally, direction is inseparable from confession as long as the soul clinging to attachment to sin, remains mostly in the purgative life. When the soul has seriously begun to advance towards fervor, it becomes easier to give direction distinct from confession. Certain priests, in order to make sure that the two will not be confused will only give direction after the absolution, and ordinarily grant it only once a month to those who confess once a week.

It is not part of the program of this volume to develop the method of giving direction. However, since we are convinced that many priests ought to take this spiritual art more seriously, we admit that it would give us great pleasure to attempt to offer certain of our confreres, who balk at the study of ponderous tomes, a short and practical synthesis of the best that has been said on the subject.[75] This *compendium* will not only

---

75. Bibliography on Spiritual Direction.

   Special works:

   English Readers will find the following easily accessible: *The Spiritual Life*, A. Tanquerey, Society of St. John the Evangelist; *Growth in Holiness*, Fr. Faber (Ch. xviii); *The Graces of Prayer,* Poulain, Kegan Paul, London; *Spiritual Director and Physician*, V. Raymond, O.P.; *Catholic Encyclopedia*, Art. "Direction"; *The Degrees of the Spiritual Life*, Abbe Saudreau, London, Burns Oates; *Christian Perfection and Contemplation*, Garrigou-Lagrange, O.P.

   Among other authors who have treated of Spiritual Direction: Cassian, Conferences, C, II, 1–13; St. Gregory the Great; St. Bernard; St. Bonaventure; St. Vincent Ferrer; St. John Climacus, *Ladder of Paradise*, 4th Deg., 5–12; St. Theresa of Avila, especially in her *Autobiography*; St. John of the Cross, *Ascent of Mount Carmel*.

   La Direction Spirituelle, Ven. Libermann, Oeuvre de Saint Paul, Paris; *L'Esprit d'un Directeur des âmes*, M. Olier, Poussielgue, Paris; *La Charité Sacerdotale*, P. Desurmount, Paris, Sainte-Famille; The various works of Fr. Timon-David, see page 55; *La pratique progressive de la confession et de la direction*, Fr. Saudreau, and other works on moral and religious formation, Paris, Lib., Saint Paul; Direction des Enfants, Simon, Paris, Téqui: *Pratique de l'Education*, Monfat, Paris, Téqui; *L'Educateur Apôtre Guibert*, Gigord, Paris.

   Also: *L'Ascétisme Chrétien*, Ribet. Paris, Poussielgue; works of Fr. Meynard, O.P., and of Mgr. Gay; *L'Ideal de l'âme fervente, La Voie*

facilitate the diagnosis and classification of souls but will also give precise information on the methods suggested to help souls in every state to *launch out into the deep*, and strive after serious progress.

Every soul is a world by itself. It has its own shades of difference. Still, as an ordinary rule, we may classify Christians in various groups. We have thought fit to attempt such a classification here below, testing souls on one hand by sin and imperfection, and on the other by their degree of prayer. Let us hope that this classification may lead some of our respected confreres to think over the necessity of studying these things, in order to learn the practical rules for directing each soul according to its state.

In the first two categories, the priest may not be able to work directly upon the souls in question but if he is a good director he will be able to give much more effective guidance to those relatives and friends who have set their hearts on winning back these dear ones, even though they may be hardened in sin, before they are entirely rejected by God.

---

qui mène a Dieu. Manuel de Spiritualité, by Saudreau; *Principes de la Vie Spirituelle*, Fr. Schryvers, C.SS.R., Brussels, De Vit; *St. François de Sales Directeur d'âmes*, F. Vincent; *Direction de Conscience*, Agnel et Espiney; *Lacordaire apôtre et directeur de jeunes gens*, H. Noble, O.P.; *Traité de l'obéissance*, Tronson, Pt. II., *Praxis Theol. Mysticae.* Lib. viii, c.1., Godinez; *Instit. Theol. Myst.*, Pt. II, c.i., Nos. 327–353, Schram; also the works of Garrigou-Lagrange, O.P., incl. *Les Trois Ages de la Vie Interieure.*

In short, a serious study of Fr. Desurmont's *Charité Sacerdotale*, of Lagrange's *Christian Perfection and Contemplation*, or Sandreau's *Degree of the Spiritual Life*, will . . . [sentence incomplete in orginal].

1. Hardened in Sin

Mortal sin. Stubborn persistence in sin, either out of ignorance or because of a maliciously warped conscience.

Prayer. Deliberate refusal to have any recourse to God.

2. Surface Christianity

Mortal sin. Considered as a trifling evil, easily forgiven.
The soul easily gives way and commits mortal sin at every
possible occasion or temptation.—Confession almost without
contrition.

Prayer. Mechanical; either inattentive, or always dictated
by temporal interest. Such souls enter into themselves very
rarely and superficially.

3. Mediocre Piety

Mortal sin. Weak resistance. Hardly ever avoids occasions but seriously regrets having sinned, and makes good
confessions.

Venial sin. Complete acceptance of this sin, which is considered as insignificant. Hence, tepidity of the will. Does
nothing whatever to prevent venial sin, or to extirpate it, or to
find it out when it is concealed.

Prayer. From time to time, prays well. Momentary fits of
fervor.

4. Intermittent Piety

Mortal sin. Loyal resistance. Habitually avoids occasion.
Deep regrets. Does penance to make reparation.

Venial sin. Sometimes deliberate. Puts up a weak fight. Sorrow only superficial. Makes a particular examination of conscience, but without any method or coherence.

Prayer. Not firmly resolved to remain faithful to meditation. Gives it up as soon as dryness is felt, or as soon as there is business to attend to.

5. Sustained Piety

Mortal sin. Never. At most very rare, when taken suddenly and violently by surprise. And then, often it is to be doubted if the sin is mortal. It is followed by ardent compunction and penance.

Venial sin. Vigilant in avoiding and fighting it. Rarely deliberate. Keen sorrow, but does little by way of reparation. Consistent particular examen, but aiming only at avoidance of venial sin.

Imperfections. The soul either avoids uncovering them, so as not to have to fight them, or else easily excuses them. Approves the thought of renouncing them, and would like to do so, but makes little effort in that direction.

Prayer. Always faithful to prayer, no matter what happens. Often affective. Alternating consolations and dryness, the latter endured with considerable hardship.

6. Fervor

Venial sin. Never deliberate. By surprise, sometimes, or with imperfect advertence. Keenly regretted, and serious reparation made.

Imperfections. Wants nothing to do with them. Watches over them, fights them with courage, in order to be more pleasing to God. Sometimes accepted, however, but regretted at once. Frequent acts of renunciation. Particular examen aims at perfection in a given virtue.

Prayer. Mental prayer gladly prolonged. Prayer on the affective side, or even prayer of simplicity. Alternation between powerful consolations and fierce trials.

7. Relative Perfection

Imperfections. Guards against them energetically and with much love. They only happen with halfadvertence.

Prayer. Habitual life of prayer, even when occupied in external works. Thirst for self-renunciation, annihilation, detachment, and divine love. Hunger for the Eucharist and for Heaven. Graces of infused prayer, of different degree. Often passive purification.

8. Heroic Perfection

Imperfections. Nothing but the first impulse.

Prayer. Supernatural graces of contemplation, sometimes accompanied by extraordinary phenomena. Pronounced passive purifications. Contempt of self to the point of complete self-forgetfulness. Prefers suffering to joys.

9. Complete Sanctity

Imperfections. Hardly apparent.

Prayer. Usually, transforming union. Spiritual marriage. Purifications by love. Ardent thirst for sufferings and humiliations.

Few and far between are the souls that belong to the last

two, even to the last three categories. Nor is it hard to understand that a priest will wait until he actually comes across such a penitent before making a study of what the best authors have to say, in order that his direction may then be prudent and safe.

But is there any excuse for a confessor who should prove too lazy to learn and to apply what is proper to the four classes of *mediocre piety*, *intermittent piety*, *sustained piety*, and *fervor*, and for that cause allow souls to moulder in their ghastly tepidity or to come to a standstill far below the degree of the interior life destined for them by God?

*   *   *

As for the points to be taken up in the direction of beginners in piety, one might reduce them, as a general rule, to the four following:

1. PEACE. Find out if the soul has *genuine* peace, not simply the peace which the world gives, or the peace that results from absence of struggle. If it has none, try to give the soul a relative peace, in spite of all its difficulties. This is the foundation of all direction. *Calmness*, *recollection*, and *confidence* also come in here.

2. A HIGH IDEAL. As soon as you have collected enough material to *classify* the soul and to recognize its weak points, as well as its strength of character and temperament and its degree of striving for perfection, find out the best means of reviving its desire to live more seriously for Jesus Christ and of breaking down the obstacles which hinder the development of grace in it. In a word, what we want here is to get the soul to aim higher and higher all the time: always *excelsior*.

3. PRAYER. Find out how the soul prays, and in particular, analyze its degree of *fidelity to mental prayer*, its method of mental prayer, the obstacles met with, and the profit drawn from it. What value does it get out of the Sacraments, the liturgical life, particular devotions, ejaculatory prayers, and the practice of the presence of God?

4. SELF-DENIAL. Find out on what point, and especially how the *particular examen* is made, and in what manner self-denial is practiced, whether through hatred of sin or love of God. How well is custody of the heart kept: in other words, what amount of vigilance is there in the spiritual combat, and in preserving the spirit of prayer throughout the day?

All the essentials of direction come down to these four points. Take all four, if you will, as the basis for a monthly examination, or confine yourself to one at a time if you do not wish to take too long.

In this way the priest will paralyze the deathgerms in the soul and revive the elements of life, and in his zeal he will come to have a passion for the exercise of this supreme art, and the Holy Ghost, whose faithful minister he is, will not be sparing in dispensing those unutterable consolations which make up, here below, one of the great joys of the priesthood. He will pour them out upon him *in proportion to his devotion* in applying to souls the principles he has studied. Did anyone ever taste the joys of the apostolate more than St. Paul? Yet, on the other hand, what a burning fire had to consume him to make him write: "For three years I ceased not with tears to admonish every one of you night and day."[76]

---

76. *Per triennium nocte et die non cessavi cum lacrymis monens unumquemque vestrum* (*Acts* 20:31).

Once I heard a prelate address the following admiring and grateful words to a doctor who had fought hard to pull him through the crisis of a mortal illness, and who was now rapidly restoring strength to his body:

"My dear doctor, I know that your son is going to be a priest. If he and his confreres, when the time comes for them to take care of souls, model themselves upon your devotion and professional conscientiousness in diagnosing sicknesses and in prescribing remedies and a diet to bring the sick man back to vigorous health, then neither Jews nor Freemasons nor Protestants will be able to prevent the triumph of the faith among us."

Apply your *knowledge:* be *devoted* to duty, and you will receive the blessing of God. Of this there can be no doubt.

And yet, take these two factors, and see what *superhuman* power they acquire when the priest who uses them is one of those to whom the priesthood is incomprehensible unless it *means progress towards sanctity.*

What holy revolution would sweep the world if in every parish, in every mission, for every community, and at the head of every Catholic group there was a real director of souls! Then, indeed, even in institutions where mediocre subjects have to be retained (such as orphanages, asylums, and homes) you would always find the whole program of activities based on this principle of *the formation of a select group, isolated as far as possible from the ordinary run of the members, until such time as they can be trained to exercise a discreet but fervent apostolate upon the rest!*

Anyone who wants to compare various Catholic enterprises in terms of the results that Christ expects from them, will be forced to come to the conclusion that wherever there is a center of genuine spiritual direction, there is no need of those wonderful "crutches" for rapid and easy progress to be made. Yet at the same time, you can take all the most fashionable "crutches" at once, and use them all in the same enterprise at the same time, and you will never be able to do anything but thinly disguise the lack of direction, without ever diminishing the crying need for it.

The more zealous priests become in perfecting themselves in the art of spiritual direction, and in devoting themselves to it, the more will they realize how unnecessary are certain exterior means which might, it is true, have some use to begin with, in establishing contact with the faithful, and drawing them in, grouping them, arousing their interest, holding on to them, and keeping them under the influence of the Church. But the Church, faithful to her true end, will never be fully satisfied until souls are *intimately incorporated* into Jesus Christ.

g. *The Entire Success of the Apostolate Depends on One Thing: An Interior Life Centered on the Blessed Eucharist*

The aim of the Incarnation, and, therefore, the aim of every apostolate, is to raise humanity to a divine level. "Christ became man that man might become God."[77] "The only-begotten Son of God, desiring us to be sharers of His Divinity, assumed our nature, in order that having become man, He might make men gods."[78] Now it is in the Eucharist, or, more accurately, in the Eucharistic life, that is in a substantial

---

77. *Christus incarnatus est ut homo fieret deus* (St. Augustine).
78. *Unigenitus Dei Filius suae divinitatis volens nos esse participes, naturam nostram assumpsit, ut homines deos faceret, factus homo* (St. Thomas, Office of Corpus Christi).

inner life, nourished at the divine Banquet, that the apostle assimilates the divine life. We have Our Lord's own words. They are absolutely clear, and leave no room for equivocation: "Unless you eat the flesh of the Son of man and drink His blood, you shall not have life in you."[79] The Eucharistic life is simply the life of Our Lord in us, not only by the indispensable state of grace, but also by the superabundance of His action. "I am come that they may have life, and have it more abundantly."[80] If the apostle is going to overflow with divine life and pour it out upon the faithful, and if the richest source for divine life he can find is the Eucharist, how can we get away from the conclusion that his works will have little efficacy except through the action of the Eucharist on those who are to be, either directly or indirectly, dispensers of that life through these works.

It is impossible to meditate upon the consequences of the dogma of the Real Presence, of the Sacrifice of the Altar, and of Communion without being led to the conclusion that Our Lord wanted to institute this Sacrament in order to make it the *center of all action, of all loyal idealism, of every apostolate* that could be of any real use to the Church. If our whole Redemption gravitates about Calvary, all the graces of the mystery flow down upon us from the Altar. And the gospel worker who does not draw all his life from the Altar utters only *a word that is dead*, a word that cannot save souls, because it comes from a heart that is not sufficiently steeped in the Precious Blood.

It was not without a profound purpose that Our Lord uttered the parable of the vine and the branches, right after the Last

---

79. *Nisi manducaveritis carnem Filii hominis et biberitis ejus sanguinem non habebitis vitam in vobis* (*Joan.* 6:54).
80. *Veni ut vitam habeant, et abundantius habeant* (*Joan.* 10:10).

Supper, in order to bring out with emphasis and precision how useless it would be for men to attempt any active ministry without basing it upon the interior life. "As the branch cannot bear fruit itself . . . so neither can you, unless you abide in Me."[81] But He goes on at once to show how powerful will be the action of an apostle who lives by the interior, Eucharistic life. "He that abideth in Me, and I in him, the same beareth much fruit."[82] *The same*, but he alone. God exercises His powerful action through him, not through others. The reason is, says St. Athanasius, "we are made gods by the flesh of Christ." When a preacher or catechist retains in himself the warm life of the Precious Blood, when his heart is consumed with the fire that consumes the Eucharistic Heart of Jesus, what life his words will have: they will burn, they will be living flames! And what effects the Eucharist will have, radiating throughout a class for instance, or through a hospital ward, or in a club, and so on, when the ones God has chosen to work there have nourished their zeal in Holy Communion, and have become *Christ-bearers!*

Whether the fight be against the demon with all his wiles, enmeshing souls in ignorance, or against the spirit of pride and impurity, trying to make souls drunk with pride or to drown them in the mire, the Eucharist, the life of the true apostle, will have an influence beyond compare against the enemy of salvation.

Love is made perfect by the Eucharist. This living memorial of the Passion revives the divine fire in the soul of the apostle when it seems on the point of going out. It makes him relive Gethsemani, the scene in the Pretorium, Calvary, and

---

81. *Sicut palmes non potest ferre fructum a semetipso . . . sic nec vos nisi in me manseritis* (*Joan.* 15:4).

82. *Qui manet in me, et ego in eo, hic fert fructum multum* (*Joan.* 15:5).

teaches him the science of sorrow and humiliation. The apostolic worker will then be able to speak to the afflicted in a language that will make them share the consolations he has drawn from this sublime source.

He speaks the language of the virtues of which Jesus is the only exemplar, because every one of his words is like a drop of the Eucharistic Blood falling upon souls. But for this reflection of the Eucharistic life the active worker will produce no other effect, by his words, than a passing enthusiasm. It will be merely a matter of captivating the secondary faculties, and occupying the outworks of the fortress. But the stronghold itself, that is the heart, the will, will generally remain impregnable.

The efficacy of an apostolate almost invariably corresponds to the degree of Eucharistic life acquired by a soul. Indeed, the sure sign of a successful apostolate is when it makes souls thirst for frequent and fruitful participation in the divine Banquet. And this result will never be obtained except in proportion as the apostle himself really makes Jesus in the Blessed Sacrament the source and center of his life.

Like St. Thomas Aquinas, who practically entered the Tabernacle, so to speak, when he wanted to work out a problem, the apostle also will go and tell all his troubles to the Divine Guest, and his action upon souls will be simply his conversations with the Author of Life put into practice.

Our wonderful Father and Pope, Pius X, the Pope of Frequent Communion, was also the Pope of the interior life. "Re-establish all things in Christ"[83] was the first thing he had to say, above all to active workers. It summarizes the program of an apostle who lives on the Eucharist and who sees that the

---

83. *Instaurare omnia in Christo* (*Eph.* 1:10).

Church will gain successes only in proportion as souls make progress in the Eucharistic life.

So many enterprises in our time, and yet so often fruitless: why is it that they have not put society back on its feet? Let us admit it once again: they can be counted in far greater numbers than in preceding ages, and yet they have been unable to check the frightful ravages of impiety in the field of family life. Why? Because they are not firmly enough based on the interior *life*, the Eucharistic *life*, the liturgical *life*, fully and properly understood. Leaders of Catholic Action, at the head of these enterprises, have been full of logic, and talent, and even of a certain piety. They have poured forth floods of light, and have managed to introduce some devotional practices: and that, of course, is already something. But because they have not gone back nearly enough to the Source of life, they have not been able to pass on to others that fervor which tempers wills to their great task. Vain have been their attempts to produce that hidden but powerful devotion to the cause, that *active* ferment working through whole groups of men, those centers of supernatural attraction for which there is no substitute and which, without noise, unceasingly spread the fire around about them and slowly but surely penetrate all classes of persons with whom they come into contact. These results are beyond such apostles because their life in Christ is too weak.

Infection from the ills of former ages could well enough be countered, and souls preserved in health, by a merely ordinary piety. But the virulence of the pestilence in our own times, a hundred times more deadly and so quickly caught from the fatal attractions of the world, must be fought with a much more powerful serum. And because we have had no laboratories in which to produce any effective antitoxins,

Catholic Action has either done little more than produce

a certain fervor of the feelings, great spasms of enthusiasm which sputter out as quickly as they burst into flame, or else, in cases where it is effective in itself, Catholic Action has reached little more than a small minority. Our seminaries and novitiates have not turned out the armies of priests, religious, and nuns, inflamed with the wine of the Eucharist, that we might have expected from them. And therefore the fire which these chosen souls were supposed to spread among the pious lay people engaged in Catholic Action, has remained latent. No doubt some pious apostles have been given to the Church. But only very rarely has she received from us workers who possess by their Eucharistic lives that total, uncompromising holiness based on custody of the heart and on ardent, active, generous, and practical zeal, all of which goes by the name of the interior life.

Sometimes we hear a parish spoken of as good or even *wonderful* because, in it, the people take off their hats to the priest, speak to him with respect, and show a certain liking for him, even going so far as to do him a favor, and gladly, if need be: and yet in that parish the majority work instead of going to Sunday Mass, the Sacraments are abandoned, ignorance of religion is widespread, intemperance and blasphemy reign supreme, and morals leave everything to be desired. A heart-rending spectacle! Is that what you call an excellent parish? Can these people, whose lives are totally pagan, be called Christians?

Men of Catholic Action, we who deplore these sad results, why have we not been more frequent in our attendance at that school where the Divine Word instructs His preachers? Why have we not drawn deeper draughts from that intimacy of love which brings us close to the God of the Eucharist, the Word of life? God has not spoken by our lips. That is our fatal weakness. Let us no longer be astonished, then, if our human words have proved almost entirely sterile.

We have not appeared to souls as a reflection of Christ, and His life in the Church. Before the people could believe in us, there had to be about our brow something of the sheen of Moses' halo when he came down from Sinai and approached the children of Israel. In the eyes of the Hebrew people, this halo bore witness to the intimacy of God's ambassador with the One by Whom he was sent. And the success of our own mission demanded not only that we be known as men of honor and conviction, but also a ray of glory from the Eucharist, to give to the people some intimation of the living God, Whom none can resist. Orators, leaders, lecturers, catechists, and professors: we have all had nothing but a mediocre success simply because there has not been, about us, a strong enough reflection of nearness to God.

We apostles who bewail the futility of our works: did we not know all along that in the last analysis the only thing that moves men is the desire of happiness? Let us ask ourselves, then, whether anybody has seen in us the *reflected light of the eternal and infinite happiness of God* which we might have secured by union with Him Who, though concealed in the Tabernacle, is nevertheless the delight of the heavenly court.

Our Master, for His part, did not forget to feed His Apostles with this indispensable food of joy. "These things I have spoken to you that My joy may be in you, and your joy may be filled,"[84] He said, right after the Last Supper, to remind them to what an extent the Eucharist was going to be the source of all the great joys of this life.

---

84. *Haec locutus sum vobis ut gaudium meum sit in vobis et gaudium vestrum impleatur* (*Joan.* 15:11).

We ministers of the Lord, for whom the Tabernacle has become mute and silent, the stone of consecration cold, the Host a venerable, but lifeless, memento: we have been unable to turn souls from their evil ways. How could we ever draw them out of the mire of their forbidden pleasures? And yet we have talked to them about the joys of religion and of good conscience. But because we have not known how to slake our own thirst at the living waters of the Lamb, we have mumbled and stuttered in our attempts to portray those ineffable joys, the very desire of which would have shattered the chains of the triple concupiscence much more effectively than all our thundering tirades about hell. God is, above all, Love: yet we have only been able to present to souls the picture of a stern Lawgiver, a Judge as inexorable in His judgments as He is terrible in His chastisements. Our lips have been unable to speak the language of the Heart of Him Who loves men, because our converse with Him has been as infrequent as it has been cold.

Let us not try to shift all the blame onto the profoundly demoralized state of society. After all, we have only to look, for example, at the effect on completely de-Christianized parishes of the presence of sensible, active, devoted, capable priests, but priests who were, above all, lovers of the Eucharist. In spite of all the efforts of Satan's minions, these priests, a terror to the demons, *facti diabolo terribiles*[85] drawing their power from the source of all power, the furnace of the Tabernacle, have found a way to temper the steel of invincible

---

85. *Tamquam leones igitur ignem spirantes ab illa mensa recedamus facti diabolo terribiles* (St. John Chrysostom, *Hom.*, 61 ad Pop. Ant.).

   Let us therefore go down from that Table breathing fire, like lions, and terrible to the demons. (This passage of St. Chrysostom is used in Lessons ii and iii of the nocturn of the Votive Office of the Blessed Sacrament in the Cistercian Breviary).

weapons which the conspiring demons have been powerless to break. But such priests are, alas, all too rare.

And yet, for such as these, mental prayer before the altar has ceased to be a fruitless and barren affair, because they have become capable of understanding these words of St. Francis of Assisi: "Prayer *is the source of grace. Preaching is the channel that pours out the graces we ourselves have received from Heaven. The ministers of the word of God have been chosen by the Great King to carry to the people of the earth what they themselves have learned and gathered from His lips, especially before the Tabernacle.*"

Our one great hope is the fact that the present day has seen the genesis of a brand of Catholic Action, in our own generation, which is no longer satisfied merely to get people to go to Communion for the sake of appearances, but works at the formation of real and generous communicants.

PART FIVE

PRINCIPLES AND HINTS FOR THE INTERIOR LIFE

1. TO ACTIVE WORKERS: HINTS ON THE INTERIOR LIFE

If our readers were to admit now that the doctrine put forward in this book is a matter of considerable *importance*, we would already be achieving a good result; but that is not enough.

The real purpose of this work is to get the reader to resolve: "I am going to live according to this doctrine."

Consequently, it is time to say to the worker in Catholic Action, to the apostle who has just read these pages, especially if he has read them on retreat: "Your approval of the subject matter will have little or no effect unless it be united to a firm resolution to intensify your interior life."

And so the aim of this fifth part is to help those on retreat to strengthen those dispositions which are *absolutely necessary* for an interior life that will make Catholic Action get results.

Convictions

Zeal will only get results in so far as it is united to the action of Christ Himself.

Christ does all the work; we are only His instruments.

Our Lord does not give His blessings to any enterprise in which men place trust in human means alone.

He does not give His blessings to enterprises that are kept going solely by natural activity.

Jesus does not give His blessing to an enterprise in which self-love is working in the place of divine love.[1]

Woe to the man who refuses to do the work to which he is called by God!

Woe to the man who worms his way into an enterprise without finding out what God wills for him!

Woe to the man who, in his work, wants to run things without really depending on God!

Woe to the man who lives an active life without taking steps to preserve or to regain the interior life!

Woe to the man who does not know how to make the interior life and the active life harmonize, so that neither suffers from the other!

Principles

1ST PRINCIPLE. Do not plunge headlong into Catholic Action from mere *natural zest for activity*, but consult God and make sure you are doing what you do under the inspiration of grace, and with the morally certain guarantee that it is *His will*.

---

1. Fr. Desurmont. C.SS.R.

2ND PRINCIPLE. It is rash and dangerous to remain too long engaged in work so heavy that it *might make the soul incapable of performing the essential to the interior life*. In such a case all, but especially priests and religious, should apply, even to the holiest of works, the text: "Pluck it out and cast it from thee."[2]

3RD PRINCIPLE. Draw up a *schedule* allotting to each activity a fixed time, and get it approved by a wise and experienced priest, of interior life. And then do violence to yourself, if necessary, to keep it, and control the flood of your activities.

4TH PRINCIPLE. For your own profit and for the profit of others, it is essential that you develop your interior life, before all else. *The busier you are*, the more you need the interior life. And therefore, the more you ought to desire it, and the more you ought to take steps to prevent this desire from becoming one of those futile longings which the devil so often uses to drug souls and hold them fast in their illusions.

5TH PRINCIPLE. If it happens by accident, and really as a result of God's will, that the soul is under great stress of work, and finds it morally impossible to give more time to prayer, what then? There is a thermometer that never lies, and always tells us whether we are *truly* fervent, in spite of it all. Simply ask yourself if you really thirst for the interior life, and if, with all good will, you seize every possible opportunity to perform at least its *essential practices?* It so, you may remain at peace, and you can count on very special graces. God holds them in reserve for you; and they will give you the strength you need to continue your advance in the spiritual life.

---

2. *Erue eum et projice abs te* (*Matt.* 5:29). Cf. the passage from St. Bernard quoted above, page 77.

6TH PRINCIPLE. As long as the active worker has not reached the point where he is *habitually recollected* and habitually *dependent upon grace*—a dependence and recollection which accompany him everywhere he goes—he is still *not in a satisfactory state* of the interior life. But in working for this necessary recollection, strain must absolutely be avoided. A simple, habitual *glance* of the heart rather than of the mind, is all that is necessary. This glance will be *sure, accurate, penetrating*, and will tell us clearly whether we are still under the influence of Jesus in the midst of our work.

Practical Suggestions

1. Let the following conviction become deeply impressed upon your mind; namely, that a soul *cannot* lead an interior life without the *schedule* we have referred to, and without the *firm resolution* to keep it all the time, especially where the rigorously fixed *hour of rising* is concerned.

2. Base your interior life on its absolutely necessary element: *morning mental prayer.* St. Theresa said that, "The person who is fully determined to make a half hour's mental prayer every morning, cost what it may, has already traveled half his journey." Without mental prayer, the day will almost unavoidably be a tepid one.

3. *Mass, Holy Communion*, and the recitation of the *Breviary* are liturgical functions which offer inexhaustible resources for the interior life and are to be exploited with an ever increasing faith and fervor.

4. The *particular and general examinations of conscience*, should, like mental prayer and the liturgical life, help us to

develop *custody of the heart* in which *"watching"* and *"praying"* (*"Vigilate et orate"*) are combined. The soul that pays attention to what is going on inside itself, and is sensitive to the *presence of the Most Holy Trinity* within it, acquires an almost instinctive habit of turning to Jesus in every situation, but especially when there appears to be some danger of becoming dissipated or weak.

5. This leads to a need for incessant prayer by means of *spiritual Communions* and *ejaculatory prayers* which are so easy, to one who wants to practice them, even in the thick of the most absorbing occupations, and which offer themselves in such a pleasing variation, appropriate to the particular needs of every *present moment*, to the present situation, dangers, difficulties, weariness, deceptions, and so on.

6. Devout *study of Sacred Scripture*, especially of the New Testament, ought to find a place each day, or at least several times a week in the life of a priest. *Spiritual reading* every afternoon is a daily duty which no generous soul will ever neglect. The mind needs to be brought face to face with supernatural truths, with the dogmas that generate piety, and with their moral consequences, so easily forgotten.

7. Thanks to this custody of the heart, which will serve as its remote preparation, *weekly confession* will *infallibly* be imbued with sincere contrition, with true sorrow, and with an ever more loyal and more resolutely firm purpose of amendment.

8. The *yearly retreat* is very useful, but it is not enough. A *monthly retreat* (taking up an entire day, or at least half a day), devoted to a serious effort to recover the equilibrium of the soul is almost indispensable to the active worker.

2. MENTAL PRAYER: A NECESSARY ELEMENT OF INTERIOR LIFE, AND CONSEQUENTLY OF THE APOSTOLATE

No results may be expected from a vague desire for the interior life, conceived after the hurried reading of some book.

This desire must *take shape* in a *precise, fervent*, and *practical* resolution.

Many active workers have asked us to help them on their way to carry out their project of an interior life by stating a few general resolutions.

The answer to their requests means adding a kind of appendix to the present volume.

However, we are glad to accede to their desires, since we are convinced that no active worker, priest or layman, will have truly profited by the reading of what has been said so far, unless he is fully determined to set apart a certain time, every morning, for mental prayer; and that, on the other hand, no priest who wishes to make progress in the interior life can neglect to use the liturgical life or to practice custody of the heart.

It seems to us more practical to present these three points in the form of personal resolutions.

We make no pretense of originating a new method of mental prayer, but merely attempt to extract the pith of the best methods.

I. Fidelity to Mental Prayer

Resolution on Mental Prayer[3]

I firmly resolve to practice mental prayer every morning.

1. *Is this fidelity to mental prayer absolutely necessary?*

I am a *priest;* I heard, on my ordination retreat, the grave words: *Sacerdos alter Christus.* I then understood that if I do not make Christ in a special manner the source of all my life, I will not be a priest according to His Heart, I will not be a priestly soul. As a *priest* I must live in intimacy with Christ. That is what He expects of me. "I will not now call you servants . . . but I have called you friends."[4]

But *my life with Christ*—Principle, Means, and End—will develop in proportion as He is the *light* of my reason and of all my interior and exterior acts, the love that regulates all the affections of my heart, my *strength* in time of trial, in my struggles, in my work, and the *food* of that supernatural life which makes me share even in the life of God.

Fidelity to mental prayer will guarantee this life with Christ. Without mental prayer it is morally *impossible.*

Shall I dare to insult, by my refusal, the Heart of Him who offers me the *means to live* in friendship with Him?

Another important, though negative, aspect of the *necessity* for mental prayer: in the economy of the divine plan, it is a *sure defense* against the dangers inherent in my weakness, in my relations with the world, and in certain of my duties.

If I practice mental prayer, I am clad, as it were, in steel

---

3. Each of these resolutions is to be slowly meditated, or rather divided up into several meditations. Merely reading through them will not be of much benefit.

4. *Jam non dicam vos servos, vos autem dixi amicos (Joan.* 15:15).

armor and am *invulnerable* to the shafts of the enemy. Without mental prayer, I will *certainly* be wounded. Hence, there
will be many faults which I will hardly notice, if at all, and yet
they will be imputed to me as their cause.

"A priest in constant contact with the world faces the
choice between *mental prayer or a very great risk of damnation*," said the pious and learned and prudent Fr. Desurmont,
without any hesitation: and he was one of the most experienced preachers of ecclesiastical retreats.

Cardinal Lavigerie, in his turn, said: "For an apostle, there
is no halfway between sanctity, if not acquired, at least *desired
and pursued* (especially by means of daily mental prayer), and
gradual corruption."

Every priest can apply to his meditation the words with
which the Holy Cross inspired the Psalmist: "Unless THY
LAW had been my *meditation* I had then perhaps *perished*
in my abjection."[5] Now this law goes so far as to oblige the
priest to reproduce the spirit of Our Lord.

A Priest Is as Good as His Mental Prayer

Two Classes of Priests

1. Priests whose resolve is so firm that they will not even allow
their mental prayer to be delayed by pretexts of social nice-
ties, business, and so on. Only a *very rare* case, of absolute
impossibility, will make them postpone it until some other
half-hour, later in the morning. Nothing more.

These true priests set their hearts on getting definite *results*
in their mental prayer, which they insist on keeping *distinct*

---

5. *Nisi quod lex tua meditatio mea est, tunc forte periisem in humilitate
    mea* (*Ps.* 118:92).

from their thanksgiving after Mass, from all spiritual reading, and, a *fortiori*, from the composition of a sermon.

They possess sanctity, by virtue of their *efficacious* desire for it. As long as they persevere in this course, their *salvation is morally certain.*

2. Priests who make nothing but a half-hearted resolution and who *put off*, and so easily omit, their mental prayer altogether, *distort its object,* or make no real effort to succeed in it.

What can they look forward to? Inevitable tepidity, subtle illusions, a drugged or distorted conscience—*and these are steps on the slippery path to hell.*

To which of these two classes do I want to belong? If I hesitate to make my choice, *my retreat has been a failure.*

All these things go together. If I give up my halfhour of mental prayer, even Holy *Mass*—and therefore my Communion—will soon give me *no personal profit* and may even be imputed to me as a *sin.* The laborious and almost mechanical recitation of my *Breviary* will no longer be the warm and joyous expression of my liturgical life. No *vigilance*, no recollection, and hence, no ejaculatory prayers. Alas! No more *spiritual reading.* My apostolate will be less and less fruitful. No frank and sincere *examination* of faults—still less any particular examen. *Confession—a matter of routine, and sometimes of questionable worth* . . . The next step will be *sacrilege!*

The citadel, less and less well defended, lies open to the assault of a legion enemies. The walls are full of holes . . . soon the whole place will be in *ruins.*

II. What Mental Prayer Ought to Be

Ascensio mentis in Deum.[6] "*To ascend thus,*" says St. Thomas, "since *it is an act not of the speculative but of the practical reason, implies acts of the will.*"

Consequently:

Mental prayer is *real hard work*, especially for beginners. Work to get detached, for a few minutes, from all that is not God. Work to remain for half an hour *fixed in God*, and to gather yourself for a *new effort* to reach perfection. This work is no doubt hard, in the beginning, but I am going to accept it with generosity. Besides this work will be quickly rewarded by great consolations here on earth, by peace in friendship, and union with Jesus.

"*Mental prayer,*" says St. Theresa, "*is nothing but a friendly conversation in which the soul speaks, heart-to-heart, with the One Who we know loves us.*"

A *loving conversation*. It would be blasphemous to imagine that God, Who makes me feel the need and at times the attraction of this converse, and, what is more, makes it an obligation for me, should not want to make it easy for me. Even if I have long neglected it, Jesus calls me tenderly to mental prayer, and offers me *special help* in speaking this language of *faith*, *hope*, and *love*, which, as Bossuet says, is precisely what my mental prayer ought to be.

Am I going to resist this appeal of a Father Who calls even the prodigal to come and listen to His word, to talk to Him as a son; to open his heart to Him and to listen to the beatings of His own?

A *simple conversation*. I will be myself. I will speak to God of my tepidity, or my sins. I will speak to Him as a prodigal,

---

6.   The ascent of the mind to God.

or from the heat of my fervor. With the simplicity of a child, I will put my state of soul before Him, and I will only use words that express what I really am.

A *practical conversation*. When the smith plunges the iron into the fire, he is not just trying to make it hot and glowing; he wants to make it *malleable*. So too, the only reason why mental prayer is to give light to my mind and warmth to my heart is to make my soul *pliant* so that it can be hammered into a new shape, so that the faults and form of the old man may be hammered out, and the form and virtues of Jesus Christ imparted to it.

Thus the result of my conversation will be to *elevate my soul to the level of the sanctity of Christ*,[7] so that He may be able to fashion it in His own likeness. "*Thou, Lord Jesus, Thou Thyself, with Thine own most gentle and most merciful, yet most powerful hand, dost FORM and MOULD my heart.*"[8]

III. How Am I Going to Make My Mental Prayer?

To make a practical application of the definition of mental prayer and the notion of its object, I will follow this logical advance. I will put my mind, especially my faith and my heart, in the presence of Our Lord *teaching* me a truth or a virtue. I will intensify my *thirst* to bring my soul into harmony with the ideal under consideration. I will deplore what is opposed to it, in me. Foreseeing the various obstacles, I will *make up my mind* to overcome them. But, convinced that by myself I will get nowhere, I will obtain, by my *earnest prayers*, the grace to succeed.

---

7.   A definition, by Alvarez de Paz, of the object of mental prayer.
8.   *Tu, Domine Jesu, Tu Ipse, Manu mitissima, misericordissima, sed tamen fortissima, formans ac pertractans cor meum* (St. Augustine).

I am a traveler, exhausted, breathless; I seek to quench my thirst. At last, VIDEO:[9] I see a spring. But it is flowing from a sheer cliff. SITIO: the more I look at this limpid water that would enable me to continue my journey, the more my desire to quench my thirst increases, in spite of all the obstacles. VOLO: at all costs, I wish to reach this spring, I will to make every effort to get there. Alas! I have to admit that I am helpless. VOLO TECUM: a guide comes up. All that is required to enlist His help is that I ask Him. He carries me even where the going is hardest. Soon I am quenching my thirst in long draughts.

And that is the way it is with the living waters of grace that flow from the Heart of Jesus.

My spiritual reading, in the evening—so precious an element in the spiritual life—rekindles my desire for *mental prayer the following morning. Before going to bed* I foresee *briefly*, but in a *clear* and *forceful* manner, the subject of my meditation,[10] as well as the special fruit I want to draw from

---

9. VIDEO, I see. SITIO, I thirst. VOLO, I wish. VOLO TECUM, I wish with Thee.

10. A book of meditations is almost necessary to keep the mind from drifting around in a fog.

There are plenty of works, old and new, that have everything that is demanded in a true book of meditations, as distinct from spiritual reading. Each point contains some striking truth presented in a clear, forceful, and concise manner, in such a way that once we have reflected upon it, we are inevitably led on into a loving and practical conversation with God.

A single point is plenty for half an hour; it should be summed up in a biblical or liturgical text, or in some fundamental idea proper to my state. Above all, we must meditate upon the last things, and sin, at least once a month; after that on our vocation, on the duties of our state, the capital sins, the principal virtues, God's attributes, the mysteries of the Rosary or other scenes from the Gospel, especially the Passion. The feasts of the Liturgy suggest their own subjects.

it, and in the presence of God I stir up my desire to profit by it.

Now it is time for my meditation.[11] It is my desire to tear myself away from the earth, and compel my imagination to present a living and speaking picture, which I am to substitute for my preoccupations, distractions, and so on.[12] This picture will be a quick sketch, in a few bold lines, but it must be striking enough to *grip my attention* and *place me in the presence of God*, Whose activity, which is all love, seeks to surround and penetrate me. Thus I come into contact with a *living*[13] *interlocutor, who commands all my adoration and love.*

At once I fall into profound adoration of Him. That is obvious, *inescapable.* I annihilate myself. I am filled with contrition, I make every protestation of complete dependence on Him, and offer up humble and confident prayer that this conversation with my God may be blessed.[14]

---

11. *Clauso ostio* (the doors being shut) as we read in the Gospel suggests that I should prefer that place in which I shall be least likely to be disturbed—the church, my room, the garden, etc.

12. For instance, Our Lord showing His Sacred Heart and saying: "I am the Resurrection and the Life"—or "Behold this Heart which has so loved men"—or else some scene from His life, Bethlehem, Thabor, Calvary, etc. If after a sincere and brief attempt we do not succeed in visualizing the scene, drop it and pass on; God will make up for it.

13. The whole success of mental prayer depends often enough on how attentively we consider the fact that the One to whom we speak is actually living and present before us; we must cease to treat Him as though He were far away, and passive; that is, little more than an abstraction.

14. We need to be thoroughly convinced of the fact that all God asks of us, in this conversation, is good will. A soul pestered by distractions, but who patiently comes back, each day, like a good child, to talk with God is making first-rate mental prayer. God supplies all our deficiencies.

Video

Gripped by the sense of *Your living presence*, Dear Lord, and so detached from the purely natural order of things, I begin to talk to You in the *language of Faith.* Faith is much more fruitful than all the analyzing my reason can do. And so, I carefully read over, or turn over in my memory, this point of meditation.

Jesus, You are the One Who is talking to me, in this truth. You are the One teaching it to me. I want to get a livelier and greater faith in this truth which You are presenting to me as a thing of absolute certainty, since it is based on Your own veracity.

As for you, my soul, do not cease to repeat: "I BELIEVE." Say it again, with even greater conviction. Be like a child going over a lesson; repeat *over and over again* that you cling to this doctrine and to all its consequences for your eternity.[15]

Jesus, this is true, absolutely true, I believe it. I *will* that this ray from the sun of revelation shall serve as the beacon of my journey. Make my faith more ardent. Fill me with a vehement desire to live this ideal, and a holy anger against all that stands in its way. I want to *devour* this food of *truth*, and make it a part of me.

But if, after I have spent several minutes in stirring up my faith, I still remain cold to the truth presented to me—no use straining. I will simply turn to You like a child, my good Master, and tell You how sorry I am for this helplessness, and beg You to make up for it.

---

15. That is the way to make convictions take a firm hold on your soul and to prepare for the gifts of the spirit of lively faith and supernatural insight.

Sitio

The more frequent are my acts of faith, and above all the more power they have (and they are a true participation in the light of the Divine Intelligence), the more intense will be the response of my heart—*the language of affective love.*

Affections, in fact, spring up all by themselves, or called forth by my will, and are cast like flowers before the feet of Jesus by my childlike soul as He speaks to me. Adoration, gratitude, love, joy, attachment to the Divine Will, and detachment from everything else, aversion, hatred, fear, anger, hope, abandonment.

My heart selects *one or more* of these sentiments, and goes into them in all their depths, tells them to You, Jesus, repeats them to You *over and over again*, tenderly, with loyal trust, but in great simplicity.

If my *feelings* offer their assistance, I accept it. It may be useful, but it is not necessary. A calm, profound love is much better than surface emotions. These last do not depend on me, and are never a sure standard by which to tell if my prayer is genuine and faithful. But what is *always in my power to accomplish* and is the most important thing is the *effort* to shake off the torpor of my heart and to make it say: My God I *want* to be united to You. I want to *annihilate* myself before You. I *want* to sing my gratitude and my joy to carry out Your Will. I want it to be true, and no longer a lie, when I tell You that I love You, and that I hate what offends You, and so on.

No matter how sincerely I try, it may happen that my heart remains cold and expresses these affections with languor. In that case, Dear Lord, I will tell You in all simplicity, how I am humbled and how much I desire to do better. I will be very glad to go on for a long time lamenting my deficiency, convinced that by complaining of my dryness to You I acquire a special right to a most efficacious, though arid, cold, and dark, union with the affections of Your Divine Heart.

What a wonderful Ideal is that which I behold in You, my Jesus. But is *my life* in *harmony* with that perfect Exemplar? That is what I now *set out to discover*, under Your earnest gaze, O my Divine Companion. Now You are all Mercy; but when I come before You in the Particular Judgment—then at a single glance You will take in all the secret motives underlying the smallest acts of my life. Am I living according to this Ideal? Jesus, if I were to die right now, would You not find that my life is in *contradiction* with it?

Good Master, *what are the points* that You want me to correct? Help me to find out the *obstacles* that prevent me from imitating You and then the internal or external causes, and the near or remote *occasions* of my faults.

When I see all my failings and my difficulties, O my Redeemer, whom I adore, my heart cries out to You in confusion, pain, sorrow, bitter regret, and with a burning thirst to do better, and with a generous and uncompromising oblation of all that I am. *Volo placere Deo in omnibus.*[16]

Volo

I pass on into the school of *willing*.

Now it is the *language of effective love*. Affections have given me the desire to correct myself. I have seen what stands in my way. Now it is up to my will to say: "I *will* get them out of the road. Jesus, my ardor in saying over and over again "*I*

---

16. "I wish to please God in all things." In these words. Suarez gives us the pith of all his ascetical treatises. These acts of sitio make the soul ready for a resolution never to refuse God anything.

will" springs from the fervor with which I repeat "*I believe, I love, I regret, I detest.*"

If it sometimes happens, dear Lord, that this Volo does not spring forth with all the power I would like it to have, I will deplore this weakness of my will, and far from letting this discourage me, I will tell You over and over again, never tiring, how much I would like to have part in Your generosity in serving Your Father.

Besides the *general* resolution to work for my salvation, and to progress in the love of God, I will also add another, to apply my prayer to the difficulties, temptations, and dangers *of this day*. But what I want most of all is to intensify in the fires of a more fervent love, *the resolution*[17] which is the object of my particular examen (in which I concern myself with some defect I need to overcome, or some virtue to be gained). I will fortify this resolution with motives drawn from the Heart of the Master. Like a true strategist, I will be very clear as to the *means* that will insure success, anticipate the occasion, and prepare for the fight.

If I anticipate some special occasion of dissipation, immortification, humiliation, temptation, or some important decision to be made, I will face the approach of this moment with vigilance, strength, and, above all, in union with Jesus, and depending on Mary.

If, in spite of all my precautions, I fall again, what a world of difference there will nevertheless be between this surprise fault and my other lapses! No more discouragement now, because I know that God receives more glory from these

---

17. It is better to stick to the same resolution for months at a time, or from one retreat to the next. The particular examen, in the form of a short conversation with Our Lord, completes the meditation, and by noting our progress or regress, greatly assists our advance.

ever-repeated new beginnings, by which I become more resolute, more mistrustful of myself, and more dependent upon
Him. Success is to be had only at this price.

Volo tecum

*"To make a lame man walk without a limp is less absurd than
to try and succeed without Thee, my Savior"* (St. Augustine).
Why do my resolutions bear no fruit? It can only be because
my belief that "I can do all things" is not followed by; "in Him
Who strengtheneth me."[18] And this brings me, then, to that
part of my prayer which is in certain respects *the most important of all: supplication,* or the *language of hope.*

Without Your grace, Jesus, I can do nothing. And there
is absolutely nothing that entitles me to it. Yet I know that
my ceaseless prayers, far from irking You, will determine the
amount of help You will give me, if they reflect a thirst to
belong to You, distrust in myself, and an unlimited, not to say
mad, confidence in Your Sacred Heart. Like the Canaanite
woman, I cast myself at Your feet, O infinite goodness. With
her persistence, full of humility and hope, I ask You not for a
few crumbs but a full share in this banquet of which You said:
"My meat is to do the will of Him that sent Me."

Grace has made me a member of Your Mystical Body, and
so I share in Your life and merits, and it is through You, O
Jesus, that I pray. Father all-holy, I am praying to You by
the Precious Blood that cries out for mercy; can You refuse
to hear my prayer? It is the cry of a beggar, going up to You,
Who are inexhaustible wealth: "Hear me, for I am needy and

---

18. *Omnia possum . . . in eo qui me confortat* (*Phil.* 4:13).

poor."[19] Clothe me in Your strength, and in my weakness glorify Your power. Your goodness, Your promises, my Jesus, and my misery and my confidence are the only titles on which I base my request that I may obtain, through union with You vigilance and strength throughout this day.

If any obstacle comes up, or any temptation, or some sacrifice to be exacted from one or other of my faculties, some text or thought which I take along with me as a *spiritual bouquet*, will help me breathe the fragrance of prayer which surrounded my resolution, and once again, at that time, I will renew my cries of powerful supplication. This *habit*, a fruit of my mental prayer, will also be the true test of its value: "*By their fruits you shall know.*"

When I get to the point where I LIVE BY FAITH, and in the CONSTANT THIRST FOR GOD, then alone the labor of the VIDEO stage of prayer will sometimes be omitted; SITIO and VOLO will spring from my heart at the very beginning of the meditation, which will then be spent in eliciting affections and in offering sacrifices, in strengthening my resolute will, and then in begging from Jesus, either directly or through Mary Immaculate, the angels, or the saints, a closer and more constant union with the Divine Will.

Now it is time for the Holy Sacrifice. Mental Prayer has made me ready. My participation in Calvary, in the name of the Church, and my Communion, will follow, as it were, naturally, as a kind of continuation of my meditation.[20] In my thanksgiving I will extend my demands to all the needs of the Church, to the souls in my care, to the dead, to my work, my relatives, friends, benefactors, enemies, and so on.

---

19. *Exaudi me, quoniam inops et pauper sum ego.* (*Ps.* 85).
20. See Appendix.

The recitation of the various hours, in my beloved Breviary, in union with the Church, for her and for myself, as well as ardent ejaculatory prayers, spiritual communions, particular examen, visit to the Blessed Sacrament, Rosary, general exa-men, and so on, will all be friendly landmarks along my road. They will give me new strength and will preserve the initial momentum that began with the morning meditation, and will guarantee that nothing escapes the action of Our Lord. Thanks to the momentum, recourse to Jesus, *frequent* at first, and then *habitual*, either directly or through His Mother, will wipe out all the contradictions between my admiration of His teachings and my free-and-easy life; between my pious beliefs and my actual conduct.

*　　　*　　　*

At this point the writer must curb the desires of his heart which, in its anxiety to be of use to active workers, would like to devote a special resolution, at this point, to the *particular examen*.

He fears, however, that if he gives in to his notion, he will make the book over long. And yet, the reading of Cassian, and of several Fathers of the Church, as well as St. Ignatius, St. Francis de Sales, and St. Vincent de Paul, persuades us that the particular and general examinations are *absolutely neces-sary* adjuncts of mental prayer, and are closely linked with *custody of the heart*.

Following the guidance of the director, the soul is now resolved to take a *more direct aim*, in meditation and during the course of the day, at some *special defect* or some *special virtue* which is the chief source of other defects and virtues.

Many are the steeds that draw the chariot. And the eye is

on them all at once, constantly. Yet in the midst of the team there is one that occupies all the care of the driver. In point of fact, if this one charger veers too much to the right or left, the whole team will be thrown off the track.

The analysis of the soul, by particular examination, to see if there has been progress, regression, or stagnation with regard to a certain *specifically chosen point*, is simply one of the elements of custody of the heart.

3. THE LITURGICAL LIFE IS A SOURCE OF THE INTERIOR LIFE: THEREFORE IT IS A SOURCE OF THE APOSTOLATE

Resolution on the Liturgical Life

I want to use my Mass, Breviary, and other liturgical functions to unite myself more and more, both as MEMBER and AMBASSADOR, to the life of the Church, and thus more fully to put on Christ, and Christ crucified, especially if I am His MINISTER.

I. What Is the Liturgy?

It is You, Jesus, that I adore as Center of the Liturgy. It is You Who give unity to this Liturgy, which I may define as the *public, social, official worship* given by the Church of God, or, the *whole complex of means which the Church uses especially in the Missal, Ritual, and Breviary, and by which she expresses her religion to the adorable Trinity, as well as instructs and sanctifies souls.*

O my soul, you must go into the very heart of the Adorable Trinity and contemplate there the *eternal Liturgy* in which the three Persons chant, one to another, their divine Life and infinite Sanctity, in their ineffable hymn of the generation of the Word and the procession of the Holy Spirit. *Sicut erat in principio . . .*

God desires to be praised outside of Himself. He created the angels, and heaven resounded with their joyous cries of *Sanctus, Sanctus, Sanctus*. He created the visible world and it magnifies His power: "The heavens announce the glory of God."

Adam comes to life and begins to sing, in the name of creation, a hymn of praise in echo of the everlasting Liturgy. Adam, Noah, Melchisedech, Abraham, Moses, the people of God, David, and all the saints of the Old Law vied in chanting it. The Jewish Pasch, their sacrifices and holocausts, the solemn worship of Jehovah in His Temple, gave this praise, especially since the fall. "Praise is not seemly in the mouth of a sinner."[21]

You, Jesus, You alone are the perfect hymn of praise, because You are the true glory of the Father. No one can worthily glorify Your Father, except through You. *Per Ipsum, et cum Ipso et in Ipso est tibi Deo Patri . . . omnis honor et Gloria.*[22]

You are the *link* between the Liturgy of earth and the Liturgy of heaven, in which You give Your elect a more direct participation. Your Incarnation came and united, in a *living and substantial union*, mankind and all creation, with the Liturgy of God Himself. *Thus it is God Who praises God*, in our Liturgy. And this is full and perfect praise, which finds its apogee in the sacrifice of Calvary.

---

21. *Non est speciosa laus in ore peccatoris* (*Eccli.* 15:9).
22. By Him and with Him and in Him, all honor and glory are given to Thee, O God the Father (Canon of the Mass).

Divine Savior, before You left the earth, You instituted the *Sacrifice* of the New Law, in order to renew Your immolation. You also instituted Your *Sacraments*, in order to communicate Your life to souls.

But You left Your Church the care of *surrounding* this Sacrifice and these Sacraments with symbols, ceremonies, exhortations, prayers, etc., in order that she might thus pay greater honor to the Mystery of the Redemption, and make it more understandable to her children, and help them to gain more profit from it while exciting in their souls a respect full of awe.

You also gave Your Church the mission of *continuing* until the end of time the prayer and praise which Your Heart never ceased to send up to Your Father during Your mortal life and which It still goes on offering to Him, in the Tabernacle and in the splendor of Your glory in heaven.

The Church, who loves You as a Spouse, and who is full of a Mother's love for us, which comes to her from Your own Heart, has carried out this twofold task. That is how those wonderful collections were formed, which include all the riches of the Liturgy.

Ever since, the Church has been uniting her praises to those which the angels and her own elect children have been giving to God in heaven. *In this way, she already begins to do, here below, what is destined to occupy her for all eternity.*

United to the praises of the man-God, this praise, the prayer of the Church, *becomes divine* and the Liturgy of the earth becomes one with that of the celestial hierarchies in the Court of Christ, echoing that everlasting praise which springs forth from the furnace of infinite love which is the Most Holy Trinity.

II. What Is the Liturgical Life?

Lord, the laws of Your Church do not bind me *strictly* to anything but the faithful observance of the rubrics and the correct pronunciation of words.

But is there any doubt that *You want my good will to give You more than this?* You want my mind and heart to *profit* by the riches hidden in the Liturgy and thus be more united to Your Church and come thereby to a closer union with Yourself.

Good Master, the example of Your most faithful servants makes me eager to come and sit down at the splendid feast to which the Church invites me, certain that I will find, in the Divine Office, in the forms, ceremonies, collects, epistles, gospels, and so on which accompany the holy Sacrifice of the Mass and the administration of the Sacraments, *healthful and abundant food to nourish my interior life.*

Let us dwell on the basic idea that ties all the elements of the Liturgy together, and the fruits by which progress may be recognized will preserve us from illusion.

*　　　*　　　*

Each one of the sacred rites may be compared to a precious stone. Yet how much greater will be the value and brilliance of those that belong to the Mass and Office, when I know how to enshrine them all together in that marvelous setting: the *liturgical cycle.*[23]

---

23. The Church, inspired by God and instructed by the Holy Apostles, has disposed the year in such a way that we may find in it, together with the life, the mysteries, the preaching and doctrine of Jesus Christ, the true fruit of all these in the admirable virtues of His servants and in the

When my soul lives, throughout a certain period of time, under the influence of a mystery, and is nourished by all that Scripture and tradition offer that is most instructive in this subject, and is constantly directed and made attentive to the *same order of ideas*, it must necessarily be influenced by this concentration, and find in the thoughts suggested by the Church a food as nourishing as it is delightful, and which will prepare it to receive that *special grace* which God reserves for each period, each Feast of the Cycle.

The Mystery comes to fill me not only as an abstract truth, absorbed in meditation, but *gripping my whole being*, bringing into play even my sense faculties, to stir up my heart and direct my will. It is more than a mere commemoration of some past event, or an ordinary anniversary: it is living actuality with all the character of a *present event to which the Church gives an application here and now*, and in which she really and truly takes part.

For instance, in the Christmas Season, rejoicing before the altar at the coming of the Holy Child, my soul can repeat: "Today Christ is born, today the Savior has appeared, today the angels sing on earth . . ."[24]

At each period in the liturgical Cycle, my Missal and Breviary disclose to me new rays of the love of Him Who is for

---

examples of His saints, and, finally, a mysterious compendium of the Old and New Testaments and of the whole of Ecclesiastical History. And thus, all the seasons are full of rich fruits for a Christian; all are full of Jesus Christ. In this variety, which all together leads up to that single unity recommended by Christ, the clean and pious soul will find, together with celestial pleasures, solid nourishment and an everlasting renewal of fervor. (Bossuet: Funeral Sermon on Maria Theresia of Austria).

24. *Hodie Christus natus est, hodie Salvator apparuit, hodie in terra canunt angeli* . . . (Office of Christmas).

us at the same time Teacher, Doctor, Consoler, Savior, and Friend. On the Altar, just as at Bethlehem or Nazareth, or on the shore of the Lake of Tiberias, Jesus reveals Himself as Light, Love, Kindness, and Mercy. He reveals Himself above all as *Love personified*, because He is *Suffering personified*, in agony at Gethsemani, atoning on Calvary.

And so the liturgical life gives the *Eucharistic life* its full development. And Your Incarnation, O Jesus, that brought God close to us, making Him visible to us in You, continues to do the very same thing for us all, in each of the mysteries that we celebrate.

So it is, dear Lord, that thanks to the Liturgy, I can share in the *Church's life and in Your own*. With her, every year, I witness the mysteries of Your Hidden life, Your Public life, Life of Suffering, and Life in Glory; and with her, I cull the fruits of them all. Besides, the periodic feasts of Our Lady and the Saints who have best imitated Your interior Life bring me, also, an increase of light and strength by placing their example before my eyes, helping me to reproduce Your virtues in myself and to inspire the faithful with the spirit of Your Gospel.

How am I to carry out, in my apostolate, the desire of Pius X? How are the faithful going to be helped, by me, *to enter into an active participation in the Holy Mysteries and in the public and solemn prayer of the Church*[25] which that Pope

---

25. In the very first year of his pontificate, on November 22, 1903, Pius X issued his celebrated motu proprio on Sacred Music, here quoted by Dom Chautard. The passage, in full, runs:

"We believe it our first duty to raise our voice, without further delay, to reprove and condemn everything, which in the functions of the cult and the celebration of the offices of the Church, departs from the right rule which has been laid down. For it is, in fact, our keen desire that the true Christian spirit may once more flourish, cost what it may, and be maintained among all the faithful: and to that end it is

called the PRIME AND INDISPENSABLE SOURCE *of the true Christian spirit*, if I myself pass by the treasures of the Liturgy without even suspecting what wonders are to be found therein?

If I am going to put more unity into my spiritual life, and unite myself still more to the life of the Church, I will aim at tying up all my other pious exercises with the Liturgy, as far as I possibly can. For instance, I will give preference to a *subject for meditation* which has a connection with the liturgical period, or feast, or cycle. In my *visits to the Blessed Sacrament*, I will converse more readily, according to the season, with the Child Jesus, Jesus suffering, Jesus glorified, Jesus living in His Church, and so on. *Private reading* on the Mystery or on the life of the Saint being honored at the time will also contribute much to this plan for a liturgical spirituality.

*　　*　　*

My adorable Master, deliver me from all *fake liturgical life*. It is ruinous to the interior life, above all because it weakens the spiritual combat.

Preserve me from a piety which would have the liturgical life consist in a lot of poetic thrills, or in an intriguing study of religious archaeology, or else which leads to *quietism* and

---

necessary to provide, above all, that everything be holy and dignified in the church where the faithful gather together to draw this spirit from its prime and indispensable source: the active participation in the sacrosanct mysteries and the public and solemn prayer of the Church. For it is vain for us to hope to bring down upon ourselves, to this end, the abundance of the blessings of heaven if our homage to the Most High, instead of rising in an odor of sweetness, on the contrary places in the hand of the Lord the scourge with which our Divine Redeemer once chased the vile profaners from the Temple."

its awful consequences; for quietism strikes at the very roots of the interior life: fear, hope, the desire of salvation, and of perfection, the fight against faults and labor to acquire virtue.

Make me really convinced that in this age of absorbing and dangerous occupations, the liturgical life, no matter how perfect it may be, *can never dispense anyone from morning mental prayer.*

Keep far from me all *sentimentality* and *fake piety* which make the liturgical life consist in impressions and emotions, and leave the will the slave of the imagination and feelings.

Not that You want me to remain cold to all the beauty and poetry which the Liturgy contains. Far from it! The Church uses her chant and her ceremonies to appeal to the sense faculties, and to reach, through them, the souls of her children more fully, and to give to *their wills* a more effective presentation of the true goods, and raise them up more surely, more easily, and more completely to God.

I can therefore enjoy all the changeless, wholesome refreshment of dogma thrown into relief by Liturgy, and let myself be moved by the majestic spectacle of a solemn High Mass, and esteem the prayers of absolution of the touching rites of Baptism, Extreme Unction, the Burial Service, and so on.

But I must never lose sight of the fact that all the resources offered by the holy Liturgy are nothing but means to arrive at the *sole end* of all interior life: *to put to death the "old man" that You, Jesus, may reign in his place.*

I will, therefore, be leading a genuine liturgical life *if I am so penetrated with the spirit of the Liturgy that I use my Mass, Prayers, and Official Rites to intensify my union with the Church, and thus to progress in my participation in the interior Life of Jesus Christ, and hence in His virtues, so that I will give a truer reflection of Him in the eyes of the faithful.*

III. The Liturgical Spirit

Jesus, this liturgical life means a special attraction for all that pertains to worship.

To some people, You have freely given this attraction. Others are less privileged. But if they ask You for it, and aid themselves by studying and reflecting, they too will obtain it.

The meditation I shall make, later on, upon the advantages of the liturgical life, is going to increase my thirst to acquire it at any price. At present I pause to consider the distinctive characteristics of this life, which give it such an important place in spirituality.

*   *   *

Union, even remote, together with the Church, to Your Sacrifice, by thought and intention, O Jesus: this is already a great thing. So is it to find one's prayer fused with the official and unceasing prayer of Your Church. The heart of the ordinary baptized Christian thus takes flight with more certainty towards God, carried up to Him by Your praises, adoration, thanksgiving, reparation, and petition.[26]

---

26. Union with somebody else's prayer can lead one to a high degree of prayer! Take the case of the peasant who offered to carry the baggage of St. Ignatius and his companions. When he noticed that, as soon as they arrived at some inn, the Fathers hastened to find some quiet spot and recollect themselves before God, he did as they did, and fell on his knees too. One day they asked him what he did when he thus recollected himself, and he answered: "All I do is say: 'Lord, these men are saints, and I am their packhorse. Whatever they do, I want to be doing too'; and so that is what I offer up to God." (Cf. Rodriguez, *Christian Perf.* Pt. I, Tr. 5, ch. xix).

   If this man came, by means of the continuous practice of this exercise, to a high degree of prayer and spirituality, how much more can

An active participation (Pope Pius X's own words) *in the sacro-sanct mysteries and in the public and solemn prayer:* that means assisting at this worship with piety and understanding; it means an avid desire to profit by the feasts and ceremonies; better still, it means serving Mass, and answering the prayers, or joining in the recitation and chanting of the Office. Is not all this a way to enter *more directly* into the thoughts of Your Church, and to *draw from the prime and indispensable source of the Christian spirit?*[27]

But then, O Holy Church, what a noble mission it is to present oneself each day, by virtue of ordination or religious profession, united to the angels and the elect, as your *ambassador* before the throne of God, there to utter your official prayer!

Incomparably more sublime, and beyond all power of expression, is the dignity of a sacred minister who becomes *Your other self,* O my Divine Redeemer, by administering the Sacraments, and above all by celebrating the Holy Sacrifice.

---

even a man without education advance in union with the liturgical life of the Church.

A Cistercian lay-brother of Clairvaux was watching the sheep during the night of the Assumption. He did his best, chiefly by reciting the Angelic Salutation, to unite himself to the Matins which the monks were singing in choir, the distant bells for which had reached him, out in the hills. God revealed to St. Bernard that the simple and humble devotion of this Brother had been so pleasing to Our Lady that she had preferred it to that of the monks, fervent as they were. (*Exordium Magnum Ord. Cisterciensis,* D. 4, c. xiii. Migne: Patr. Lat., Vol. 185).

27. Pius X, *Mot. Prop.* Nov. 22, 1903, on Sacred Music.

First Principle

As a member of the Church, I must have the conviction that when I take part, even as a plain Christian,[28] *in a liturgical ceremony, I am united to the whole Church not only through the Communion of Saints, but by virtue of a real and active co-operation in an act of religion which the Church, the Mystical Body of Christ, offers as a society to God. And by this notion the Church like a true Mother helps dispose my soul to receive the Christian virtues.*[29]

Your Church, Lord Jesus, forms a perfect society, whose members, closely united one to another, are destined to form an even more perfect and more holy society, that of the Elect.

As a Christian I am a member of that Body of which You are the *Head and the Life.* And that is *the point of view from which You look at me,* Divine Savior. So I give You a special

---

28. The priest, and even the bishop, is present, like any ordinary member of the faithful, only in his capacity as a plain Christian when he assists at a ceremony, when exercising no special function in it, profiting from it in the ordinary way.

29. We can better understand the efficacy of the Liturgy in making us live the life of grace and in making the whole interior life more easily accessible to us, when we recall that all official prayer, every ceremony instituted by the Church, possesses an impetratory power which is, in itself, irresistible, *per se efficacissima.* In this case the prayer that is put into operation to obtain a particular grace is more than just an individual gesture, the isolated prayer of a soul, however excellently disposed; it is also the act of the whole Church who becomes a suppliant with us. It is the voice of the dearly beloved Spouse, which always gives joy to the Heart of God, and which He always hears and answers in some way.

To sum it all up in a word: the impetratory power of the Liturgy is made up of two elements: the *opus operantis* of the soul making use of the Great Sacramental of the Liturgy, and the *opus operantis* of the Church. The two actions, that of the soul and that of the Church, are like two forces that combine and leap up, in a single momentum, to God.

joy when, in presenting myself before You, I speak to You as my Head, and consider myself as one of the sheep of that Fold of which You are the only Shepherd, and which includes in its unity all my brothers in the Church militant, suffering and triumphant.

Your Apostle taught me this doctrine which expands my soul and broadens the horizons of my spirituality. And thus it is, he says, that "*As in one body we have many members, so we, being many, are one body in Christ, and every one members one of another.*"[30] And elsewhere: "*For as the body is one and hath many members: and all the members of the body, whereas they are many, yet are one body, so also is Christ.*"[31]

There, then, is the unity of Your Church, indivisible in the parts and in the whole, all entirely present in the whole Body, and all in each one of the parts,[32] united in the Holy Spirit,

---

30. *Sicut enim in uno corpore multa membra habemus . . . ita multi unum sumus in Christo, singuli autem alter alterius membra* (*Rom.* 12:4–5).

31. *Sicut enim corpus unum est, et membra habet multa, omnia autem membra corporis cum sint multa, unum tamen corpus sunt; ita et Christus* (*1 Cor.* 12:12).

32. *Unusquisque fidelium quasi quaedam minor videtur esse Ecclesia dum salvo unitatis arcanae mysterio, etiam cuncta Redemptionis humanae unus homo suscipit Sacramenta* (St. Peter Damian, *Opusc.* xi. c. 10. Migne, *Patr. Lat.*, Vol. 145, col. 239).

    "Each one of the faithful may be called a little Church in himself, since, with the mystery of this hidden unity, one man receives all the Sacraments of man's Redemption (which were given by Our Lord to the whole Church)." This passage is taken from St. Peter Damian's beautiful treatise on the Mystical Body which is also a treatise on the Liturgy, the "Liber qui Dicitur Dominus Vobiscum," or the tract on the "Dominus Vobiscum." The present words occur in his discussion of the way each one of the faithful can say "miserere MEI Deus," and "Deus in adjutorium MEUM intende" (as it is in the psalm and at the beginning of each hour in the monastic Breviary), both in his own name and in that of the whole Church.

united in You, Jesus, and brought by this union into the unique and eternal society of the Father, Son, and Holy Ghost.[33]

The Church is the assembly of the faithful who, under the government of the *same* authority, are united by the *same* faith and the *same* charity, and tend to the *same* end, that is, *incorporation in Christ* by the *same* means, which are summed up in grace, of which the ordinary channels are *prayer* and the *Sacraments*.

The great prayer, and the favorite channel of grace is *liturgical* prayer, the prayer of the Church herself, *more powerful* than the prayer of single individuals and even of pious associations, no matter how powerful private and non-liturgical forms of social prayer may be, and no matter how much they are recommended in the Gospel.[34]

Incorporated in the true Church, a child of God and a member of Christ by the Sacraments of Baptism, I have acquired the *right* to participate in the other Sacraments, in the Divine Office, in the fruits of the Mass, and in the indulgences and prayers of the Church. I can benefit by all the graces and all the merits of my brethren.

I bear, from Baptism, an indelible mark which *commissions me to worship God according to the rite of the Christian*

---

33. St. Peter Damian, quoted by D. Gréa, *La Sainte Liturgie*, p. 51.
34. St. Ignatius Martyr writes, in his *Epistle to the Ephesians*, c. v: "Make no mistake: unless one come to the altar he is deprived of the Bread of God. Now if the prayer of one or the other of you has such great power, how much greater is the power of that prayer which is of the bishop and of the whole Church? Therefore, he who does not come to the assembly of the faithful, is puffed up with pride, and has already excommunicated and judged himself" (Migne, *Patr. Graeca*, Vol. III, 647).

St. Alphonsus Liguori preferred one prayer of the Breviary to a hundred private prayers.

religion.[35] My Baptismal consecration makes me a member of the Kingdom of God, and I form part of that "chosen *genera-tion, the kingly priesthood, the holy nation.*"[36]

And so, I participate *as a Christian* in the sacred ministry, although in a remote and indirect manner, by my prayers, by my share in the offering, by my active participation in the Sac-rifice of the Mass and in the liturgical offices, and in multiply-ing my spiritual sacrifices, as St. Peter recommends, by the practice of virtues, by accomplishing all things with a view to pleasing God and uniting myself to Him, and by making of my body a living victim, holy and agreeable to God.[37] And that is what you teach me, Holy Mother Church when, by the priest, You say to the faithful: *Orate frates* . . . "Pray, brethren, that my sacrifice and yours may be acceptable," and where the priest says also, in the Canon: *Memento Domine . . . et omnium circumstantium pro quibus tibi offerimus vel qui tibi offerunt hoc Sacrificium laudis,* "Remember Lord . . . (N. and N.) and

---

35. *Charactere sacramentali insignitur homo ut ad cultum Dei deputatus secundum ritum Christianae religionis* (Card. Billot, *De Ecclesiae Sacram.*, t. 1, thes. 2).

36. *Vos autem genus electum, regale sacerdotium, gens sancta, populus acquisitionis* (*1 Ptr.* 2:9).

37. *Sacerdotium sanctum, offerre spirituales, hostias, acceptabiles Dco per Jesum Christum* (*1 Ptr.* 2:5). It is in this sense that St. Ambrose says: "*Omnes filii Ecclesiae sacerdotes sunt; ungimur enim in Sacerdotium sanctum, offerentes nosmetipsos Deo, hostias spirituales*" (*In Lucam,* lib. iv. n. 33. Migne, Patr. Lat., vol. 15, 676). "All the children of the Church are priests, for we are anointed in a holy priesthood, offering ourselves to God as spiritual victims."

　　Sicut omnes Christianos dicimus propter mysticum Chrisma; sic omnes Sacerdotes, quoniam membra sunt unius Sacerdotis. (St. Augustine, *De Civit. Dei,* xx :10. Migne, P. L., vol. 41, col. 676).

　　"Just as we call all 'Christians' because of the mystical Chrism, so we call all 'priests' because all are members of one Priest."

all those who are here present, for whom we offer to Thee, or who offer to Thee this sacrifice of Praise." And, further on: "Receive, Lord, with Kindness, we beg of Thee, this offering which we make to Thee, I Thy servant, and Thy family."[38]

Indeed, the holy Liturgy is so truly *the common work of the entire Church*, that is of the priests and people, that the mystery of this unity is ever really present in the Church by the indestructible power of the *Communion of Saints*, which is proposed to our belief in the Apostles' Creed. The Divine Office and Holy Mass, which is the most important part of the Liturgy, cannot be celebrated without the whole Church being involved, and being mysteriously present.[39]

And so, in the Liturgy, *everything is done in common in the name of all, for the benefit of all.* All the prayers are said in the plural.

This close union between all the members, by the same faith and by participation in the same Sacraments, produces *fraternal love in their souls*, and this is the distinctive sign of

---

38. *Hanc igitur oblationem servitutis nostrae sed et cunctae familiae tuae quaesumus, Domine, ut placatus accipias* (Canon of the Mass).

"We all make this offering together with the priest, our consent is given to all that he does, all that he says. And what is it that he says? 'Pray, my brethren, that my sacrifice and yours may be agreeable to the Lord our God.' And what is your answer? 'May the Lord receive from your hands: . . . What? . . . my sacrifice and yours!' And then, again, what does the priest say? 'Remember Thy servants for whom we offer . . .' Is that all? He adds . . . 'or who offer Thee this sacrifice.' Let us, then, offer with him. Let us offer Jesus Christ, and offer up our own selves, together with the whole Catholic Church, spread over the whole earth" (Bossuet, *Medit. on the Gospel.* Last Supper, Pt. 1, 83rd day).

39. Peter Damian (also speaking of the *Hanc igitur . . .*): "By these words it is quite clearly evident that the Sacrifice which is placed upon the altar by the hands of the priest is offered by the entire family of God as a whole" (*Lib. qui Dic. Dominus Vobiscum*, cap. viii. Also see D. Grea. *La Sainte Liturgic.*, p. 51).

those who wish to imitate Christ and walk in His footsteps. *"By this shall all men know that you are my disciples, if you have love one for another."*[40] This bond among the members of the Church draws them all the closer together in proportion as they participate more fully, through the Communion of Saints, in the grace and charity of the Head who communicates to them supernatural and divine life.

These truths are the *foundation* of the liturgical life which, in its turn, brings me *constantly back to them.*

O Holy Church of God, what great love for you this thought enkindles in my heart! I am one of your members. I am a member of Christ! What love for all Christians this gives me, since I realize that they are my brothers, and that we are all one in Christ! And what love for my divine Head, Jesus Christ!

It is not possible for me to remain indifferent to anything that concerns you. Sad, if I behold you persecuted, I rejoice at the news of your conquests, your triumphs.

What a joy to think that, while I am sanctifying myself, I am also contributing to the increase of your beauty and working for the sanctification of all the children of the Church, my brothers, and even for the salvation of the whole human family!

O Holy Church of God, I wish, as far as in me lies, to make you more lovely and more holy and more full. And the splendor of your whole unity will come forth from the *perfection of each one of your children*, built on the foundation that dominated solidarity which was the thought that dominated Christ's prayer after the Last Supper and was the true testament of His Heart: "That they may be one . . . That they may be made perfect in one."[41]

---

40. *Joan.* 13:35.

41. *"Ut sint unum, ut sint consummati in unum"* (*Joan.* 17:21, 23).

O Mother, Holy Church, how moved I am with love and admiration for your liturgical prayer! Since I am one of your members, *it is my prayer too*, especially when I am present or take an active part in it. All that you have *is mine;* and everything I have *belongs to you.*

A drop of water is nothing. But united with the ocean, it shares in all that power and immensity. And that is the way it is when my prayer is united with yours. To God all things are present. He takes in, at one glance, the past, the present, and the future; and in His eyes, *my prayer is all one* with that universal chorus of praises which you have been sending up to Him ever since you began, and which will continue to rise up to the throne of His Eternal Majesty even to the end of time.

Jesus, You want my piety to take, in certain respects, a utilitarian, practical, and petitioning character.

But the order of petitions in the *Our Father* shows me how much You want my piety to be *first of all* devoted to the *praise of God*,[42] and that far from being egotistical, narrow, and isolated, it should make my supplications embrace *all the needs of my brothers.*

Help me, by the liturgical life, to arrive at this generous and exalted piety which, without detriment to the spiritual combat, gives to God, and generously, great *praise;* this *charitable, fraternal,* and *universal* (i.e. Catholic) *piety,* which takes in all souls and has all the interests of the Church at heart.

---

42. *Creatus est homo ad hunc finem, ut Dominum Deum suum laudet ac revereatur eique serviens tandem salvus fiat:* "Man was created to this end; that he should praise God and give Him reverence, and, by serving Him, be saved" (St. Ignatius, *Spiritual Exercises*).

"Our end is the service of Our Lord, and it is only in order to serve Him better that we must correct our faults and acquire virtues; sanctity is only a means to better service." Bl. P. J. Eymard.

Holy Church, it is your mission to beget, without ceasing, new children to your Divine Spouse and to bring them up "into the measure of the age of the fullness of Christ."[43] And that means that you have received all the means, in abundance, to achieve this end. And the importance you attach to the Liturgy proves how efficacious it must be to teach me how to *begin to praise God and to make spiritual progress.*

During His public life Our Lord spoke "as one having power."[44]

And that is the way you talk too, O Holy Church, my Mother. Guardian of the treasure of truth, you realize the importance of your mission. Dispenser of the Precious Blood, you well know all the means of sanctification which the Lord has put into your hands.

You do not call upon my reason, and tell me, "Examine these things, study them." But you do address yourself *to my faith*, saying, "Trust in me. Am I not your Mother? And is there anything I desire more than to see you grow, from day to day, in likeness to your divine Model? Now who is there that knows Jesus better than I do, who am His Spouse? Where, then, *will you better find the Spirit of your Redeemer than in the Liturgy*, which is the genuine expression of what I think and what I feel?"

Oh yes, dear holy Mother, I will allow myself to be led and formed by you with the simplicity and confidence of a child, reminding myself that *I am praying with my Mother.* These are her very own words, which she puts in my mouth in order that I may be filled with her spirit, and that her thoughts may pass into my heart.

---

43. *In mensuram aetatis plenitudinis Christi* (*Eph.* 4:13).
44. *Sicut potestatem habens* (*Matt.* 7:29).

With you, then, will I rejoice; yes, with you, Holy Church. *Gaudeamus exultemus!* With you will I lament: *ploremus!* With you will I praise Him: *confitemini Domino!* With you will I beg for mercy: *miserere!* With you I shall hope: *speravi, sperabo!* With you I shall love: *diligam!* I will ardently unite myself with all your demands, formulated in the wonderful prayers, in order that the life-giving movements of the mind and will that you wish to elicit by these words and sacred rites may enter more deeply into my heart, and make it more pliant to the touch of the Holy Ghost, so that my will may at last be totally absorbed into the Will of God.

Second Principle

Whenever I take part as a REPRESENTATIVE OF THE CHURCH[45] in any liturgical function, it is God's desire that I give expression to my virtue of religion by being fully conscious of the OFFICIAL MANDATE with which I am honored, and that, thus united more and more perfectly to the life of the Church, I may progress in all the virtues.

I am the representative of Your Church for the purpose of offering incessantly to God, through You, Lord Jesus, in His Name and in the name of all His children, the sacrifice of praise and supplication. Consequently, I am what St. Bernardine of Siena so beautifully called: *persona publica, totius Ecclesiae*

---

45. Those who are thus delegated by the Church are: clerics, religious obliged to recite the office, even though they only do so in private. So, too, are all those who are bound to sing office in choir in churches canonically erected, and to attend chapter of conventual masses. The same also applies to those who, without having received Orders, fulfill such functions by the tolerance of the Church, such as servers of Mass.

os, a public person, the mouth of the whole Church.[46]

And therefore, at every liturgical function, there must be in me a kind of *dual personality*, such as exists, for instance, in an ambassador. In his private life, such a one is nothing but a private citizen. But once he has put on the insignia of his office and speaks and acts in the name of his king, he becomes, at that very moment, the representative and, in a certain sense, the *very person of his sovereign*.

The same is true in my own case when I am carrying out my liturgical "functions." My individual being receives the *addition* of a dignity which invests me with a public mandate. I can and must consider myself, then, as the official deputy of the entire Church.

If I pray, or recite my office, even privately, I do so no longer merely in my own name. The words I use were not chosen by me. *It is the Church that places them upon my lips.*[47] That very fact means that it is the Church that prays with my lips, and speaks and acts through me, just as a king speaks and acts through his ambassador. And then I am truly THE WHOLE CHURCH, as St. Peter Damian so beautifully puts it.[48] *By me, the Church is united in the divine religion of Jesus Christ* and

---

46. Sermon xx.

47. *Sacerdos personam induit Ecclesiae, verba illius gerit, vocem assumit* (Gulielm. Paris., *De Sacramento Ordinis*). The priest puts on the person of the Church, he utters her words, he takes on her voice.

48. *Per unitatem fidei, sacerdos Ecclesia tota est et ejus vices gerit.* "Through the unity of faith, the priest is the whole Church, and acts in her behalf."

   Quid mirum si sacerdos quilibet . . . vicem Ecclesiae solus expleat . . cum per unitatis intimae Sacramentum, tota spiritualiter sit Ecclesiae? "What wonder is it, then, if any priest . . . stands in the place of the whole Church, since by the Sacrament of intimate union, he is, spiritually speaking, the whole Church" (St. Peter Damian, *Lib. qui dic. Dominus Vobiscum*, c. x. Migne, P.L. vol. 145, col. 239).

addresses to the Most Holy Trinity adoration, thanksgiving, reparation, and supplication.

Hence, if I have any appreciation of my dignity, how will I be able to begin my office, for instance, without there taking place within me a *mysterious activity which elevates me above myself*, above the natural course of my thoughts, to fill me and penetrate me completely with the conviction that I am, as it were, a *mediator* between heaven and earth.[49]

What a disaster if I were to forget these truths! The saints were filled with them.[50] These truths were their life. *God expects me to be mindful of them* whenever I exercise any function. By the liturgical life, the Church helps me, unceasingly, to keep in mind the fact that I am her representative, and *God demands* that I live up to this dignity, in practice, by leading an exemplary life.[51]

Oh my God, fill me with a profound esteem for this mission

---

49. *Medius stat sacerdos inter Deum et humanam naturam; illinc venientia beneficia an nos deferens, et nostras petitiones illinc perferens* (St. John Chrysostom, *Hom.* V, n. 1, *in illud, Vidi Dominum*).

   "The priest stands midway between God and human nature: he passes on to us the good things that come down from God, and lifts up to Him our petitions.

50. Why is it that the priest, when he says the office, says, even when alone, *Dominus vobiscum*? And why does he reply, *Et cum spiritu tuo*? and not *Et cum spiritu meo*? The thing is, says St. Peter Damian, that the priest is not alone. When he says Mass, or prays, he has before him the entire Church, mysteriously present, and it is to the Church that he addresses the salutation, *Dominus Vobiscum*. And then, since he represents the Church, the Church replies through his own mouth, *Et cum spiritu tuo*. (Cf. St. Peter Damian, in the *Lib. Dominus Vobiscum*, 6, 10, etc.) His thoughts on this subject are followed throughout this whole section.

51. *Laudate Dominum, sed laudate de vobis, id est, ut non sola lingua et vox vestra laudet Dominum, sed et conscientia vestra, vita vestra, facta vestra* (St. Augustine, *Enarratio in Ps. 148*, n. 2).

which the Church has entrusted to me. *What a spur it will be, to me, against cowardly sloth in the spiritual combat!* But grant me, also a true sense of my greatness as a Christian, and give me a childlike attitude before Your holy Church, so that I may profit abundantly by the treasures of interior life laid up in the holy Liturgy.

Third Principle

As a PRIEST, when I consecrate the Blessed Eucharist or administer the Sacraments, I must stir up the conviction that I am a MINISTER OF JESUS CHRIST, and therefore an *alter Christus*. And I must *hold it as certain that if I am to find, in*

"Praise the Lord, but praise Him from the very roots of your being, that is, let not only your tongues and voices praise the Lord, but also your consciences, your lives, and all that you do."

"Just as men expect you to be a saint when you present yourself among them as God's delegate, so God demands it of you when you appear before Him to intercede for mankind. An intercessor is one sent from the misery of this earth to parley with the justice of God. Now, St. Thomas says, two things are necessary, in an envoy if he is to be favorably received. The first is that he be a worthy representative of the people who send him, and the second that he be a friend of the prince to whom he is sent. You priest, who have no esteem for your sanctity, can you call yourself a worthy representative of the Christian people when you do not show forth the completeness of the Christian virtues? Can you call yourself the friend of God, when you do not serve Him faithfully?

"If this is true of the indifferent mediator, how much more so of one who is in sin ! How can words be found to express the anomalies of his appalling situation? Good souls come to you and say: "Pray for me, Father, you have credit in the sight of God." But would you like to know what efficacy there is in the protection thus piously invoked? "God is more pleased with the barking of dogs, than with the prayer of such clerics" (St. Augustine, Serm. 37: Fr. Caussette, *Manrèze du Pretre*, 1e jour, 2e discours)

the exercise of my functions, the special graces necessary to acquire the virtues demanded by my priesthood, everything depends on me.[52]

O Jesus, Your faithful children form a single Body, but in that Body "all the members have not the same office."[53] "There are diversities of graces."[54]

Since You willed to leave to the Church a visible Sacrifice, You endowed her with a priesthood whose *principal end* is to continue Your immolation on the altar, and then to distribute Your Precious Blood by the Sacraments and to sanctify Your Mystical Body by communicating to it Your divine Life.

Sovereign Priest, You decided *from all eternity* to choose and consecrate me as Your minister in order to *exercise Your Priesthood through me.*[55] You communicated to me Your powers in order to accomplish by my co-operation,[56] a work *greater than the creation of the universe*, the miracle of Transubstantiation, and in order to remain, by this miraculous means, the Host and the Religion of Your Church.

What meaning I find, now, in the exuberant terms with which the Fathers of the Church seek to express the magnitude of the priestly dignity.[57] Indeed, their words logically compel

---

52. What is said here regarding priests also applies, in due proportion, to deacons and subdeacons.

53. *Omnia autem membra non eundem actum habent (Rom.* 12:4).

54. *Divisiones gratiarum sunt (1 Cor.* 12:4).

55. *Ipse est principalis Sacerdos, qui, in omnibus et per omnes Sacerdotes novi Testamenti, offert. Ideo enim quia erat Sacerdos in aeternum instituit Apostolos Sacerdotes, up per ipsos suum Sacerdotium exsequeretur* (De Lugo, *De Euchar.*, Disp. xix, Sec. VI, n. 86).

56. *Dei adjutores sumus (1 Cor.* 3:9).

57. The Holy Fathers seem to have exhausted their eloquence in speaking of the dignity of the priest. Their thoughts may be summed up in a word, if we say that this dignity outstrips everything else in creation: God alone is greater.

me to consider myself by virtue of Your priesthood, communicated to me, as Your other self, *Sacerdos alter Christus.*

Is there not, in fact, an *identification* between You and me? After all, Your Person and mine are so truly one that when I pronounce the words: *Hoc est Corpus meum, Hic est calix Sanguinis mei,* You make them Your own?[58]

Sublimitas sacerdotis nullis comparationibus potest adaequari. "The sublimity of the priest can be expressed by no comparison" (St. Ambrose, *De Dign. Sacerd.,* c. ii).

Qui sacerdotem dicit, prorsus divinum insinuat virum. When you say "priest," you are speaking of a man who is altogether divine (St. Dionysius, the "Areopagite").

Praetulit vos regibus et imperatoribus, praetulit vestrum ordinem ordinibus omnibus, imo ut altius loquar, praetulit vos Angelis et Archangelis, Thronis et Dominationibus. "He has placed you above kings and emperors, he has placed your order above all other orders, indeed, to go higher still. he has placed you above the angels and archangels, Thrones and Dominations" (St. Bernard, Serm. *ad Past. in Syn.,* an apocryphal work, Migne, P.L., vol. 184. col. 1086).

Perspicuum est illam esse illorum sacerdotum functionem qua nulla major excogitari possit. Quare merito non solum angeli, sed dii etiam, quia Dei immortalis vim et numen apud nos teneant, appellantur.

"It is evident that this is that function of priests, than which no greater can be conceived. Wherefore they are rightly called not only angels, but even gods, because they hold, among us, the power and might of the undying God" (*Cat. Rom. de Ord.,* 1).

58. *Reliqua omnia quae dicuntur in superioribus a sacerdote dicuntur. . . .*

Ubi venitur ut conficiatur venerabile Sacramentum jam non suis sermonibus utitur sacerdos, sed utitur sermonibus Christi. Ergo sermo Christi conficit hoc Sacramentum. Quis est sermo Christi? Nempe is quo facta sunt omnia.

"All the other words, uttered in the prayers up to this point in the Mass, are spoken by the priest in his own person. . . . But when the time comes to confect the adorable Sacrament, the priest now no longer uses his own words, but utters the words of Christ. And therefore this Sacrament is confected by the word of Christ. What is the Word of Christ? It is that Word by which all things were created" (St. Ambrose, *De Sacramentis,* Lib. iv, c. 4, n. 14).

I lend You my lips, since I can say, without lying: *My Body, My Blood.*[59] All that is necessary is for me to *will* to make this consecration, and You will it also. Your will is fused with mine. In the greatest act which You can perform here below, *Your soul is tightly bound together with mine.* I lend You what is most mine, my will. And at once *Your will and mine are fused.*

So true is it that You act through me, that if I dared to say, over the matter of the Sacrifice, "This is the Body of Jesus Christ," instead of "this is My Body," the Consecration would not be valid.

The Blessed Eucharist is Your very Self, Jesus, hidden under the appearances of bread. And does not *every Mass* make it *more strikingly clear to me* that You yourself are the

---

Ecce Ambrosius no solum vult sacerdotem loqui in persona Christi sed etiam non loqui in propria persona, neque illa esse verba sacerdotis. Quia, cum sacerdos assumatur a Christo ut eum repraesentet, et ut Christus per os sacerdotis loquatur, non decuit sacerdotem adhuc retinere in his verbis propriam personam.

"See how Ambrose would have the priest not only speak in the person of Christ, but also not to speak in his own person: nor would he have these words be the priest's at all. For, since the priest is assumed by Christ, to represent Him, and in order that Christ may speak through the mouth of the priest, it is not fitting that the priest should, when uttering these words, retain his own person" (De Lugo, *De Euch.*, disp. xi, sec. v, n. 103).

59. *Ipse est, (Christus) qui sanctificat et immolat. . . . Cum videris sacerdotem offerentem, ne ut sacerdotem esse putes, sed Christi manum invisibiliter extentam. . . . Sacerdos linguam suam commodat*

"It is Christ Himself who sanctifies and immolates. . . When you see the priest offering the Holy Sacrifice, do not think that it is as a priest that he does so, but as the hand of Christ, invisibly extended. . . . The priest lends his tongue" (St. Chrysostom, *Hom.* 86, in Joan. n. 4).

Priest;[60] for You are the only Priest; and it is You that are concealed under the appearances of the one You have chosen as Your minister.

Alter Christus! I re-live that phrase every time I confer one of the other Sacraments. You alone are able to say, in Your quality of Redeemer, *"Ego te baptizo," "Ego te absolvo,"* thus exercising a power *no less divine than that of creation itself.* I too utter these same words. And the angels are more attentive to them than to the *fiat* which made worlds spring forth where there was nothingness,[61] since (and what a miracle it is, too!) they are capable of forming God in a soul, and producing a Child of God who participates in the intimate life of the Divinity.

At every priestly function, I can almost hear You saying to me: "My son, how is it possible for you to imagine that after I have made you, by these divine powers, *another Christ,* I should *tolerate that in your practical routine of living you should be WITHOUT CHRIST or even AGAINST CHRIST?"*

"What! In the exercise of these priestly functions, you have just acted as one whose being has been melted into My very own Being. And a few minutes later, Satan comes and *takes My place* and makes you, by sin, a sort of Antichrist, or hypnotizes you to such a degree of torpor that you deliberately *forget* the obligation to imitate Me, and to strive, as My Apostle says, to "put Me on"?

"Absit! You can count on My mercy when human weakness *alone* is the cause of your daily faults, which you *right away*

---

60. *"Nihil aliud Sacrifex quam Christi simulacrum":* "The sacrificer is simply an image of Christ" (Petr. Bles., *Trac. Ryth de Euch.* c. viii).

61. *Majus opus est ex impio justum facere quam creare coelum et terram:* "It is a greater work to make a just man out of a sinner, than to create heaven and earth" (St. Augustine).

regret and for which you quickly make reparation. But *if you cooly adopt a program of systematic infidelities, and return from these to your sublime functions without any remorse, you will only arouse My anger!*

"What an abyss there is between your functions and those of the priests of the Old Law. And yet, if My prophets uttered dire threats against Sion, because of the sins of the people or the rulers, listen to what came of the prevarication of the priests: '*The Lord hath accomplished His wrath. He hath poured out His fierce anger; and He hath kindled a fire in Sion and it hath devoured the foundations thereof . . . for the iniquities of her priests.*'[62]

"With what severity, too, does my Church *forbid* the priest to approach the altar or to confer the Sacraments if there remain one single mortal sin upon his conscience!

"Inspired by Me, she goes still further. Her very rites compel you to be either *truly holy* or an *impostor*. Either you will have to make up your mind to live an interior life, or else resign yourself *to say to Me* from the beginning of Mass to the end, *things that you do not really think, and ask of Me things that you do not desire.* The sacred words and ceremonies necessarily imply, in the priest, a spirit of compunction and a desire to purify his soul of his slightest faults; therefore, custody of the heart. They imply a spirit of adoration, and, therefore, of recollection. They imply a spirit of faith, hope, and love, and, therefore, a supernatural trend in everything that you say or do during the day, and in all your works!"

---

62. *Lam. Jerem.* 4:11–13.

O Jesus, I fully realize that to put on the sacred vestments without being *firmly resolved* to strive to acquire the virtues which they symbolize, is only a kind of *hypocrisy*. It is my will that henceforth bows and genuflections, signs of the Cross and other ceremonies, and all the formulas of prayer may never be a *hollow fraud* hiding emptiness, coldness, indifference for the interior life, and adding to my faults that of a lying mummery under the very eyes of the Eternal God.

Let me then tremble with a holy fear every time I draw near to Your dread mysteries, every time I put on the liturgical vestments. Let the prayers with which I accompany this act, the formulas of the Missal and Ritual, so full of unction and strength, *move me to scrutinize my own heart and find out whether it is truly in harmony with Yours, O Jesus;* that is to say, whether I have a loyal and practical desire *to imitate You by leading an interior life.*

O my soul, get rid of all those compromises which might lead me to consider it enough to be an *"alter Christus"* only during my sacred functions, and to believe that after them, provided I am not actually *against Christ*, I can dispense myself from working to *put on Jesus Christ.*

Here I am, not merely an ambassador of *Jesus Crucified*, but actually His other Self. Can I attempt to get away with an *easy-going piety*, and content myself with *commonplace virtues?*

Useless for me to try and persuade myself that the cloistered monk is bound, more than I am, to strive after the imitation of Christ and to acquire an interior life. It is a *grave error*, based upon a misunderstanding.

The religious is obliged to tend to sanctity by the *use of certain special means;* that is, vows of obedience and poverty, and keeping his rule. As a priest, I am not restricted to these means; but I am obliged to pursue and to realize *the same end*, and I am so obliged by *many more considerations* than the consecrated soul who does not have the responsibility of distributing the Precious Blood.[63]

---

63. *Vos estis lux mundi, vos estis sal terrae. Quod si sal evanuerit in quo salietur?* "You are the light of the world . . . You are the salt of the earth. But if the salt loses its savor, wherewith shall it be salted?" (*Matt.* 5:13).

Exemplum esto fidelium in verbo, in conversatione, in caritate, in fide, in castitate. "Be thou an example of the faithful in word, in conversation, in charity, in faith, in chastity" (*1 Tim.* 4:12).

In divino omni quis audeat aliis fieri nisi secundum omnem habitum suum factus sit Deo formissimus et Deo simillimus. "In all divine things, who is there that would dare to show the way to others unless in all his habits he himself first be most closely patterned on God, and most like to God ?" (S. Dionysius. *De Eccles. Hier.*).

Sacerdos debet vitam habere immaculatam, ut omnes in illum, veluti in aliquod exemplum excellens, intueantur. "The priest should lead a life that is without blemish, in order that everyone may look to him for a perfect example" (St. John Chrysostom, *Hom.* x, in *Tim.*).

Nihil in sacerdote commune cum multitudine. Vita sacerdotis praeponderare debet, sicut praeponderat gratia. "The priest has nothing in common with the multitude. The life of the priest should excel as grace excels" (St. Ambrose, *Epist. 82*).

Aut caeteris honestiores, aut fabula omnibus sunt sacerdotes. "Priests are either better than everybody else, or else a scandal to everybody else" (St. Bernard, *De Consideratione*, Lib. iv, c. 6).

Sicut illi qui Ordinem suscipiunt, super plebem constituuntur qradu Ordinis, ita et superiores sint menito sanctitatis. "Just as they who receive Holy Orders are constituted above the crowd by the degree of their Order, so too they ought to stand out by virtue of their holiness" (St. Thomas, *Suppl.*, q. 35).

Sic decet omnes clericos in sortem Domini vocatos, vitam moresque suos omnes componere, ut habitu, gestu, incessu, sermone, aliisque omnibus rebus nihil nisi grave, moderate ac religione plenum prae se ferant. "Thus it is fitting that all clerics called to the service of the Lord should order their life and manners in such wise that in their dress, their gestures, their gait, their speech, and in all other things they should display nothing but what is grave and proper and full of religion" (Council of Trent, sess. 22, c. 1, de reform.).

Woe to me, then, if I lull myself to sleep with an illusion that is beyond doubt *culpable* since it could have easily been dispelled by a *glance at the teaching of the Church and of her saints:* an illusion whose falsity will be brought home to me on the threshold of eternity.

Woe to me if I do not know how to take advantage of my liturgical functions to discover what You *demand* of me, or if I remain deaf to the voices of all the holy objects that surround me: the altar, the confessional, the baptismal font, the vessels, linen and vestments. *Imitamini quod tractatis*—"imitate what you handle."[64]

"Be ye clean you that carry the vessels of the Lord."[65]

Si religiosus careat Ordine, manifestum est excellere praeeminentiam Ordinis quantum ad dignitatem, quia per sacrum Ordinem aliquis deputatur ad dignissima ministeria, quibus ipsi Christo servitur in Sacramento altaris; ad quod requiritur major sanctitas interior quam requirat etiam religionis status. "In the case of a religious who has not received Holy Orders, it is clear that the Holy Orders have a far superior dignity (to the vows of religion) since by Orders a man is deputed to the most noble of all ministries; namely, that by which Christ Himself is served in the Sacrament of the Altar; and this demands a greater interior sanctity than is required even by the religious state" (St. Thomas, 2a 2ae. q. 184).

Vix bonus monachus facit bonum clericum. "A good monk will not necessarily be a good cleric" (St. Augustine. *ad Val.*).

Nullam ascensus et deificationis mensuram agnoscant. "Let them know no limit to spiritual progress, nor to likeness to God" (St. Greg. Naz.).

Pares Deo conentur esse sanctitate, ut qui viderit ministrum altaris Dominum veneretur. "Let them attempt to be equal to God in sanctity, in order that whosoever sees the minister of the altar may revere God in him" (St. Ambrose. *de Offic.*, c. 5).

64. Roman Pontifical: Rites of Ordination.
65. *Mundamini qui fertis vasa Domini* (*Is.* 52:12).

"For they offer the burnt-offering of the Lord and the bread of their God and therefore they shall be holy."[66]

I would be all the less excusable, Jesus, for turning a deaf ear to these appeals, inasmuch as *each one* of my functions is the occasion of an *actual grace* which You offer me to form my soul to Your image and likeness.

It is the Church that solicits this grace. It is her heart full of jealous eagerness to fulfill Your expectations, that cares for me like the apple of her eye. It is She who, before my ordination, tried to make me see what immensely important consequences were involved in this identification of me with You.

Impone, Domine, capiti meo galeam salutis . . . praecinge mecingulo puritatis . . . Ut indulgeris omnia peccata mea. Fac me tuis semper inhaerere mandatis et a te numquam separari permittas, etc.,[67] it is no longer I that make these petitions for myself. They are being made by all the true faithful, all the fervent souls consecrated to You, all the members of the Ecclesiastical heirarchy who made my poor prayer their prayer. Their cry rises to Your throne. It is the voice of Your Spouse that You hear. *And when Your priests are resolved to lead an interior life, and therefore bring their hearts into harmony with their liturgical functions, You always grant these entreaties made for them by the Church.*

Instead, then, of excluding myself by my voluntary negligence from these suffrages which I address to Your Father for the faithful at large, when saying Mass or administering the Sacraments, *I want to profit by these graces*, Jesus. *At each* one of my priestly acts I will *open my heart wide to Your action.* Then You will fill it with light consolation and power

---

66. *Incensum et panes offerunt Deo, et ideo sancti erunt* (*Levit.* 21:6).

67. From the prayers said by the Priest while vesting, and also just before Communion in the Mass.

which, in spite of all the obstacles, will *enable me to iden-tify my judgments with Yours, my affections and desires with Yours, just as my Priesthood identifies me with You,* Eternal Priest, when, through me, make Yourself a Victim upon the altar, or Redeemer of souls.

*   *   *

A few words to sum up the three principles of the liturgical life.

Cum ecclesia

When *I unite with the Church as a simple Christian,* this very union impels me to fill myself with her thoughts and her aspirations.

Ecclesia

When the Church herself is represented in my person, so that I, so to speak, *am* the Church, and so act as her *ambassador* before the throne of God, I am all the more powerfully drawn to make her aspirations my own, in order to be less unworthy to address myself to His Thrice Holy Majesty, and, by means of *official prayers*, to exercise a more efficacious apostolate.

Christus

But when, by virtue of my participation in the Priesthood of Christ, I am an *alter Christus*, what terms can express the insistence with which You call me, Jesus, to take on more and more of Your divine likeness, and that I may thus manifest

You to the faithful and move them, by the *apostolate of good example* to follow You?

IV. The Advantages of the Liturgical Life

a. It Helps Me to Be Permanently Supernatural in All My Acts

How hard it is for me, O my God, to base the ordinary run of my actions upon a supernatural motive! Satan and creatures conspire with my self-love to lure my soul and faculties away from their dependence upon Jesus living within me.

How many times, in the course of the day, this purity of intention which so *greatly affects* the merit of my actions and the efficacy of my apostolate is ruined *through lack of vigilance or of fidelity!* Only continual effort will obtain for me, with God's help the power to ensure that most of my actions may have *grace as their vivifying principle, and be directed by grace, towards God, as their end.*

I cannot make these efforts without mental prayer. Yet what a difference it makes, when this striving for purity of intention has, for its background, the liturgical life! Mental prayer and the liturgical life are two sisters who help each other. Mental prayer, before my Mass and Office, puts me *in a supernatural atmosphere*. The liturgical life makes it possible to *transmit the fruits of my mental prayer to all the actions of the day*.[68]

*   *   *

---

68. "I make a good meditation in order to be able to say Mass well and I say Mass and my Office with devotion in order that I may make a good meditation the following morning" (Fr. Olivaint).

O Holy Church, when you are teaching me, *how easy it is for me to acquire the habit* of giving to my Creator and Father at all times the worship that is His due! You are the Spouse of Him Who is Adoration, Thanksgiving, Reparation, and Meditation in the highest degree, and, by your Liturgy, you give me *that thirst*, which Jesus had, to glorify His Father; and this is the *first end* you had in view when you established the Liturgy.

Is it not obvious that if I live the liturgical life I will become steeped in the *virtue of religion*, since the whole Liturgy is nothing but the continuous and public exercise of that virtue, which is the most excellent of all virtues after Faith, Hope, and Charity?

If I make use of the light of faith, it is quite true hat I can *manifest the dependence of all my faculties upon God*, as well as piety, vigilance, and valor in the spiritual combat. But what great need there is for this human being of mine, composed of body and soul, to receive the assistance of its every faculty in order to fix the mind upon eternal values, and fill the heart with an eager enthusiasm to profit by them, and excite the will to ask for them repeatedly and to strive, without respite, to possess them!

The Liturgy *grips my entire being*. The whole complex of ceremonies, genuflections, bows, symbols, chants, texts, appealing to the eye, the ear, the feelings, the imagination, the intellect, and the heart— by means of all these, the Church reminds me that everything that is in me: *os, lingua, mens, sensus, vigor*,[69] all must be directed to God.

All the means used by the Church to show me what are *God's rights* and His claims to the worship of my filial homage

---

69. The mouth, the tongue, the mind, the senses, and all our strength (from the Hymn sung daily at Terce).

and to the total ownership of my being develop in me the virtue of religion, and, by that very fact, the supernatural spirit.

Everything in the Liturgy *speaks to me of God*, of His *perfections*, His *mercies*. Everything *takes me back to God*. Everything tells me how His *Providence* is ever holding out to my soul means of sanctification in every trial, every assistance from on high, every warning, encouragement, promise, light, yes, even in His threats.

Also, the Liturgy keeps me ceaselessly *talking to God* and expressing my religion under the most varied forms.

If, with an earnest desire to profit by it, I submit to this liturgical formation, how is it possible that the virtue of religion should not strike deeper and deeper roots into my being, after all the manifold exercises that follow, each day, from my functions as a minister of the Church? I am bound to form a habit, a *mental state*, and that means a genuine inner life.

* * *

The Liturgy is a *school of the presence of God;* and teaches us to stay in the presence of our God as He was manifested to us in the Incarnation! Call it rather a *school of the presence of Jesus, and of love!*

Love is fed by the knowledge of the attractions of the One loved, by the proofs He has given us of His love, but above all, says St. Thomas, by His presence.

Now the Liturgy reproduces, explains, and applies these various manifestations of the life of Jesus among us. *It keeps us permanently in a supernatural and divine atmosphere*, by prolonging, so to speak, the life of Our Lord, and by displaying to us, in all His mysteries, how kind and lovable is His Heart.

Dear Lord, it is You Yourself Who continue to teach us, through the Liturgy, Your great lesson, and to show us the great revelation of Your love. I see you clearer and clearer: not through the eyes of a historian, that is, behind the veil of centuries, nor in the way You are so often known by the theologian, as the object of laborious speculations. You are right *close to me*. You are ever *Emmanuel*, God with us, with Your Church, and so, *with me*. You are someone that every member of Your Church *lives* with, and Whom the Liturgy shows me at all times *in the forefront of my life*, as the model and object of my love.

By the cycle of Your Feasts, by the lessons chosen from Your Gospel and from the writings of Your Apostles, and by the splendor with which she causes Your Sacraments to shine forth especially the Blessed Eucharist, the Church *makes You live among us, and lets us hear the beating of Your Heart.*

To believe that Jesus lives in me; that He wants to work in me if only I do not stand in His way! When prayer has filled me with the conviction of this truth, what a mighty source of strength I possess, in my supernatural life! But when frequently throughout the course of the day, using all the varied and sensible means offered by the Liturgy, I nourish my mind and heart with the *dogma of grace*, of Christ praying and acting with every one of the members whose life He is supplying for their deficiencies, and, hence, for mine; then I am really maintaining myself under the permanent influence of the supernatural, I am getting to live in union with Jesus, and to find an established place in His love.

Love of complacency, of benevolence, of preference, of hope—all these forms of love shine forth in the wonderful collects, in the psalms, the ceremonies, the prayers. And they penetrate my soul.

How strong and generous the interior life becomes, with this method of contemplating *Jesus as living and ever present!* And when some act of detachment or of abnegation may be required to keep my life supernatural when some difficult task is to be performed, some pain or insult to be endured, how quickly the spiritual battle, the virtue, the trial will lose their painful and repugnant aspect of instead of looking at the bare Cross, I look at You nailed there, O my Savior; and if I hear You ask me, as You show me Your wounds, for this sacrifice as a proof of love.

Then, too, the Liturgy gives me strong support in another way by repeatedly reminding me that my love is not acting in isolation. *I am not alone* in the fight against these natural impulses that are ever threatening to engulf me. The Church is alive to the fact of my incorporation in Christ and *follows me like a mother*, giving me a share in all the merits of the millions of souls with whom I am in communion, and who speak the same official language of love as I do; and she renews my powers of endurance by assuring me that Heaven and Purgatory are here with me, for my encouragement and assistance.

Nothing is so effective as the *mindfulness of eternity* in keeping the soul directed to God in all its acts.

Now everything in the Liturgy reminds me of *my last end*. The expressions *vita aeterna, coelum, infernum, mors, saeculum saeculi*, and others like them are of frequent recurrence.

Prayers and offices for the dead, funerals bring before my mind death, judgment, rewards and unending punishments, the value of time and the purifications that have to be gone through, willynilly, either here below or in Purgatory, if I am going to get in to Heaven.

The *feasts of the saints* speak to me of the glory of those who were before me here on earth, and show me the crown which is in store for me if I follow in their footsteps and conform to their example.

By these lessons the Church is ceaselessly crying out to me: "Beloved soul, consider the eternal years, and you will remain faithful to your motto, '*God in all things, all the time, everywhere!*'"

O divine Liturgy: if I want to acknowledge all the benefits you bring us, I must enumerate all the virtues! Thanks to the chosen Scripture texts which you place before me at all times, thanks to the rites and symbols which express the divine Mysteries to me, my soul is *constantly raised above this earth and directed* now towards the theological virtues, now towards the fear of God, the horror for sin and for the spirit of this world, with detachment, compunction, confidence, or spiritual joy.

b.   It Is a Most Powerful Aid in Conforming My Interior Life to That of Jesus Christ

O my adorable Master, there are three sentiments which hold sway in Your Sacred Heart: complete *dependence* upon Your Father, and therefore perfect *humility;* then secondly a *burning and universal love* for men; and finally the *spirit of sacrifice.*

Perfect Humility

When You came into the world, You said, "Father, *behold, I come to do Thy will.*"[70] You often remind us that Your whole inner life may be summed up as a continual desire *to*

---

70. *Ingrediens mundum dicit: Hostiam et oblationem noluisti . . . Tunc dixi: Ecce venio . . . ut faciam, Deus, voluntatem tuam* (*Heb.* 10:5–7).

do always the things that please Your Father.[71] O Jesus, You are obedience itself, *"obedient unto death, even to the death of the Cross."*[72]

Even now, You obey Your priests. At the sound of their voice, You come back to the earth: *"The Lord obeying the voice of a man."*[73]

What a school the Liturgy is, in which to learn to imitate Your subjection, if my heart will only become *supple and responsive to the smallest rites* with a desire of forming a spirit of dependence upon God, and of unflinchingly taming this "ego" of mine, so thirsty for liberty, and of *bending* my judgment and my will, so quick to refuse allegiance, Lord, to the *fundamental spirit* which You came to teach by Your example: the Worship of the Will of God!

Every time I thrust my own personality into the background in order that I may obey the Church as I would obey You Yourself, and *act in her name, and unite myself with her*, hence unite myself to You, I am receiving a priceless training that shapes my soul. This fidelity to the smallest prescriptions and rubrics will bear fruit in an immensely increased self-mastery when it comes to *putting down my pride* on more difficult occasions![74]

What is more, since the Liturgy constantly reminds me of the *infallible truth that You are living within me*, and of the *necessity of Your grace* if I am to draw fruit from even the

---

71. *Ego quae placita sunt ei, facio semper* (*Joan.* 8:29). *Meus cibus est ut faciam voluntatem ejus qui misit me* (*Joan.* 4:34). *Descendi de coelo non ut faciam voluntatem meam, sed voluntatem ejus qui misit me* (*Joan.* 6:38).
72. *Factus obediens usque ad mortem, mortem autem crucis* (*Philipp.* 2:8).
73. *Obediente Domino voci hominis* (*Jos.* 10:14).
74. *Qui fidelis est in minimo in majori fidelis est* (*Luc.* 16:10). He that is faithful in that which is least is also in that which is greater.

simplest thought, it is at war with all presumption and with that self-satisfaction which, between them, would be enough to ravage every vestige of interior life. The *Per Dominum Nostrum* that comes at the end of almost every prayer in the Liturgy, would be enough to recall to my mind, were I able to forget it, that by myself I can do nothing, absolutely nothing, except sin or perform acts that have no merit. Everything convinces me of the *necessity to run to You for help at all times*. Everything keeps telling me that You demand this suppliant dependence, that my life may not wander off the track in pursuit of a lying mirage.

Through her Liturgy, the Church insists with great solicitude on this question of supplication, in order to convince her children of its necessity. She makes this Liturgy a true *school of prayer*, and therefore of humility. By her formulas, by the Sacraments and Sacramentals, she teaches me that *everything comes to me through Your Precious Blood*, and that the great means of reaping Its fruit is to unite myself, by humble prayer, to Your desire to apply them to us.

Let me profit, then, O Jesus, by these continual lessons, in order to increase the vivid awareness of my own littleness and to convince myself that *I am nothing but a tiny particle in the Host which is Your Mystical Body, and that in the immense chorus of praise conducted by You, I am nothing but a thin and feeble voice.*

Let me, thanks to the Liturgy, see more and more clearly that humility can make that voice more *and more* pure and clear, and that particle whiter and *ever whiter*.

Universal Charity

Your Heart, Lord Jesus, embraced all men in Its mission of Redemption.

At Your death, You cried out upon the world, *"I thirst,"* and You do still, upon our altars and in the Tabernacle and in the very depths of Your glory. In all our souls, yes, even that of the plain Christian, that cry must be answered by a similar thirst: *the strong desire to spend ourselves for our brothers; the burning thirst for the salvation of all men, and for the diffusion of the Gospel; a mighty zeal for the encouragement of priestly and religious vocations; and finally, tireless prayers that the faithful may come to comprehend the extent of their duties, and that souls consecrated to God may realize how necessary, for them, is the interior life.*

How much more powerful an effect these desires should have, then, upon Your priests, constantly reminded, by their rites, that You have given them a special place in Your Mystical Body in order that they may *incorporate* as many souls as possible into You, and that they are co-redeemers, mediators, whose function it is to weep, *"inter vestibulum et altare."*[75] for the sins of the world, and sanctify themselves, not only for their own sake, but in order *to be able to sanctify others*, to form, and instruct and guide souls and make Your life course through their veins. "And for them do I sanctify myself, that they also may be sanctified in truth."[76]

Holy Church of the Redeemer, Mother of *all* my brethren, your children, how can I live your Liturgy without sharing the strong desire in the Heart of your Divine Spouse for

---

75. *Joel* 2:17.
76. *Ego sanctifico meipsum ut sint et ipsi sanctificati (Joan.* 17:19).

the salvation of His creatures and for the deliverance of the souls that groan in Purgatory?

Of course, I share in the fruits of my Mass, my Office. But it is your intent that the *first share* should go, *before all else*, to the whole group of souls which are in your care: *in primus quae tibi offerimus pro Ecclesia sancta tua Catholica*.[77] You take a thousand means to insure that my heart will expand with love and my interior life will grow like to that of Jesus.

O my beloved liturgical life, increase in me the *filial love for Holy Church* and for the common Father of all the faithful. Make me more devoted, more submissive to my superiors in the hierarchy, and more united to them in all their cares and desires. Help me *never to forget that Jesus lives in every person with whom I come in daily contact*, and that He carries them all in His heart. Make me radiate, among them, a spirit of indulgence, of support, of patience, and of service, that I may thus reflect the meekness of the sweet Savior.

Keep me firmly rooted in the conviction that the only way I can get to Heaven is *by the Cross*, and that my praises, adoration, sacrifices, and all my other acts have no value, for heaven, except through the *Blood of Christ*, and it is *in union with all the other Christians* that I must gain Heaven, since *it is with all the elect* that I am to enjoy it, and to continue, with them, through Christ, for all eternity, the chorus of praises in which I have part here on earth.

---

77. Which we offer Thee first of all for Thy Holy Catholic Church (Canon of the Mass).

A Spirit of Sacrifice

Lord Jesus, You knew that mankind could only be saved by sacrifice, and You made Your whole life on earth a perpetual immolation.

Identified with You, acting as Priest with You, when I celebrate Mass, O my Crucified God, I desire to be a *victim* with You. *Everything in You revolves around Your Cross. Everything in me has to revolve around my Mass. It will be the center, the sun of my days, just as Your Sacrifice is the central act of the Liturgy.*

And the Liturgy will become, to me, a *school of the spirit of sacrifice*, because the altar and the Tabernacle will ever be taking me back to *Calvary*. By making me share in the thoughts and aspirations of Your Church, the Liturgy will communicate Your own sentiments to me, O Jesus, and thus will the words of St. Paul be fulfilled in me: "Let this mind be in you which was also in Christ Jesus,"[78] along with those other words that were spoken to me at my ordination: *Imitamini quod tractatis.*[79]

The Missal, Ritual, and Breviary constantly recall to me in many different ways, were it only by the countless Signs of the Cross, that sacrifice has become, since the fall, *the law of the human race*, and that it has no value except insofar as it is united with Your Sacrifice. Hence, I shall render unto You *victim for victim*, O my divine Redeemer. *I will offer up to You a total immolation of my whole self, an immolation that shall MERGE with the Sacrifice once consummated by You on Golgotha and renewed many times, every second by the Masses which are said in unending succession all around the world.*

---

78. *Hoc sentite in vobis quod et in Christo Jesu* (*Philipp.* 2:5).
79. Imitate what you perform (Roman Pontifical.).

The Liturgy will render this obligation of myself much easier and will enable me to make a greater contribution towards
*filling up those things that are wanting of Your sufferings for
Your Body, which is the Church.*[80]

I will thus bring my share and join it to that great Host
made up of the *sacrifices of all Christians.*[81] And this Host
will rise up to Heaven to expiate the sins of the world and
bring down upon the Church militant and suffering the fruits
of Your Redemption.

In this way, I will lead a true liturgical life. For when I
"put You on," O my crucified Jesus, and unite myself in a
practical way with Your Sacrifice by carrying out Your counsel to *deny myself,* thus making of myself a holocaust; is not
that, O my Savior, the end to which Your Church would lead
me in filling me with Your thoughts by her prayers and holy
ceremonies, and bringing *into my heart that which in You*

---

80. *Adimpleo quae desunt passionum Christi pro corpore ejus, quod est
Ecclesia (Coloss. 1:24).*

81. *Tota ipsa redempta Civitas, hoc est congregatio societasque sancto-
rum, universale Sacrificium offertur Deo per Sacerdotem magnum, qui
etiam obtulit in Passione pro nobis, ut tanti capitis corpus essemus . . .
Cum itaque nos hortatus esset Apostolus ut exhibeamus corpora nostra
hostiam viventem . . . Hoc es Sacrificium Christianorum: multi unum
corpus in Christo. Quod etiam Sacramento altaris, fidelibus noto, fre-
quentat Ecclesia, ubi et demonstretur quod in ea re, quam offert, ipsa
offeratur* (St. Augustine, *City of God,* Bk. ix, c. vi).

   "All the whole redeemed city, that is the congregation and society of the saints is offered to God as a universal Sacrifice by that
High Priest, Who even offered it in His Passion, for us, that we might
become the body of so noble a Head . . . Now therefore the Apostle,
having exhorted us to give up our bodies as a living sacrifice. . . . This
is the Christian Sacrifice: we are one Body with Christ, as the Church
celebrates in the Sacrament of the Altar, so well known to the faithful, wherein it is shown to the Church that she herself is offered in the
Victim which she offers."

dominated everything: the Spirit of Sacrifice?[82]

Thus will I become one of those carefully chosen living stones, polished by tribulations, "by the blows of the life-giving chisel, by ceaseless, relentless work of the mason's hammer."[83] and destined to enter into the construction of the heavenly Jerusalem.

c. The Liturgical Life Makes Me
   Live the Life of the Saints and
   Blessed in Heaven

Conversatio nostra in coelis est,[84] said St. Paul. And where will I find a better way to carry out what he here expresses, than in the Liturgy? This Liturgy we have here on earth is simply an imitation of the *celestial Liturgy* which the Beloved Disciple, John, describes for us in his Apocalypse. When I sing or recite my Office, what else am I doing but carrying out

---

82. *Tunc demum sacerdoti hostia proderit si, seipsum hostiam faciens, velit humiliter et efficaciter imitari quod agit* (Petr. Blesens. *Epist.* cxxiii).

   Then alone will the Mass be of profit to the priest if, making of himself a host, he is willing to imitate in a most humble and practical manner the Sacrifice he performs.

   Qui Passionis Dominicae mysteria celebramus, debemus imitari quod agimus. Tunc ergo vere pro nobis Hostia erit Deo, cum nosmetipsos hostiam fecerimus (St. Gregory the Great, *Dialogues*, iv, c. 59).

   We who celebrate the mysteries of the Lord's Passion ought to imitate what we perform. And then will it truly be an offering to God that will make us pleasing to Him, if we make of ourselves victims also.

83. *Scalpri salubris ictibus*
   Et tunsione plurima
   Fabri polita malleo.
   (*Roman Brev.* Hymn at Vespers, from the *Common of the Dedication of a Church*).

84. *Philipp.* 3:20.

the same function upon which the angels pride themselves, before the Throne of the Almighty?

More than that, does not the doxology of every Psalm and hymn, the conclusion of every prayer cast me down *prostrate in adoration before the Most Holy Trinity?*

The countless *feasts of the Saints* make me live, as it were, intimate companionship with my brothers in Paradise who are my protectors and who pray for me. The Feasts of *Our Blessed Lady* remind me that I possess, in Heaven above, a most loving and powerful Mother who will never rest until she beholds me safe at her feet in the Kingdom of Her Son. Is it possible that all these feasts, that all the *mysteries* of my sweet Savior—Christmas, Easter, and especially the Ascension—should not make me HOMESICK FOR HEAVEN, which St. Gregory considered as a token of predestination?

V. The Practice of the Liturgical Life

Good Master, You have deigned to give me some understanding of what the liturgical life is. Am I going to try and offer the duties of my ministry as a pretext for avoiding the *effort* which You demand, in order that I may put all this into practice? Surely You would answer that *it will take no more time* to fulfill my liturgical functions in the way You desire me to, than it does already to get through them mechanically. You would tell me to consider the *example* of so many of Your servants, like Bl. Fr. Perboyre, among others[85] who charged by You with unceasing and deeply absorbing occupations to a degree of the highest intensity, was nevertheless a most perfect example of a "liturgical soul."

---

85. Cf. his *"Life,"* Bk. iii, ch. 8 and 9 (Paris, 1890).

a.   Remote Preparation

Dear Savior, turn my desire for a liturgical life into a powerful SPIRIT OF FAITH with respects to everything that has to do with divine worship.

Your angels and saints see You face to face. Nothing can distract their minds from the august functions which go to make up one of the elements of their incomparable bliss. But I, on the other hand, still a prey to all the weaknesses of human nature, simply cannot *keep myself in Your presence*, when I unite with the Church in addressing You, unless You develop in me the gift of Faith which I received at Baptism.

May I never come to regard my liturgical functions as a burdensome duty, to get over and done with as soon as possible or something to be put up with for the sake of the fee! Never, I hope, will I dare to speak of the Thrice Holy God or carry out His rites with *careless familiarity and insulting negligence* which I would be ashamed to manifest to His most humble servant. *May I never give scandal in those things which were expressly designed to edify!* And yet, can I forsee how far I will fall if I once cease to watch myself in this matter of the spirit of Faith?

O my God, if I am already sliding down this perilous incline, have mercy, pull me back! Or rather, give me so lively a Faith that I will be *gripped by the importance that all liturgical acts really possess in Your sight*, and will rejoice to feel their sublime wonders flood my will with an ever-growing enthusiasm.

Can it be said that I have the slightest spirit of Faith if I take no trouble to know the RUBRICS and to observe them? This is a neglect for which not even the most lofty and appreciative intuitions about the Liturgy can compensate in Your sight, O my God! What difference does it make if I feel no natural attraction for this task? It is enough for me to know that *my obe-dience* is pleasing to You, and that it will *gain me great merit*.

On my retreats, I must never fail to *examine myself on this point, with regard to the Missal, Ritual, and Breviary*.

Your Church, O Jesus, has chiefly drawn upon the treasures of the PSALMS for her cult. If I have any liturgical spirit, my soul will be able to see You, in passages from the Psalter, especially in *Your life of suffering*. And I will be able to realize that the words, the deep thoughts which came forth from the secret depths of Your Heart and rose to up God during Your mortal life, are to be found written down in very many of the prophetic verses with which You inspired Your Psalmist.

And there I will be able to discern gathered together in a most marvelous synthesis, *a forecast of the chief teachings of Your Gospel*.

Under these same veils, I will detect the *voice of the Church* as she carries on Your life of trials and expresses to God, in the midst of all her sufferings and triumphs, sentiments that echo those of her Divine Spouse; sentiments which may also be appropriated in all temptations, reverses, combats, sorrows, discouragement, deceptions, as well as in victory and consola-tion, by *every soul* in whom Your life can be manifested.

If I set aside part of my *reading* time for *Holy Scripture* exclusively, I shall develop my taste for the Liturgy and make it easier to keep my mind on its words.[86]

Reflective observation will show that every liturgical

---

86. *Plus lucratur qui orat et intelligit quam qui tantum lingua orat. Nam qui intelligit reficitur quantum ad intellectum et quantum ad affectum* (St. Thomas, in. *1 Cor*. 14:14).

One who prays with understanding profits more than one who prays with the tongue alone. For he who understands receives nourish-ment as to the intellect and the will.

composition has a *central idea* about which the various teachings are grouped.

Oh *what weapons*, my soul, will you thus forge, *against thy ever roving imagination*, especially if you know how to learn from SYMBOLS.

The Church makes use of symbols to speak to the senses a language which captivates them, making the truths that are represented sensible. *Agnoscite quod agitis* (realize what you are doing), she told me at my ordination. *Ceremonies, sacred linen, holy objects, vestments*, all speak with a meaningful voice, given them by the Church, my Mother. How am I ever going to enlighten the understandings and reach the hearts of the faithful that the *Church wants* to capture by her naive and grandiose speech if I myself do not possess the key to such instruction?

b. Immediate Preparation

"Before prayer, prepare thy soul."[87] Just before Mass, and every time I take up the Breviary, I should make a firm, calm act of *recollection*, in order to *free myself* from all that has no connection with God, and to *fix* my attention upon Him. The One I am about to talk to is God.

But He is also my Father. Therefore, I shall unite that *reverence and awe* which even the Queen of Angels herself retains, when she speaks to her Divine Son, with the ingenuous candor which gives even an old man, when he talks to God's infinite Majesty, the *soul of a little child*.

This simple and childlike attitude before my Father will artlessly reflect my conviction that I am united to Jesus Christ,

---

87. *Ante orationem praepara animam tuam* (*Eccli.* xviii 23).

that no matter how unworthy I may be, I represent the Church, and that I am certain beyond a doubt that the soldiers of the celestial army are standing at my side as I pray: "I will sing praise to Thee in the sight of the angels."[88]

As for you, my soul: this is no longer the time to be reasoning, meditating. Become, once again, the *soul of a child*. When you arrived at the age of reason, you accepted, as the expression of absolute truth everything that mother told you. So must you also with the same simplicity and artlessness receive from your *Mother the Church all* that she is about to give you to nourish your faith.

This *renewal of youth* is indispensable to the soul! The more I make myself the *soul of a child* the more I will profit by the riches of the Liturgy, and will allow myself to be possessed by the poetry that lives in it. And that will be the measure of my progress in the liturgical spirit.

Then it will be easy for my soul to *enter into adoration*, and *stay there* all through whatever function (ceremony, Office, Mass, Sacraments, etc.,) engages me, whether as member of the Church or as her ambassador, as the minister of God.

The way I *enter into adoration* will determine, to a great extent, not only the profit and merit of my liturgical act, but also the consolations which God makes contingent upon its perfect accomplishment and which will give me strength to carry on my apostolic labors.

And so I am going to *adore*. I desire, by an act of my will, to spring up even unto union with the adorations of the Man-God, that I may offer His prayer together with mine to God. This must be a swift upward *flight of the heart:* not an effort of the mind.

---

88. *In conspectu angelorum psallam tibi* (*Ps.* 137).

I will and desire this with Your grace, Lord Jesus! And I will ask this grace for instance, in my Office, by saying with purpose and recollection my *Deus in adjutorium*, or, in the same manner, the *Introibo* of my Mass.

I will it. It is this filial and loving will, strong and humble, united with an earnest desire for Your help, that *You demand of me.*

If it should happen that my intellect opens up some fine expansive vista to my faith, or if my sensibilities contribute some holy emotion, well and good; my will shall *take advantage of them* to make adoration easier. But I will always remember the principle that *in the last analysis union with God dwells in the summit of the soul, in the will,* and even though darkness and aridity fall to its lot, the will, though dry and cold, will take her flight on the wings of *pure faith.*

c. Doing My Liturgical Work

To do well my liturgical work is a gift of Your bounty, O my God! *Omnipotens et misericors Deus, de cujus munere venit ut tibi a fidelibus tuis digne et laudabiliter serviatur.*[89] O Lord, please grant me this gift. I want to *remain in adoration* all during my liturgical function. *That sums up all the methods in one word.*

My will casts down my heart at the feet of the Majesty of God, and keeps it there. All its work is now contained in the three words, *digne, attente, devote* . . . from the prayer *Aperi,* and they most aptly express what must be the attitude of my body, of my mind, and of my heart.

---

89. Almighty and most merciful God, Whose gift it is that Thy faithful should pay Thee fit and laudable service (Collect for the 12th Sun. after Pent.).

DIGNE. A respectful position and bearing, the precise pronunciation of the words, slowing down over the more important
parts. Careful observance of the rubrics. My tone of voice, *the
way in which I make signs of the Cross, genuflections, etc.; my
body* itself: all will go to show not only that *I know Whom I
am addressing, and what I am saying,* but also that *my heart is
in what I am doing.* What an APOSTOLATE I can sometimes
exercise.[90]

---

90. Apostolate or Scandal. There are many souls who look at religion
   through a hazy intellectualism or ritualism, and to such persons, a
   whole sermon by a second-rate priest has far less meaning than the
   apostolate of a genuine priest whose great faith, piety, and compunction shine forth in his ministrations at a Baptism, Funeral, or, above all,
   at Mass. Words and rites are arrows that strike deep into such hearts.
   When the Liturgy is thus lived, they see in it the certitude of the mystery expressed. The invisible begins to exist for them, and they are
   prompted to invoke Jesus, Whom they hardly know at all, but with
   Whom they sense that the priest is in close communication. But only
   weakening or total loss of their faith follows when the spectacle before
   them merely turns their stomach, and moves them to cry out: "Why,
   you can't tell me that priest believes in a God or fears Him! Look at
   the way he says Mass, administers Baptism, recites his prayers, and
   performs his ceremonies!" What responsibilities! Who would dare
   to maintain that such scandals will not be visited with the strictest of
   judgment?
      How the faithful are influenced by the way a priest acts; whether it
   be that he displays deeply reverential fear, or an insolent nonchalance
   in his sacred functions!
      Once when studying in a university graduate school, into which no
   clerical influence entered at all, I chanced to observe a priest reciting
   his Breviary, he being unaware that he was the object of my attention.
   His bearing, full of respect and religion, was a revelation to me, and
   produced in me an urgent need to pray from then on, and to pray in the
   way this priest was praying. The Church appeared to me, concretized,
   so to speak, in this worthy minister, in communion with his God.
      But a faithful Catholic soul recently admitted to me: "When I saw
   the way my parish priest rushed through his Mass at high speed, I was

In the courts of earthly kings, a simple servant considers the least function to be something great, and unconsciously takes on a majestic and solemn air in performing it. Cannot I acquire some of that *distinctive bearing* which will show itself by my *state of mind* and by the dignity of my bearing when I carry out my duties in my capacity as member of the guard of honor of the King of Kings and of the God of all Majesty?

ATTENTE. My mind will be eager to go foraging through the sacred words and rites in order to get everything that will nourish my heart.

Sometimes my attention will consider the *literal sense* of the texts, whether I follow every phase or whether, while going on with my recitation of the prayers, I take time to meditate on some word that has struck my attention, until such time as I feel the need to seek the honey of devotion in some other flower: in either case, I am fulfilling the precept *Mens concordet voci*.[91]

At other times, my intellect may occupy itself with the *mystery of the day* or the *principal idea* of the liturgical season.

But the part played by the mind will remain in the background compared to the role of the will. The mind will serve only as the will's *source of supply*, helping it to *remain in adoration or to return to that state.*

As soon as distractions arise it shall be my will to return to the act of adoration; but I shall make this movement of the will without irritation or harshness, without a sudden violent

---

completely upset, and found it hard to believe that he had any faith. Soon I lost all power to pray, even to believe, and a kind of disgust, caused by the fear that I would have to continue to see this priest say Mass, caused me, from then on, to avoid the parish church."

91. Let mind and voice agree (*Rule of St. Benedict*).

jerk, but *peacefully* (since everything that is done with Your aid, Lord Jesus, is peaceful and quiet), yet *powerfully* (since every genuine desire to co-operate with Your aid, Lord, is powerful and strong).

DEVOTE. This is the most important point. Everything comes back to the need of making our Office and all our liturgical functions *acts of piety*, and, consequently, acts that come *from the heart.*

"Haste kills all devotion." Such is the principle laid down by St. Francis de Sales in talking of the Breviary, and it applies a *fortiori* to the Mass. Hence. I shall make it a hard and fast rule to devote *around half an hour to my* MASS in order to ensure a devout recitation not only of the Canon but of all the other parts as well. I shall reject without pity all PRETEXTS for getting through this, the principal act of my day, in a hurry. If I have the habit of mutilating certain words or ceremonies, I shall apply myself, and go over these faulty places *very slowly and carefully*, even exaggerating my exactitude for a while.[92]

With all due proportion, I shall also apply this resolution to all my other liturgical functions: administrations of the Sacraments, Benediction, Burials, and so on.

As far as the Breviary is concerned, I shall carefully *decide in advance when I am to say my Office.* When that time comes, I shall compel myself, cost what it may, to drop everything else. *At any price, I want my recitation of the Office to be a real prayer from the heart.* O my Divine Mediator! Fill

---

92. A certain author of the nineteenth century, as notorious for his impiety as he was famous for the realism of his descriptions, once found no better simile by which to give a caricature of a person speaking very volubly without knowing what he was saying, than to describe that person as talking "like a priest gabbling his Mass."

my heart with detestation for all haste in those things where I stand in Your place, or act in the name of the Church! Fill me with the conviction that haste paralyzes that *great Sacramental*, the Liturgy, and makes impossible that spirit of prayer without which, no matter how zealous a priest I may appear to be on the outside, I would be lukewarm, or perhaps worse, in Your estimation. Burn into my inmost heart those words so full of terror: "*Cursed be he that doth the work of God deceitfully.*"[93]

Sometimes I will let my heart soar, and take in by a panoramic *synthesis of Faith*, the general meaning of the mystery which the liturgical Cycle calls to mind; and I will feed my soul with this broad view.

At other times, I will make my Office a *long, lingering act* of Faith or Hope, Desire or Regret, Oblation or Love.

Then again, just to remain, *in simplicity*, LOOKING at God will be enough. By this I mean a loving and continuous contemplation of a mystery, of a perfection of God, of one of Your titles, my Jesus, of Your Church, my own nothingness, my faults, my needs, or else my dignity as a Christian, as a priest, as a religious. Vastly different is this simple "looking" from an act of the intellect in the course of theological studies. This "look" will increase Faith, but will give even greater and more rapid growth to Love. It is a reflection, no doubt a pale one, but still a reflection of the beatific vision, this "looking" and it is the fulfillment of what You promised even here below to pure and fervent souls: "Blessed are the clean of heart for they shall see God."[94]

---

93. *Maledictus qui facit opus Dei fraudulentur (Jer. 48:10).*
94. *Beati mundo corde, quoniam ipsi Deum videbunt (Matt. 5:8).*

*   *   *

And thus every ceremony will become *a restful change* because it will bring my soul a real breathing spell and relieve it from the stifling press of occupations.

Holy Liturgy, what sweet fragrance you will bring into my soul by your various "functions." Far from being a slavish burden these functions will become one of the greatest consolations of my life.

How could it be otherwise when thanks to your constant reminders I am ever coming back to the fact of my dignity as a child and ambassador of the Church, as member and minister of Jesus Christ, and am ever being more and more closely united to Him Who is the "*Joy of the elect.*"

By my union with Him I shall learn to get profit out of the crosses of this mortal life, and to sow the seeds of my eternal happiness and by my liturgical life, which is far more effective than any apostolate, I will see that other souls have been drawn to follow after me in the ways of salvation and sanctity.

4. CUSTODY OF THE HEART IS THE KEYSTONE OF THE INTERIOR LIFE: HENCE IT IS ESSENTIAL IN THE APOSTOLATE

Resolution on Custody of The Heart

Oh Jesus, it is my desire that my heart acquire a habitual solicitude to PRESERVE ITSELF from every stain and to BECOME MORE AND MORE UNITED to Your Heart in all my occupations conversations, recreations, and so on.

The negative, but essential element of this resolution

demands that I absolutely refuse to contract any stain in my motives and in the way my acts are carried out.[95]

The positive element drives my ambition on to the point of seeking to intensify the Faith, Hope, and Love with which the action was begun.

This resolution is going to be the real barometer by which to measure the *practical value* of my morning mental prayer and my liturgical life. For my interior life will be what my

---

95. PURITY OF INTENTION

Q: How is purity of intention to be acquired?

A: It is acquired by close attention to ourselves at the beginning and above all during the course of our actions.

Q: Why is this attention necessary at the beginning of our actions?

A: Because if these actions are pleasing, useful, or in harmony with our natural attractions, nature at once moves to perform them of its own accord, attracted by pleasure and self-interest alone. But we must pay great attention to ourselves, indeed we must have great command over ourselves, if we are to prevent the will from being rushed off its feet, so to speak, by the appeals of natural motives with their flattery, solicitations, and attractions.

Q: Why do you add that this attention is above all necessary during the course of our actions?

A: Because even when a person has the strength to repudiate, at the outset, every seductive appeal of sense and self-love, in order to follow in all things nothing but the direction of faith, in all purity of intention; nevertheless if he forgets, later on, to keep a close watch on himself, the actual enjoyment of the pleasure that makes itself felt, or of the advantages that accrue during the course of certain actions keep piling up new impressions and appeals, and the heart yields little by little, so that nature, although mortified by the first refusals, comes to life again and regains its ascendancy. Pretty soon, self-love subtly and almost without our being aware of it, begins to insinuate its selfish motives, and substitutes them for the good motives with which our actions were taken up and begun. From this fact, it many times happens, as St. Paul says, that what began in the spirit ends up in the flesh, that is in low and worldly and selfish views. —Fr. de Caussade, S.J.

custody of the heart is. "With all watchfulness keep thy heart, because life issueth out from it."[96]

Mental prayer gives me back the verve with which I run on towards divine union. But it is *custody of the heart* which is going to enable the traveler to gain strength from the nourishment he took before his journey began, or takes along the way, so that he will always maintain the same lively pace with which he started out.

This custody of the heart means nothing else but *the HABITUAL, or at least frequent solicitude to preserve all our acts, as we perform them, from everything that might corrupt their MOTIVE or their ACCOMPLISHMENT.*

This solicitude will be calm, peaceful, free of all strain, at once humble and strong, because its basis is filial recourse to God and trust in that recourse. Here my heart and my will do much more work than my mind, which must remain free to carry out my various obligations. Far from impeding my activity, custody of the heart will make it all the more perfect by bringing it into line with the Spirit of God, and adjusting it to the duties of my state.

Now this exercise is something that I want to practice at every moment of the day. It will consist in a glance from the heart, upon the present action, and a moderate attentiveness to all the various parts of the action as I perform them. It amounts to carrying out, with all exactitude, the precept: *Age quod agis.*[97] My soul, like an alert sentinel, will keep a vigilant watch over all the movements of my heart, over everything that goes on within me, all my impressions, intentions,

---

96. *Omni custodia serva cor tuum, quia ex ipso vita procedit* (*Prov.* 4:23).
97. Do what you are doing—that is to say: apply yourself totally to the matter in hand.

passions, inclinations, and, in a word, over all my interior and exterior acts, all my thoughts, actions, and words.

Obviously this custody of the heart *demands* a certain amount of recollection, and it cannot be practiced if my soul is dissipated.

However, the frequent practice of this exercise will help me to acquire the *habit* that will make self-custody easy.

Quo vadam et ad quid?[98] What would Jesus do; how would He act in my place? What would He advise? What does He ask of me at this moment? Such are the questions that will come spontaneously to my mind, hungry for interior life.

When I feel myself drawn to Jesus through Mary, this custody of the heart will quickly become far more effective. My heart will soon feel, as it were, an incessant need for recourse to so good a Mother. And this is how we actualize the precept, "ABIDE *in Me and I in you.*"[99] which sums up all the other principles of the interior life.

What You have declared, O Jesus, to be the fruit of the Eucharist, "he abideth in Me and I in him." is what my soul is out to get, by means of custody of the heart, which will unite me with You.

He abideth in Me. Yes, I shall see myself as truly in my home, in Your divine Heart; with every right to dispose of all Your wealth, by using the unlimited treasures of sanctifying Grace, and the inexhaustible mine of Your actual Graces.

And I in him. But, thanks to my self-custody, You also, My Lord, will be truly at home in my heart. For, bending every effort to insure the continual exercise of Your sovereignty

---

98. Where am I going, and for what? St. Ignatius of Loyola used frequently to ask himself this, and it is alluded to in the *Spiritual Exercises.*

99. *Manete in Me et Ego in vobis* (*Joan.* 15:4).

over the operation of all my faculties, not only will I be careful never to do anything without You, but my ambition will go so far as to desire to put into every one of my actions an ever increasing power of love.

The habit of interior recollection, of spiritual combat, of a busy and well regulated life, and the incalculable increase of my merits will all result from my self-custody.

And thus, O Jesus, my *indirect* union with You through my works, that is my relations, according to Your will, with creatures, will become the sequel to my *direct* union with You through mental prayer, the liturgical life, and the Sacraments. In both these cases, this union will proceed from Faith and from Charity and will be formed under the influence of Grace. In the direct union, it is You *Yourself, O My God*, and *You alone*, that I have in view. In the indirect union I apply myself to other things. But since it is in obedience to You that I do so these objects to which I have to give my attention become *the means willed by You* to achieve my union with You. I leave You in order to find You. *It is always You* that I am seeking, and with just as much love, but now I seek You *in Your Will*. And this divine Will of Yours is the one and only beacon light upon which self-custody fixes my constant gaze, that I may direct all that I do to Your service. And so in either case I am able to say: "It is good for me to adhere to my God."[100]

It is therefore a great MISTAKE to imagine that in order to become united to You I must *put off my active work or else wait for it to get done*. It is a mistake to imagine that certain kinds of work, because of their very nature, or because of the time they involve, might *so dominate my life or cramp my freedom* that it would become impossible for me to be united

---

100. *Mihi adhaerere Deo bonum est* (*Ps.* 72:28).

to You. Not at all: You want me to be free. You do not want activities to imprison me beneath their weight. You want me *to be the master* and not the slave of activity. And to that end You offer me Your grace, on condition that I am faithful in the custody of my heart.

And so, from the moment a supernatural practical sense tells me, through the many events and circumstances and details arranged by Your Providence, that such and such activity is really bound up with Your will, I have the twofold duty of *not trying to get out of it* but also of *not doing it merely for the pleasure it may give me.* I must take on the job, and carry it out *solely in order to do Your Will.* Otherwise selflove might step in and corrupt its worth, and diminish my merit.[101] And if I find out what it is You will, Dear Lord, and see how You want it done, *Quod, et quomodo Deus vult,* and then go ahead and do it simply because it is Your Will, *Et quia Deus vat,* then my union with You, far from diminishing, will only be intensified.

---

101. "Good actions," says Fr. Desurmont, C.SS.R., "conceal within themselves delights, honors, glory and a certain indefinable something which human nature finds extremely tasty, and which it often likes far more than sinful pleasure. And the soul is not on its guard against this gnawing worm, this refined egoism which kills actual grace.

"The Lord, out of kindness toward us as well as out of jealousy for His glory, declares Himself to be, as far as He is concerned, indifferent to all particular goods. And He has decided that one thing alone shall be pleasing to Him, namely His own Will. In such a way that a mere nothing, performed in conformity with His Will, can merit Heaven, while wonders worked without it remain unrewarded. And consequently what we have to do is to aim, in all things, not only at what is simply good, but at the good that is willed by God, that is, His Will" (*Le Retour Continuel à Dieu*).

I. The Need for Self-Custody

My God, You are Holiness itself, and here on earth You only admit a soul to intimacy with You *in the measure in which it applies* itself to destroy or to avoid everything that can soil or stain it in any way.

And yet I can find myself SWARMING LIKE AN ANT-HILL WITH VENIAL SINS or deliberate imperfections, which deprive my soul of all the abounding graces which You held in store for me from all eternity. Consider a few of these sins—like the failure through spiritual laziness, to raise up my soul to God; an inordinate love of creatures; hasty temper and impatience; nursing a grudge; being capricious and changeable; getting soft, loving whatever is easy and gives pleasure; always talking without any cause about the faults of other people; dissipation, and a lot of curiosity about things that have nothing whatever to do with the glory of God; spreading scandal, gossiping, and making rash and stupid judgments of others; vain self-complacency; contempt of others, and constant criticism of their conduct; always looking for admiration and praise, and doing things with these in view; showing off anything that is to my credit; presumption, stubbornness, jealousy, lack of respect for superiors, murmuring; no mortification in eating, drinking, and so on.

Can my mental prayer and my liturgical life be any good if they do not bring me, bit by bit, to such a state of recollection that my soul will be wakeful against even faults of *plain weakness*; if they do not help me to pick myself up again *right away* as soon as my will begins to give in; and even if they do not, in certain cases, lead me to impose certain sanctions upon myself?

What a thought, Dear Lord! If I do not watch myself, I can *paralyze* Your activity in me!

Masses, Communions, Confessions, my other pious exercises, the special protection of Divine Providence with my eternal salvation in view, the tender concern of my Guardian Angel, and, worse still, even your motherly watchfulness over me, Sweet Immaculate Mother, *all this can be paralyzed, canceled out, by my fault!*

If I am lacking in good will to impose upon myself that constraint which You were talking about, Dear Lord, when You said: "the violent bear it away,"[102]

Satan will ever be trying to catch me by surprise and lead me astray, and weaken me, and he will even go so far as to pervert my whole conscience with his illusions.

O my soul! Some of those falls which you think are mere weakness are perhaps already much more than that in the eyes of God. If you do not practice custody of the heart and if you do not forge ahead in carrying out the program of *keeping all the motives of my actions purely for Jesus alone*, how can you escape from that conclusion?

If I do not resolve upon custody of the heart, not only will I pile up a long and fearsome debt for Purgatory, but even though I may yet avoid mortal sin, I will be on the incline that inevitably leads to it. Have you thought of that, O my soul?

II. Self-Custody Begins With the Practice of the Presence of God

O Holy Trinity, if I am in the state of Grace, and I hope I am, then *You are dwelling in my heart*, with all Your glory and all

---

102. *Violenti rapiunt illud* (*Matt.* 11:12).

Your infinite perfections, just as You dwell in Heaven; but here You are hidden by the veils of Faith.

There is not a single moment when *Your eyes are not upon me*, seeing all that I do.

Your Justice and Your Mercy *are always at work in me*. In response to my infidelities, You take away Your special graces, or else You no longer dispose events with maternal care in such a way that they turn out to my advantage: at other times, to bring me back to Yourself, You load me down with fresh kindness.

If I really looked upon this indwelling in me as the most wonderful of all facts and *the most worthy of my attention*, would I be so often and for such long periods oblivious of it?

Is it not this failure to attend to the *fundamental fact* of my existence that is the reason for such poor success up to the present in all my attempts to practice self-custody?

A constant succession of *ejaculatory prayers* all through the day ought to be keeping this loving indwelling of God ever in my conscious thoughts. *Up until now, my soul, have you really taken the trouble to fill your life with these little landmarks as you go along; have you even remembered to make these aspirations* ONCE IN AN HOUR? Have you drawn enough profit from your daily meditation and from your liturgical life to enter from time to time, even if it is only a few seconds, into the inner sanctuary of your heart, there to adore the infinite Beauty, the Immensity, the All-Power, the Sanctity, the Life, and the Love, in a word, the *Supreme and Perfect Good* Who deigns to dwell there and Who is *your Beginning and your End?*

How about *Spiritual Communions?* What kind of a part do they play in my daily life? And yet they are right at hand, not only to remind me of the indwelling of the Most Holy Trinity within me, but also to *increase that indwelling by a new in pouring of the Precious Blood into my soul.*

Up to now, how much importance have I attached to these riches that I find all along my road? All I needed to do was bend down and pick up diamonds and place them in my diadem. What a far call it is from me to those souls who, *in the thick of their work or their conversations* return a thousand times a day to their Divine Guest! They have acquired this habit, and *their hearts are fixed where their treasure is.*

III. Self-Custody Aided by Devotion to Our Lady

O my Immaculate Mother, when, on Calvary, the words of Your Son made me also a child of yours, it was in order that you might then aid me to keep my heart united, through Jesus, to the Holy Trinity.

I want my *ever more frequent invocations* to you, to aim above all at this custody of my heart, so that I may purify all its tendencies, intentions, affections, and desires.

I desire no longer to close my ears to your sweet voice that urges me: "Stop that, my child! *Get your heart back on the right path again!* Do not think that, in what you are now doing, you are seeking only God's glory, and nothing else." How often have you not interrupted my dissipation, my somewhat questionable occupations, with this motherly appeal! And how often, alas, have I drowned out the sound of your voice!

Sweet Mother, from now on I am going to hear YOUR HEART REMINDING ME OF THE TRUTH, and my fidelity will correspond to it by *firmly and decisively putting on the brakes.* Maybe it will only be a momentary halt, like a lightning flash in the course of my activity, but it will be all

I shall need to ask myself one of these questions: *For whom am I doing this? How would Jesus be acting in my place?* Now when I acquire the habit of always putting to myself this question in the depths of my heart, I am practicing custody of the heart. And this is what is going to enable me even in the smallest details, to keep my faculties and all their impulses in an ever more perfect *habit of dependence* upon God living within me.

IV. Learning Self-Custody

It is a torment to me, to remain out of the presence of God for long intervals during the course of my work. I am filled with sorrow by the realization that all during this time when I am pouring myself out in activities, numerous faults escape me, irrespective of the state of my soul, whether I display a mixture of fervor and imperfections, or whether I am frankly tepid. And hence I want to start to remedy matters today by practicing custody of the heart.

In the morning, when I am making my meditation, I shall determine *very precisely and firmly upon a certain moment in my work* when I shall attempt, even while carrying on busily the work willed by God, to live *as perfect an interior life as I can*, to practice self-custody, that is, to be in Your presence, dear Lord, and at the same time keep an eye on myself, always having recourse to You, acting *just as if* I had made the vow always to do what is most perfect.

I shall begin by doing this for five minutes, or even less, morning and evening,[103] and shall concern myself much more

---

103. This is practically the same as what Bossuet called the "moment of loving solitude which we should at all costs set aside during the day." It is also what St. Francis de Sales so strongly recommended under

with making it perfect than with making it long. I shall also try to make it better and better all the time, and strive to have the purity of intention, the custody of my heart and of all my faculties, and the generosity, that you would expect to find in a saint, in a word: to act in all things as *Christ Himself would have acted* in doing the same work, and to do all this *in the midst of my work, EVEN, or rather ABOVE ALL if it is very ABSORBING.*

This will prove *an apprenticeship for a practical interior life.* It will be a protest against my habits of dissipation and my *wandering mind.* I want Jesus. I want His Kingdom. And when the time for external work arrives I want His Kingdom to go on just the same in myself. I do not want my soul to go on being a public hallway open to every wind, in which it becomes impossible to live united to Jesus, vigilant, suppliant, and generous.

During this brief moment, I shall keep my eyes directed, without strain, upon all the motives of my soul's acts, and I shall forgive no fault. My good will, too, will be frevently determined to let nothing slip through that might make my living less perfect during this interval, brief as it is! And then my heart also, will be resolved to have frequent recourse to Our Lord, to keep going in this WORKOUT IN SANCTITY.

This practice is going to be *hearty, and happy, and done with great expansion of soul.* Of course vigilance and

---

the name of spiritual retreats. "Devotion's principal work lies in this exercise of the spiritual retreat and in ejaculatory prayers. Here is an exercise that can make up for the lack of all the other forms of prayer, but the lack of this one is practically irreparable by any other means. Without it, it is impossible to lead the active life otherwise than badly . . . and work will always be an obstacle to us" (*Intro. to the Dev. Life,* Pt. ii, ch. 3).

mortification will be necessary if I am going to keep in the presence of God and deny my faculties and senses everything that smacks of nature. But I am not going to be satisfied with this merely negative side. I shall try above all to *put into this exercise that intensity of love* which, by making me more careful in the practice of *Age quod agis*, first of all the purity of intention and then with an ever increasing ardor and impersonality and generosity, will give my works all their perfection and value.

In the evening, at my general examination of conscience (or at the particular examen, if I make this exercise its subject), I shall make a rigorously close analysis of the way these few minutes of strict and unreserved self-custody before Jesus turned out. Then I will impose a sanction, some little penance (cut out a few cigarettes or take a little less dessert, unnoticed by anyone else, or else pray a little while with the arms out in the form of a cross, or give myself a few smart blows on the fingers with a ruler or some hard object), if I observe that I have not been sufficiently vigilant, or fervent, or suppliant, or loving during this tryout in self-custody, that is, in the union of *interior and active life*.

What wonderful results can be obtained from this practice! *What a school of self-custody!*

What *new light* it will throw on sins and imperfections of whose existence I was not even aware!

These blessed moments will come *gradually to exercise a VIRTUAL influence on the moments that come after*. Nevertheless, I shall not prolong them until I have just about gone as far in them as I can, in holiness and perfection of execution, and intensity of love.

I am going to aim at quality rather than extent. My thirst to take more than just a few minutes at this practice will grow stronger in proportion as I see more correctly what I am and what You expect of me, Dear Lord. And thus gradually getting familiar with this salutary exercise I shall *contract a real need for it, and it will become a habit*, and then You will make known to my soul, thus purified, the secrets of the life of union with You.

V. Self-Custody: Under What Conditions?

The whole trend of my life is almost all more or less imperfect. This CONVICTION, which Satan tries to keep out of my mind, is going to be the basis of *mistrust* of myself and of creatures. And this element, *united to my desire to belong to Jesus* will necessarily produce:

Vigilance, loyal and exact, gentle, peaceful, confident in grace, and based on the repression of dissipation and of the excesses of natural enthusiasm. A frequent *renewal* of my resolution. Tireless *new beginnings*, ever full of confidence in the mercy of Christ for the soul that really puts up a fight to acquire self-custody. An ever increasing certitude that *I am not fighting alone* but united to Jesus living in me, to Mary His Mother, to my Guardian Angel, and to the Saints. A conviction that these powerful allies are helping me at *every moment* as long as I keep striving for self-custody: as long as I do not put myself out of reach of their assistance. Finally, a *cordial and frequent recourse* to all these divine helps, that I may be able with their aid to do *quod Deus vult* and do it *quomodo Deus vult* and *quia Deus vult*.[104]

Oh! what a transformation will take place in my life, Dear Lord, if I keep my heart united to You! My mind may be

---

104. What God wants . . . the way God wants it . . . because God wants it.

completely absorbed in the *business in hand*. And yet there is something I have observed in souls that are extremely busy, and who yet never cease *to live and breathe in You:* and that is what I want to arrive at, in the course of even my most absorbing work.

If I have well understood what self-custody means, far from diminishing *the freedom of action required by my faculties* if they are to carry out all the duties of my state, my soul, breathing in the atmosphere of love which is Yourself, Jesus, will *increase that liberty* and make my life serene, joyful, powerful, and full of fruit.

Instead of being the slave of my pride, of my selfishness or of my laziness; instead of groaning beneath the yoke of my passions and feelings, I shall become more and more free. And with this increase in my liberty I shall be able, O my God, to give You more and more frequent homage of dependence. Thus I shall be strengthened in *true humility*, the foundation without which the interior life would simply be an illusion. And so I shall develop in myself that basic spirit of submission: *Submisso ad Deum*,[105] which sums up the whole inner life of Our Savior.

Participating in the flame of love which made You always so attentive and docile to Your Father's good pleasure, Jesus, I shall merit a share, in Heaven, of the glory which Your Humanity enjoys as a reward for its wonderful dependence of humility and love: "Becoming obedient . . . for which God also hath exalted Him. . . ."[106]

---

105. Humility consists chiefly in the submission of man to God (St. Thomas Aquinas).

106. *Factus oboediens . . . propter quod et Deus exaltavit ilium* (*Phil.* 2:9).

5. THE APOSTLE MUST HAVE AN ARDENT DEVOTION TO MARY IMMACULATE

As a member of the Cistercian Order, so completely consecrated to Mary, and as a child of that great saint who was, for
half a century, the apostle of Europe, St. Bernard, how can
we forget that the holy abbot of Clairvaux attributed to Mary
all his progress in union with Jesus, and all his success in the
apostolate?

Everybody knows what tremendous effects were produced
by the apostolate of this saint, who remains the most illustri-
ous of the sons of St. Benedict: an apostolate that embraced
nations and kings, Councils and even Popes.

On all sides we hear the praises of the sanctity, the genius,
the deep knowledge of Holy Scripture, and the penetrating
unction of the writings of this the last of the Fathers of the
Church.

But one title above all others sums up all the admiration of
the ages for this holy doctor: *Cytharista Mariae*, "the Harpist
of Mary."

This "Bard of Mary" has never been surpassed by any of
those who have proclaimed the glories of the Mother of God.
St. Bernardine of Siena and St. Francis of Sales, as well as
Bossuet, St. Alphonsus, St. Grignon de Monfort, and so on,
all draw largely upon the treasures of St. Bernard when they
want to speak of her, and find arguments to support that great
truth which the holy Doctor so emphasized: "Everything
comes to us through Mary."

"See, my brethren, with what sentiments of devotion God
has desired us to honor Mary, He Who has placed in her the
fullness of all good. If there is in us any hope, any grace, any

pledge of salvation, let us admit that all this overflows upon us from her who is flowing with delights. . . . Suppose you were to take away the sun, which enlightens the world: what would become of the day? Take away Mary, that star of the sea, of our huge, vast sea, what is left but deep obscurity, the shadow of death, pitchy blackness? Therefore it is from the depths of our hearts, from the very vitals of our being, and with all our mind and will that we must honor the Virgin Mary: for such is the will of Him Who willed us to have all through Mary."[107]

Strong with the strength of this doctrine we will not hesitate to lay down as a principle that *no matter what the apostle may do to ensure salvation and spiritual progress and the fruitfulness of his apostolate, he runs the risk of finding that he has built on sand if his activity does not rest on a very special devotion to Our Lady.*

a. For His Personal Interior Life

The apostle cannot claim to have a sufficient devotion to Our Lady if his confidence in her is not enthusiastic, and if his homage to her is almost entirely external. Like her Son, *intuetur cor*, she only looks at our hearts, and judges us to be her true children only by the power with which our love corresponds to hers.

She looks to find a heart that is firmly convinced of the glories and privileges and offices of her who is at the same time the Mother of God and the Mother of men:

A heart that is convinced of this truth: that the fight against faults, the acquisition of virtues, the Kingdom of Christ in

---

107. *Sermon on the Nativity of Our Lady*, called "de Aquaeductu" (St. Bernard).

souls, and consequently all guarantee of salvation and sanc- ity, are in proportion to the degree of our devotion to Mary;[108]

A heart that is gripped with the thought that everything is easier, more delightful, and progresses more rapidly in the interior life when we act in union with Mary;[109]

A heart full to overflowing of filial confidence, come what may, in her whose gentle tact, and wise anticipation of our needs, and whose tenderness and mercy and generosity we know by experience;[110]

A heart ever more and more on fire with love for her who is associated with all our joys, united with us in all our trials, and through whom all our affections pass.

All these sentiments give us a good picture of St. Bernard, who may be taken as the model for active workers. Who does not know the words that leaped forth from the soul of this holy abbot when, in his exposition of the Gospel *"Missus est,"* for the benefit of his monks, he cries out:

"O you who in the ebb and flow of this age are aware that you are tossed in the midst of storms and tempests rather than walking upon the earth, keep your eyes fixed on this star, so that you may not perish in the gale. If the winds of temptations are let loose, if you are striking on the rocks of tribulation, look to the star, call upon Mary. If you are flung about by the

---

108. No one is saved except through thee, Mother of God. No one receives the gift of God except through thee, O full of grace! (St. Germain).

    Holiness increases in proportion to the devotion that one pro- fesses for Mary (Fr. Faber).

109. With Mary, we make more progress in the love of Jesus in one month than we could in years of living less united to this good Mother (St. Grignon de Montfort).

110. *Filioli, haec mea maxima fiducia est, haec tota ratio spei meae.*

    My little children, she it is who is the foundation of all my trust and the whole reason for all my hope (St. Bernard).

waves of pride, of ambition, of scandal, of jealousy, look on the star, call upon Mary. If anger or avarice or evil desires attack the frail bark of your soul, lift up your eyes to Mary. If, crushed under the enormity of your sins, in confusion at the horrible wounds of your conscience, alarmed by the horror of the judgment, you begin to be drawn into the whirlpool of sadness and despair, think of Mary. In dangers, in anguish, in doubt, think of Mary, invoke Mary. Let Mary never be far from your lips, never far from your heart; and to obtain the support of her prayers, do not forget the example of her life. In following her you shall not go astray; by praying to her you shall not despair; in contemplating her you shall not go wrong. With her support you fall not; under her protection you fear not; under her guidance, you do not grow weary; if she is propitious to you, you will reach the port."

Obliged to limit this work, and yet desirous of offering our confreres in the apostolate a sort of summary of the advice St. Bernard gives to those who would like to become true children of Mary, we believe there is no better course for us to take than to offer the suggestion that they read with attention the solid and valuable little book of Fr. Lhomeau, "The Spiritual Life as Taught by Bl. Grignon de Montfort."[111]

Along with the words of St. Alphonsus and Fr. Desurmont's commentaries, the writings of Fr. Faber and of Fr. Giraud of La Salette, this book of Fr. Lhomeau gives an unusually complete exposition of the teaching of St. Bernard, whom it quotes at every turn. It has that strong foundation of dogma, that unction and practical character, and everything else that goes to achieve the result which the abbot of Clairvaux was

---

111. *La Vie Spirituelle à l'Ecole du Bienheureux Grignon de Montfort,* Librairie Oudin. Fr. Lhomeau was Superior General of the congregation which St. G. de Montfort founded.

always striving to obtain: namely to form the hearts of his children after the image of his own and give them what was the outstanding characteristic of all the great Cistercian writers: *the need for habitual recourse to Mary and to lead a life of union with her.*

Let us bring this to a close with the consoling words which the great Cistercian, St. Gertrude, whom Dom Guèranger calls Gertrude the Great, heard from the lips of the Most Blessed Virgin:

"They ought not to call my sweetest Jesus my only Son, but rather my first-born Son. I conceived Him first in my womb, but after Him, or rather, through Him, I conceived every one of you to be His brothers and to be my children, adopting you in the womb of my maternal charity." Everything in the writings of this saint, the patroness of the Trappistine nuns, reflects the spirit of her Holy Father St. Bernard with regard to the life of union with Mary.

b. *For an Effective Apostolate*

Whether it be the task of the active worker to rescue souls from sin or to make virtues put forth flowers in their souls, his first objective must always be, as was St. Paul's, to bring forth Our Lord in them. Now Bossuet says that God, having once willed to give us Jesus through the Most Blessed Virgin, there is no further change in that order. It was she who brought forth the Head, and so it is she too who is to bring forth the members.

To isolate Mary from the apostolate would be to misconstrue one of the most vital parts of the divine Plan. "All the elect," says St. Augustine, "are, in this world, hidden in the womb of the Most Blessed Virgin, where they are cherished and nourished and fostered and reared by this good Mother until such time as she brings them forth to glory after their death."

And St. Bernardine of Siena justly concludes that, since the Incarnation, Mary has acquired a sort of jurisdiction over every temporal mission of the Holy Ghost, in such a way that no creature receives any graces but through her hands.

But the man with true devotion to Mary becomes all-powerful over the Heart of his Mother. And so, what apostle can doubt the efficacy of his Apostolate when, by his devotions, he can control the all-powerful mediation of Mary in the distribution of the merits of the Precious Blood?

Hence we observe that all great converters of souls are filled with an unusually powerful devotion for the Blessed Virgin. Are they out to free a soul from sin? What persuasive warmth is theirs, identified as they are by their horror for evil and their love of purity, with her who has applied to herself the name of the Immaculate Conception!

It was by the voice of Mary that the Precursor recognized the presence of Jesus, and leaped in the womb of his mother. What persuasive accents will Mary give to her true children, that they may open to Jesus hearts hitherto locked!

What words come to the minds of those who are intimately united to the Mother of Mercies when they want to prevent souls that have long abused grace, from falling into despair!

Some unfortunate man does not know Mary. The assurance with which the apostle shows her to be a true Mother and Refuge of sinners will open out new horizons to such a one!

The Holy Curé of Ars sometimes ran across sinners, blinded by delusions, who relied on some external practice of devotion to the Blessed Virgin to quiet their consciences, and let them sin with greater freedom, without fear of the everlasting flames of Hell. In such cases, his words were of tremendous effect, both in bringing the guilty one to realize the monstrosity of this presumption, so insulting to the Mother of Mercy, and to make him use that act of devotion to implore the grace to get free from the crushing coils of the infernal snake.

But in a similar situation an apostle without much devotion to Mary will only succeed, by his wounding, frigid words, in making the poor drowning wretch let go of the last straw that might have turned into a force strong enough to keep him afloat until he reached safety.

When Mary is living in the heart of her apostle, he will be guaranteed the use of the persuasive eloquence of Our Blessed Mother herself, speaking in him, and moving souls with whom all else has failed. It is apparent that Our Lord, in a most beautiful delicacy of feeling, has left to the mediation of His Mother the most difficult conquests of the apostolate desiring that they should be accorded to no one but those who live in intimate union with her. "Through thee He has reduced our enemies to nought": *Per te ad nihilum redegit inimicos nostros.*

Never will the true son of Mary run out of arguments, of means or even of expedients when it becomes necessary, in almost hopeless cases, to strengthen the helpless and give consolation to those who cannot be consoled.

The Decree that added the invocation *Mater Boni Consilii* (Mother of Good Counsel) to Our Lady's Litany, goes back to the titles of "Treasuress of Heavenly Graces," and "Universal Consoler" (*Coelestium gratiarum Thesauraria, Consolatrix universalis*), which are Mary's due. "Mother of Good Counsel," she only gives to those who are truly devoted to her, as she did at Cana, the secret of obtaining from God the wine of strength and of joy to distribute to men.

But it is above all when the time comes to speak to souls of the love of God that this Ravisher of Hearts, *Raptrix Cordium*, as St. Bernard called her, the Spouse of Substantial Love, places upon the lips of her intimates the words of fire that enkindle love of Christ, and bring into being, through that love every other virtue.

We apostles are bound to have a passionate love for her whom Pius IX calls *Virgo Sacerdos*, the Priestly Virgin, and whose dignity, in every respect, outstrips that of any priest or pontiff. And this love gives us the right never to give up any work as fruitless if we have once begun it with Mary, and are ready to keep on going, in it, with her. For Mary, as a matter of fact, is at the base and at the final peak of perfection of all things that have to do with the Kingdom of God through her Son.

But let us be careful never to delude ourselves that we are working *with her* if all we do is to erect altars and have a few hymns sung in her honor. What she is looking for, from us, is a devotion that will allow us to affirm, in all sincerity, that we live *habitually* united to her, that we have recourse to her counsel, that our affections pass through her Heart and that our petitions are frequently made through her. But the thing that Mary most of all expects of our devotion is the imitation of all the virtues that we admire in her and the unreserved abandonment of ourselves into her hands that she may clothe us with her Divine Son.

On this condition of *habitual recourse* to Mary, we will imitate that general of the army of the people of God, who, before marching against the enemy told Deborah: "If thou wilt come *with me*, I will go; if thou wilt not come with me, I will not go." Not only will she be concerned in the principal decisions of our lives, but also with every detail of their execution, even the most unforeseen.

United with her whose invocation *Our Lady of the Sacred Heart* sums up all her titles, we will never run the risk of ruining our works by allowing them to obstruct our interior life, to become a danger to our souls, and serve more for our own glory than for that of our God. On the contrary, we will go through our works to the interior life, and hence to an ever more and more intimate union with her who will guarantee us the possession of her Son for all eternity.

EPILOGUE

So now we lay down this little book before the throne of Mary Immaculate.

There is an old sixth century Byzantine painting of the Most Blessed Virgin that gives a perfect subject of meditation; the Heart of Mary as the consummate ideal of the apostolate.

The figure of Our Blessed Lady is shown carrying in Her Bosom the Incarnate Word surrounded by a circle of light. Like the Eternal Father she ever keeps within herself the Word she has given to the world. As Rohault de Fleury said: "The Savior shines in the midst of her breast like the Eucharist with all the veils torn away." Jesus lives in her. He is her Heart, her life-breath, her center, and her life: this is an image of the interior life.

But the Divine Child is there carrying out the work of His apostolate. His attitude, the scroll of His Gospel which He holds in His left hand, the gesture of His right hand, His expression, everything shows clearly that He is teaching. And the Blessed Virgin is united to His word. The expression on her face seems to tell us that she too would like to say something. Her wide-open eyes are looking for souls to whom she may communicate her Son: and that represents the active life of preaching and instruction.

Her hands oustretched like those of the "*orantes*," or praying women depicted on the walls of the Catacombs, or of the Priest offering the Holy Victim, tell us that it is above all by prayer and union to the Sacrifice of Christ that our interior life will have depth and our apostolate fecundity.

She lives in Jesus, through Jesus, by His life, His love, and by union with His Sacrifice; and Jesus speaks in her and through her. Jesus is her life, and she is the Word-carrier, she amplifies His voice, she serves as His monstrance.

In the same way the soul that is dedicated to the greatest and most perfect of all works, the apostolate, must live in God in order to be able to talk about Him meaningfully and with effect; and, let us repeat it once again, the active life can and must only be, in any soul, the overflow of the interior life.

TEN AIDS TO MENTAL PRAYER

Mental prayer is a furnace, in which the watchfires of vigilance are constantly rekindled.

Fidelity to mental prayer gives life to all our other pious exercises. By it, the soul will gradually acquire vigilance and a spirit of prayer, that is, a habit of ever more frequent recourse to God.

Union with God in mental prayer will lead to intimate union with Him, even in the midst of our most absorbing occupations.

The soul, thus living in union with God, by custody of the heart, will draw down into itself, more and more, the gifts of the Holy Ghost, the infused virtues, and perhaps God will call it to a higher degree of prayer.

Dom Vital Lehodey's splendid *"Ways of Mental Prayer"* (Paris, Lecoffre. Eng. Transl. Dublin, M. H. Gill) presents a clear and forceful summary of all the essentials of the ascent of the soul, through the various degrees of prayer, and gives rules by which we can ascertain whether a higher type of prayer is really a gift of God or the product of illusion.

Before speaking of affective prayer, the first degree of the comparatively advanced prayer to which God ordinarily only calls souls who have *attained* custody of the heart by means of meditation, Fr. Rigoleuc points out in his fine book of "*Spiritual Works*" (Avignon, 1843, p. 17ff.) ten ways of conversing with God when, *after a sincere attempt*, one finds it morally impossible to make a set meditation upon a subject prepared the evening before.

We here summarize the suggestions of this holy writer:

FIRST WAY. Take some spiritual book (*New Testament, Following of Christ*), read a few lines, pausing long in between— meditate a little on what you have read, trying to get the full meaning and to impress it on your mind.—Draw some holy affection, love, contrition, etc., from the reading.

Avoid reading or meditating too much.—Every time you pause, remain as long as your mind finds it pleasant or useful to do so.

SECOND WAY. Take some text of Holy Scripture, or some vocal prayer, like the *Pater, Ave,* or *Credo,* and say it over, stopping at each word, drawing out various holy sentiments, upon which you may dwell as long as you like.

At the end, ask God for some grace or virtue, depending on what has been the subject of your meditations.

Do not stop on any one word if it wearies or tires you. When you find no more matter for thought or affections, leave it and pass on quietly to the next.

But when you feel yourself moved by some good sentiment, remain there as long as it lasts, without going to the trouble of passing on to something else.—There is no necessity to be always making new acts; it is often quite enough to remain in the presence of God silently turning over in your mind the words you have already meditated upon, or savoring the affections they have aroused in your heart.

THIRD WAY. When the prepared subject-matter does not give you enough scope, or room for free action, make acts of faith, adoration, thanksgiving, hope, love, and so on, letting them range as wide and free as you please, pausing at each one to let it sink in.

FOURTH WAY. When meditation is impossible, and you are too helpless and dried-up to produce a single affection, tell Our Lord that it is your intention to make an act, for example, of contrition, every time you draw breath, or pass a bead of the rosary between your fingers, or say, vocally, some short prayer.

Renew this assurance of your intention, from time to time, and then, if God suggests some other good thought, receive it with humility, and dwell upon it.

FIFTH WAY. In time of trial or dryness, if you are completely barren and powerless to make any acts or to have any thoughts, abandon yourself generously to suffering, without anxiety, and without making any effort to avoid it, making no other acts except this self-abandonment into the hands of God to suffer this trial and all it may please Him to send.

Or else you may unite your prayer with Our Lord's Agony in the garden and His desolation upon the Cross.—See yourself attached to the Cross with the Savior and stir yourself up to follow His example, and remain there suffering without flinching, until death.

SIXTH WAY. A survey of your own conscience.— Admit your defects, passions, weaknesses, infirmities, helplessness, misery, nothingness.—Adore God's judgments with regard to the state in which you find yourself.—Submit to His holy will.—Bless Him both for His punishments and for the favors of His mercy.—Humble yourself before His sovereign Majesty.—Sincerely confess your sins and infidelities to Him and ask Him to forgive you.—Take back all your false judgments and errors.—Detest all the wrong you have done, and resolve to correct yourself in future.

This kind of prayer is very free and unhampered, and admits of all kinds of affections. It can be practiced at all times, especially in some unexpected trial, to submit to the punishments of God's justice, or as a means of regaining recollection after a lot of activity and distracting affairs.

SEVENTH WAY. Conjure up a vivid picture of the Last Things. Visualize yourself in agony, between time and eternity—between your past life and the judgment of God.— What would you wish to have done? How would you want to have lived?—Think of the pain you will feel then.—Call to mind your sins, your negligence, your abuse of grace.—How would you like to have acted in this or that situation?— Make up your mind to adopt a real, practical means of remedying those defects which give you reason for anxiety.

Visualize yourself dead, buried, rotting, forgotten by all. See yourself before the Judgment-seat of Christ: in Purgatory—in Hell.

The more vivid the picture, the better will be your meditation.

We all need this mystical death, to get the flesh off of our soul, and to rise again, that is, to get free from corruption and sin. We need to go through this purgatory, in order to arive at the enjoyment of God in this life.

EIGHTH WAY. Apply your mind to Jesus in the Most Blessed Sacrament. Address yourself to Our Lord in the Blessed Sacrament, with all the respect that His Real Presence demands, unite yourself to Him and to all His operations in the Eucharist, where He is ceaselessly adoring, praising, and loving His Father, in the name of all men, and in the condition of a victim.

Realize His recollection, His hidden life, His utter privation of everything, obedience, humility, and so on.—Stir yourself up to imitate them, and resolve to do so according as the occasions arise.

Offer up Jesus to the Father, as the only Victim worthy of Him, and by Whom we can offer homage to Him, thank Him for His gifts, satisfy His justice, and oblige His mercy to help us.

Offer yourself to sacrifice your being, your life, your work. Offer up to Him some act of virtue you propose to perform, some mortification upon which you have resolved, with a view to self-conquest, and offer this for the same ends for which Our Lord immolates Himself in the Holy Sacraments.—Make this offering with an ardent desire to add as much as possible to the glory He gives to His Father in this august mystery.

End with a spiritual Communion.

This is an excellent form of prayer, especially for your visit to the Blessed Sacrament. Get to know it well, because our happiness in this life depends on our union with Jesus in the Blessed Sacrament.

NINTH WAY. This prayer is to be made in the Name of Jesus Christ. It will arouse our confidence in God, and help us to enter into the spirit and the sentiments of Our Lord.

Its foundation is the fact that we are united to the Son of God, and are His brothers, members of His Mystical Body; that He has made over to us all His merits, and left us the legacy of all the rewards owed Him by His Father for His labors and death. And this is what makes us capable of honoring

God with a worship worthy of Him, and gives us the right to treat with God, and, as it were, to exact His graces of Him as though by justice.—As creatures, we have not this right, still less as sinners, for there is an infinite disproportion between God and creatures, and infinite opposition between God and sinners. But because we are united to the Incarnate Word, and are His brothers, and His members, we are enabled to appear before God with confidence, and speak familiarly with Him and oblige Him to give us a favorable hearing, to grant our requests, and to grant us His graces, because of the alliance and union between us and His Son.

Hence, we are to appear before God either to adore, to praise, or to love Him, by Jesus Christ working in us as the Head in His members, lifting us up, by His spirit, to an entirely divine state, or else to ask some favor in virtue of the merits of His Son. And for that purpose we should remind Him of all that His well beloved Son has done for Him, His life and death, and His sufferings, the reward for which belongs to us because of the deed of gift by which he has made it over to us.

And this is the spirit in which we should recite the Divine Office.

TENTH WAY. Simple attention to the presence of God, and meditation.

Before starting out to meditate on the prepared topic, put yourself in the presence of God without making any other distinct thought, or stirring up in yourself any other sentiment except the respect and love for God which His presence inspires.—Be content to remain thus before God, in silence, in simple repose of the spirit as long as it satisfies you. After that, go on with your meditation in the usual way.

It is a good thing to begin all your prayer in this way, and worthwhile to return to it after every point.—Relax in this simple awareness of God's presence.—It is a way to gain real interior recollection.— You will develop the habit of centering your mind upon God and thus gradually pave the way for contemplation.—But do not remain this way out of pure laziness or just to avoid the trouble of making a meditation.